The Fiberworks Source Book

YOUR MAIL ORDER GUIDE
TO SUPPLIES AND SERVICES
FOR THE FIBER ARTS

Bobbi A. McRae

BETTERWAY PUBLICATIONS, INC. White Hall, Virginia

First Printing: March, 1985

Published by Betterway Publications, Inc.
White Hall, VA 22987

Book design by Diane Nelson
Cover photography by Erin Garvey; products from
Williams Corner Bookstore, Genevieve M. Clark,
and Stenciled Interiors.
Typography by East Coast Typography, Inc.

Library of Congress Cataloging in Publication Data

McRae, Bobbi A.
   The fiberworks source book.

   Bibliography: p.
   Includes index.
   1. Fiberwork — Equipment and supplies — Catalogs.
2. Textile crafts — Equipment and supplies — Catalogs.
3. Fiberwork — Equipment and supplies — Directories.
4. Textile crafts — Equipment and supplies — Directories.
I. Title.
TT698.M37   1985   746'.028   85-1210
ISBN 0-932620-46-9 (pbk.)

Printed in the United States of America

This book is dedicated with love
and deepest appreciation
to my husband,
Michael,
and to my parents,
Barbara A. & Bobby J. Neal.

Table of Contents

Acknowledgements

Many people helped me "keep everything together" while I was working on this book, but there are always those special few who do more than their share. My special thanks goes to Stephen Blumrich, surface designer and editor of the *Surface Design Journal,* for his help in locating school and college addresses for Chapter Nine; to Anne Patterson Dee, editor of *CraftsWoman* magazine, for her professional advice, help and friendly letters; to Sharon, who is always just a phone call away; and to all of those weavers, spinners, dyers, designers, and other fiber artists who went out of their way to send information, samples and photos. Without them (and the sheep), there would be no book.

About the Author

Photograph by Michael C. McRae

Bobbi A. McRae graduated from the University of Texas at Austin in 1981 with a B.A. in Studio Art. It was there that a life-long interest in fabrics and sewing surfaced, leading her to concentrate in the fiber arts — much to the chagrin of her metal and plexiglas-loving instructors. She still lives in Austin, where she is presently working in the areas of surface design, handmade paper, and handmade felt. She is a freelance writer, and has written articles for *The Crafts Report, CraftsWoman,* and *Needle and Thread.* THE FIBERWORKS SOURCE BOOK is her first book.

Introduction

In the beginning, when *The Fiberworks Source Book* was just a germ of an idea, I sent letters to over 500 yarn suppliers, publishers, weavers, spinners, designers, and other fiber artists, telling them of my desire to put together a directory of this type. I was astounded at the response. All comments were positive. In fact, they all centered around one basic idea — the overwhelming *need* for a source book of this kind.

Although many large suppliers are listed here, the majority of the suppliers are home-based fiber artists, craftspeople, or business owners. Some are even ranchers. Many of them live outside the larger cities, and rely mostly on mail order for their own supplies and for their income. You will find a wide range of materials offered by these people, including looms, spinning wheels, wools, silks, angora rabbit fur, camel down, reindeer hair, handspun and naturally dyed yarns, natural and synthetic dyes, rubber stamps, natural fabrics, books, computer software for designers and weavers, threads, materials for making your own paper or baskets, various needlework supplies, and thousands of other supplies. Many of these people even raise their own sheep or other fiber-producing animals, shear and prepare the fibers, and then make beautiful, handspun yarns to use for weaving, knitting, or crocheting.

I hope that once you see the potential of the interesting, unique materials listed in the book, you will be inspired to try something new. I believe that this book should be about "discovery" — learn what clean wool straight from the sheep smells and feels like; discover how soft the fur from an angora rabbit can be; order a silk cocoon from one of the sources and reel your own silk thread; experience spinning your own knitting or crocheting yarns like your grandmother (or great-grandmother) once did; learn to dye your own yarns or fabrics with natural materials or synthetic dyes. Thousands of books on all aspects of the fiber arts are also offered — buy one and discover a totally new craft.

How about making handmade paper? Or making your own baskets? How about handpainting your own design on a silk blouse or dress?

Whatever you decide to do, be daring. You can be sure that working in fibers is exciting, challenging, and fulfilling. Fibers and fabrics are warm, sensuous, touchable, and take on a life of their own. Give it a try, and have fun!

How to Use This Book

The Fiberworks Source Book is your "buying guide" to fiber art supplies. It is currently the most complete and comprehensive listing of materials and services available to those who work in this area.

The name, address and phone number of each company is listed first. The next line explains what type of business the company does — whether it is a manufacturer, mail order company, or retail store. On the same line, you may find these letters: V/MC/AMEX. This stands for the type of credit cards that the company will accept, if any: Visa, Master-Card, and American Express. The date that the company was established is listed last.

The main paragraph in the entry lists as many items as possible that the company offers, and will tell you if they offer classes or workshops in their shop or studio.

Discount information appears next. If the company sells wholesale, that information also appears here. Many of the companies do give nice discounts to their customers. The drawback, however, is the minimum order requirement that a company may require. In this case, it would be to your advantage to get together with several friends and order your supplies at one time.

The price (if any) of the catalog and/or samples is listed last. Even though some of the prices may seem high, the samples are usually well worth the price, and lots of them can be used in your smaller projects.

A "S.A.S.E." is a self-addressed, stamped envelope.

Some of the suppliers do not have formal, printed catalogs. All of them, however, will respond to a simple note for prices or information. There are a lot of nice, friendly people listed in this book, and they will be happy to help you find the things you need, if at all possible.

By the way, most of these companies carry more than one type of supply. For example, a yarn company will most likely also offer natural or synthetic dyes, so that company may be listed in two chapters —Chapter 4 and Chapter 5, depending on how complete the selection is. Your best bet is to check the Index where all page numbers are listed for an item.

If you do not see your favorite yarn company or fiber supplier listed, it may be that they did not return my Information Sheet. Only information received was included in the book.

 NOTE TO READERS

I would definitely like to hear your thoughts and comments about the book and any of the suppliers listed that you deal with. Also, if you have a favorite company that you do business with that is not listed, or a favorite material that you use or would like to find, let me know. This information will be useful in preparing future editions of the book and subsequent updates.

Suppliers of fiber equipment or materials who are interested in possible listings in future editions should also contact me. And for those of you who are already listed, keep me up to date on your new products, changes of address, etc.

I'd love to hear from you all.

Write to: Bobbi A. McRae
               P.O. Box 49770
               Austin, TX 78765

CHAPTER 1   Associations and Organizations

This chapter contains addresses and basic information on the associations and organizations that represent the various areas of the fiber arts. Others can provide basic information on other related subjects.

AMERICAN CRAFT COUNCIL

401 Park Avenue South
New York, NY 10016
(212) 696-0710

THE AMERICAN CRAFT COUNCIL is a national, nonprofit educational organization founded in 1943 by Aileen Osborn Webb to promote interest in contemporary crafts. In addition to publishing *American Craft* magazine, the Council maintains the American Craft Museum in New York City and sponsors a library and nationwide audiovisual service.

Through its subsidiary, American Craft Enterprises, Inc., craft markets are presented in various parts of the country.

Membership benefits include six issues of *American Craft* magazine, free admission to the American Craft Museum and Library in New York City, discounts on ACC publications and slides, free admission to ACC craft fairs, and eligibility to apply for ACC sponsored group insurance.

Current membership dues are $35.00 per year; write for more information.

CATALYST

14 East 60th Street
New York, NY 10022
(212) 759-9700

CATALYST is the national not-for-profit organization that works within the corporate community to promote the full participation of women in business and the professions. Their three main goals are to: further the upward mobility of women, reconcile the needs of the workplace and family, and expand career awareness among students. Some of the services offered by Catalyst include a Women's Professional Groups Network, Library and Audiovisual Center, Career Publications and Audiovisual Materials, and many others.

Write for more information.

CENTER FOR THE HISTORY OF AMERICAN NEEDLEWORK

Old Economy Village
14th and Church Streets
Ambridge, PA 15003
(412) 266-6440

THE CENTER FOR THE HISTORY OF AMERICAN NEEDLEWORK (or CHAN) was founded in 1974 to develop public recognition for American needlework and textiles. Some of the services offered include: a Research Library of over 3,000 volumes, a Textile Collection of over 2,500 items, Audiovisual Programs, Exhibitions, Publications, and a Speaker's Bureau. Some of the services are included with the membership fee — others for a self-addressed, stamped envelope or a simple phone call.

Current membership dues are $15.00 per year, which includes a quarterly newsletter, discounts on reproductions of library materials and publications, bibliographies, patterns, reference materials, etc.

Write or call for further information.

CENTER FOR OCCUPATIONAL HAZARDS

5 Beekman Street
New York, NY 10038
(212) 227-6220

THE CENTER FOR OCCUPATIONAL HAZARDS (COH) is a national organization which provides research and information on health hazards in the arts. COH has a variety of services aimed at helping to eliminate hazards in the arts. These include: Art Hazards Information Center, Art Hazards Newsletter, Lecture Program, Art Hazards Course, Consultation Program with Dr. Michael McCann, and publications which cover various art hazards.

Quantity discounts are given on publications.

Send a SASE for more information and a list of available publications.

THE EMBROIDERER'S GUILD OF AMERICA

National Headquarters
6 East 45th Street
New York, NY 10017

The EMBROIDERER'S GUILD OF AMERICA is a national organization that exists to share their interest in all types of embroidery. The Guild offers a variety of services to its members, including the *Needle Arts* magazine, correspondence courses, including a Teacher's Certification course, group courses, and a Master Craftsman program. The Guild also sponsors national seminars, workshops and exhibitions.

Write for further information about the Guild or a membership application.

GRAPHIC ARTISTS GUILD

30 East 20th Street
New York, NY 10003

Members of this organization include such persons as needleartists, textile designers, illustrators, graphic designers, and others. The GRAPHIC ARTISTS GUILD offers various membership benefits, including publications, a legal referral system, insurance plans, model contracts and purchase orders, and pricing and ethical guidelines.

Write for additional information.

HANDWEAVERS GUILD OF AMERICA

65 La Salle Road
West Hartford, CT 06107

The HANDWEAVERS GUILD OF AMERICA is one of the professional organizations for weavers and spinners. In addition to publishing the magazine, *Shuttle Spindle & Dyepot,* they also sponsor the Convergence conferences, Certification of Excellence, and offer a number of publications and other services. If you weave or spin, you really should be a member of the HGA.

Send for additional information.

INTERNATIONAL SILK ASSOCIATION

P.O. Box 907
Englewood Cliffs, NJ 07632

The INTERNATIONAL SILK ASSOCIATION provides a wide variety of information on silk, how it is produced, its history, etc.

Write for more information.

NATIONAL ALLIANCE OF HOMEBASED BUSINESSWOMEN

P.O. Box 237
Norwood, NJ 07648

The NATIONAL ALLIANCE OF HOMEBASED BUSINESSWOMEN (NAHB) was founded by Marion Behr and Wendy Lazar, in order to meet the professional needs of the rising numbers of self-employed women in the United States. Ms. Behr and Ms. Lazar have also published *Women Working Home: The Homebased Business Guide and Directory,* which is available from the NAHB.

Write for more information.

NATIONAL ANGORA RABBIT BREEDERS CLUB

Black River Road
Watertown, NY 13601

The NATIONAL ANGORA RABBIT BREEDERS CLUB promotes the raising of angora rabbits across the nation. many spinners raise their own rabbits because of the luxurious, soft fur that the rabbits produce. This fur is often made into handspun yarns or sold to other spinners for their use. If you are interested in raising your own angora rabbits, this club can help you get started.

Write to Connie Cummings, Secretary of the Club, for more information.

NATIONAL COTTON COUNCIL OF AMERICA

P.O. Box 12285
Memphis, TN 38182
(901) 274-9030

The NATIONAL COTTON COUNCIL OF AMERICA can provide useful background information on cotton — how it is grown, why it is important, how it is processed, the history of cotton, etc. The Council also publishes a variety of booklets and pamphlets on various aspects of cotton.

Write for more information.

Cotton plant. Courtesy The National Cotton Council of America

NATIONAL STANDARDS
COUNCIL OF AMERICAN
EMBROIDERERS

P.O. Box 8578
Northfield, IL 60093

The NATIONAL STANDARDS COUNCIL OF AMERICAN EM-BROIDERERS is a non-profit educational organization dedicated to promoting high standards in the art of needlework, with the emphasis on "needlework as an expression of creativity." Members of NSCAE receive *The Flying Needle,* a quarterly journal containing articles on embroidery, artists and their work, exhibits, etc. Services provided by the Council include a lending library of over 1,000 volumes on needlework and design, a slide lending library, study portfolios, a directory of embroidery and textile collections in the U.S., a correspondence school, and a biennial exhibit, "Needle Expressions."

Write for membership information. Current annual dues are $15.00

SOCIETY OF CRAFT
DESIGNERS

P.O. Box 7744
Columbus, GA 31908
(404) 327-1522

The SOCIETY OF CRAFT DESIGNERS is an organization dedicated to the promotion of the individual designer in particular and the craft industry as a whole. The Society conducts educational seminars across the country, and provides a meeting place for designers, writers, manufacturers, retailers, publishers, instructors, etc. The Society also provides a listing and referral service, and serves as a showcase for members' work at an annual Fine-Craft Auction and Bazaar. A newsletter is published to keep channels of communication open among the members.

Annual dues are currently $60.00. Write for more information.

SURFACE DESIGN
ASSOCIATION, INC.

311 E. Washington Street
Fayetteville, TN 37334
(615) 433-6804

The SURFACE DESIGN ASSOCIATION is a non-profit, educational organization that exists to stimulate, promote and improve education in the area of surface design on fabrics, to improve communication and distribution of technical information to the public, to provide opportunities for the public to view exhibitions, and to provide a public forum for exchange of ideas through conferences, workshops, and publications.

The SDA sponsors a yearly national conference and regional conferences.

The SDA membership fee also includes a subscription to *The Surface Design Journal.*

Write for additional information.

THE WEAVING AND
SPINNING COUNCIL

P.O. Box 339
Sanbornville, NH 03872

The WEAVING AND SPINNING COUNCIL likes to share their enthusi-
asm for weaving and spinning by sponsoring a National Spinning and
Weaving Week. This week is set aside each year to "celebrate the timeless
crafts of weaving and spinning and to honor craftspeople past and present,
who perpetuate a legacy of fine handmade textiles."

Write to the Council for more information, and dates of upcoming Spinning and Weaving Weeks.

THE WOOL BUREAU, INC.

360 Lexington Avenue
New York, NY 10017
(212) 986-6222

THE WOOL BUREAU, INC. can provide basic information, publications,
etc. on wool and wool production.

Write for more information.

CHAPTER 2   Services

This chapter includes people and companies who provide special services or information to fiber artists and other craftspeople. Some of these services include software design programs, flameproofing, photography, editorial services, and printing, along with others.

SWEDISH LACE TEA MATS IN 10/2 PERLE COTTON 4/11/84

PROJECT LENGTH IN INCHES

160

LENGTH OF EACH WARP THREAD IN YARDS

8

SETT

24

WIDTH IN INCHES

12.5

SLEYED WIDTH

14

ACTUAL ENDS WARPED

336

TOTAL WARP YARDAGE

2688

TOTAL WARP IN POUNDS & IN (OUNCES)

0.896   (14.336-OUNCES)

PRICE OF WARP

$7.1232

PICKS PER INCH

24

WOVEN LENGTH

188

WEFT YARDAGE

1754.66667

TOTAL WEFT IN POUNDS & IN (OUNCES)

0.585   (9.35822222-OUNCES)

PRICE OF WEFT

$4.64986667

Sample printout from The Yarn Calculator.
© *Baker Computer Company*

KARI A. ARNOLD

1612 Tennessee
Lawrence, KS 66044
(913) 843-8351

Mail Order; Established in 1983

KARI ARNOLD has developed several software programs for weavers which she is willing to share with others for a very minimal price. Programs currently available are: Weave Design, Color Weave, and Weave Analysis. These three programs, which come in one package, are design and analysis programs written for the expanded Commodore Vic-20 Computer. Another of Kari's programs, Calcuweave, is a weaving calculations program written for the Vic-20 and the Commodore 64. Design programs for the Commodore 64 will be available in the near future from Ms. Arnold. She also guarantees "personal service."

Send for a free Information Sheet.

BAKER COMPUTER
COMPANY

38 Beal Street
Winthrop, MA 02152
(617) 846-3395

Mail Order; Established in 1981

Pam Baker is a weaver; Jim Baker is a computer programmer. When Pam wanted a way to simply, quickly, and neatly do calculations and keep records for her weavings, the two put their heads together. The result was BAKER COMPUTER COMPANY and The Yarn Calculator, a program for the Apple Computer. The Yarn Calculator is a versatile utility program which can compute the quantity of fibers needed to weave a certain design. The program can compute length of each warp thread in yards, total warp ends, sleyed width, weft yardage, and can also figure projects with multiple warps or wefts. Other features included in the program are five fiber conversion tables, yards-to-pounds fiber converter function, pricing function for cost of yarn usage, printout capabilities and other options. The program can be run on Apple II+, IIe, IIc, and III computers. Also, it can be used on other computers that are compatible with Applesoft Basic.

The entire software package includes a manual, one program disk, and one copy of the program disk for back-up purposes. With this program, you can spend your time weaving — not computing!

Send a SASE for free information. The User's Manual is available without program for $2.00

BALLANTYNE FLAME-
PROOFING COMPANY

2722 N. Lincoln Avenue
Chicago, IL 60614
(312) 348-7770

Manufacturer, Mail Order, Retail Shop; Established in 1941

BALLANTYNE FLAMEPROOFING carries a complete line of fire retardants for various materials, including most common fabrics, synthetics, nylons, dacrons, etc., chemicals for unfinished woods and papers, and chemicals that can be used on grass cloths and Christmas trees.

Discounts are given with a minimum order of one gallon.

No catalog is available; write for information on specific chemical applications.

BOB BARRET
PHOTOGRAPHY

RD 1, Box 219
High Falls, NY 12440
(914) 687-0716

BOB BARRETT has offered his fine photographic services to many fiber artists, and his work is included in museums and slide rental collections. His work has also been published in *American Craft, Fine Woodworking, Ceramics Monthly,* etc.

Mr. Barrett can provide two sets of five slides each for approximately $100.00 plus shipping (his minimum fee in 1984 prices). Models are extra. He accepts work shipped UPS, registered U.S. Mail or Federal Express. Prices can be estimated after Bob sees the work.

For your convenience, he also sets up his studio at various art and craft shows during the year — the ACC Springfield and Rhinebeck Fairs, for example.

Send for a current brochure.

BYTE RITE

Rt. 1, Box 768
Mount Airy, NC 27030
(919) 789-2983

Manufacturer, Mail Order; Established in 1983

BYTE RITE offers several fiber art design computer programs for the IBM PC or PCjr. The EagerWeaver program includes a drawdown system which handles up to 16 harnesses and 10 treadles. It also features full-screen editing by cursor control, CRT color and hard-copy black and white display of drawdowns, file system to store and retrieve complete weaves, individual threadings, treadlings, tie-ups and color sequences, namedrafts, and worksheets to use at your loom. System requirements for the EagerWeaver are an IBM PC or PCjr with 64K memory, one disk drive, color graphics CRT, DOS and BASICA, IBM PC Graphics printer or Epson MX80 printer.

Byte Rite also offers an EagerStriper program which designs up to 79 vertical stripe units, and a PlaidsPlanner which designs up to 39 vertical by 23 horizontal units (can be used for both plaids and stripes).

All programs come complete with instruction manuals. The company also offers IBM PC programming and consulting services on an individual basis.

Send for a set of free brochures on all programs.

COMPUCRAFTS

RFD 2, Box 216
Lincoln, MA 01773
(617) 259-0409

Mail Order; Established in 1983

COMPUCRAFTS offers two software programs for weavers and needlecraft artists, The Weaver and The Stitch Grapher, written for the Apple II+, or IIe microcomputer. The company is owned by David L. Natwig, a chemist and professional software engineer, who also happens to be married to a weaver, teacher, and cross-stitcher.

The Weaver can be used for creating new designs in seconds, creating drawdowns, creating a data-base of drafts and drawdowns, exploring alternate treadling sequences and tie-ups, and checking book errors before starting a project. The Stitch Grapher was designed to create, modify and print the necessary charts for counted cross stitch and all other graph dependant needle arts. Charts generated by the program are very clear, defined, and easy to read.

Write for more information and current prices.

CONROY SOFTWARE

3423 Southgate Road
Ottawa, Ontario
CANADA K1V 7Y5
(613) 737-0503

Mail Order; Established in 1983

CONROY SOFTWARE offers two design programs for weavers, Design-A-Draft and Design-A-Draft II. The first program is a menu-driven computer program which produces drawdowns in seconds. The program can design new drafts, retrieve previous drafts, and edit. This allows designs for 40 warp threads and 24 weft threads, and was written for the Commodore 64 with disk drive, and the Commodore or the Gemini X printer. Design-A-Draft II allows display of up to 255 warp threads and 180 weft threads, 16 harnesses and 16 treadles. This program, also written for the Commodore 64, calculates warp and weft amounts, gives a thread-by-thread draft, edits, and produces worksheets, record cards and weave analyses for your use.

Send for more information and current prices.

DAEDALUS PUBLISHING

1153 Oxford Road
Deerfield, IL 60015
(312) 945-1769

In addition to being the publisher of *Crafts Woman* magazine, Anne Patterson Dee of DAEDALUS PUBLICATIONS, INC. also provides a number of Professional Crafts Marketing Services, which include:
- Typesetting and Layout Services for your ads, catalogs, flyers, brochures, etc. The finished original is sent to you in camera-ready form, ready to take to your printer.
- News Releases — Anne can write a one-page, double-spaced news release, tailor-made for your new product or business and written in the style and format that magazine and newspaper editors prefer.
- Mailing Lists — A set of 200 peel-and-stick labels in zip code order (enough for a bulk rate mailing) addressed to the Women's or Lifestyle Editor of major newspapers all over the country.

Write for more information or cost estimates.

DONNELLY OFFSET NEGATIVES

183 St. Paul Street
Rochester, NY 14604
(716) 232-3996

Mail Order

DONNELLY OFFSET NEGATIVES, owned by John E. Donnelly, can produce negatives in 8x10, 11x14, and 12x14, to be used with photographic printing on fabrics.

Some quantity prices are given; write for details.

Send for a current price list and order form.

IHANA BRUSHING SERVICE

1037 South University
Denver, CO 80209
(303) 744-0411

Mail Order; Established in 1982

CARLA S. MOORE owns the only professional machine brushing service for handweavers in the country. The IHANA (Finnish for "lovely") finishing process gives a luxurious, even nap and professional look to your handwoven fabrics. Although brushing can be done by hand, Ihana uses a traditional small mill dressed with natural teasels. These are much gentler on your work than wire cloth.

Carla is constantly testing her brushing process on different brands and types of yarns. Her brochure states that she welcomes calls about setts, tested yarns, fabric care, etc.

The minimum order is $10.00.

Send for a free brochure and sample of brushed fabric.

**MID-WEST SCENIC AND
STAGE EQUIPMENT
COMPANY**

224 West Bruce Street
Milwaukee, WI 53204
(424) 276-2707

MID-WEST SCENIC AND STAGE CO. offers chemicals for flame-proofing, and fire-retardant fabrics.

Write for more information; enclose a SASE.

OPCODE SOFTWARE

1909½ Vine Street
Berkeley, CA 94709
(415) 525-6997

Manufacturer, Mail Order; Established in 1981

Mark Opperman of OPCODE SOFTWARE has designed a computer program called the Navette for the Apple II computer. Mark says that his program is "the most powerful, flexible, and competitively priced pattern design tool on the market today." The Navette, designed by a French handweaver, provides you with familiar visual displays of drawdowns. The program allows you to simulate different weave densities by changing the horizontal and vertical spacing of your printout (provided your printer has this capability) and the pattern character. In addition, drawdowns may be printed with or without color effects. The program also analyzes weave structures. After editing a pattern directly on the display, Navette will determine the threading, treadling, and tie-up necessary to weave it, all in a matter of seconds. Patterns requiring up to 16 harnesses can be accomodated. The program also features warp pattern repeats up to 132 threads, weft pattern repeats up to 96 shots, with up to 280 warp threads and 192 shots displayed. The program requires an Apple II, II+, or IIe with 64K and one disk drive, and an Epson or Apple dot matrix printer.

Opcode also offers "Computer Aided Drafting" workshops and classes.

Send for a free brochure and price list.

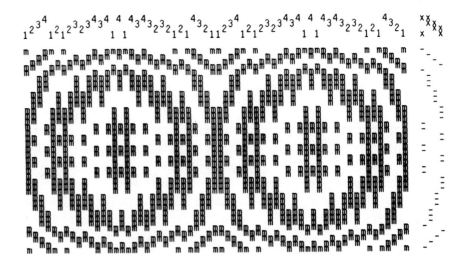

Printed drawdown from the Navette. © Opcode Software, Mark Opperman

JIM QUALIA PHOTOGRAPHY

P.O. Box 710122
Dallas, TX 75214
(214) 826-8327

Mail Order; Established in 1970

JIM QUALIA PHOTOGRAPHY has been serving the commercial photography industry in Dallas for over seven years. He has recently expanded his services, and is now working with home-based craftspeople and other creative businesses. He offers a basic photography service where you ship your products to him to be photographed. The items are photographed singly or together on a plain background. You then have the option of ordering either color transparencies, color prints, or black and white prints.

Send for a current price list and more details.

STAR*SYSTEMS

28 Topstone Drive
Bethel, CT 06801
(203) 744-0546

Mail Order, Established in 1983

STAR*SYSTEMS offers a weaving design computer program called the PC Weaver for the IBM Personal Computer. The program features four to eight harnesses, four to eight treadles, 140 warp threads, 150 weft threads, rising or sinking shed, versatile screen editor, forward and reverse repeats, forward and reverse block copy, "treadle as drawn in" command, draft file storage and retrieval, easy-to-use draft "worksheet" display, and light/dark color and weave effects. The system requirements for the program are: IBM PC with DOS 1.1, 2.0, or 2.1 operating system, 80-column display (monochrome or color), Epson MX-80, RX-80, or FX-80 printer, drive, and 64K memory.

Send for a free brochure and sample printout.

CAROL STRICKLER

1690-F Wilson Court
Boulder, CO 80302
(303) 444-0610

Publisher, Mail Order; Established in 1978

CAROL STRICKLER markets the Weft-Writer, a weaving drawdown program for the Apple PC, written by Stewart J. Strickler. The program displays drawdowns up to 280 warp threads wide, 160 wefts high, up to 24-shaft threadings with as many as 24 treadles, and automatic repeats of shorter patterns if so desired. The program allows storage of patterns for later recall for display or printing, and an editing function for changing stored patterns.

Send a long SASE for more information and current prices.

TREADLE I

18 Mildred Road
West Hartford, CT 06107
(203) 561-2299

Mail Order, Retail Hours by Appointment; Established in 1977

TREADLE I offers easy-to-read computer-aided drawdowns of weaving drafts. These include threading, tie-up and treadling directions.

Write for more information.

UNIQUITY

P.O. Box 3063
DeLand, FL 32723
(904) 736-1450

Manufacturer, Mail Order;
V/MC/AMEX; Established in
1973

Herbert and Patricia Pitts, owners of UNIQUITY, can manufacture custom-made Plexiglas display cases for your three-dimensional pieces of fiber art. The cases come in several designs, including rectangular, wall mounted, or round. The company can also make pedestals out of various materials with Plexiglas tops for your larger pieces of work.

Other options and services offered by Uniquity include custom designs to your specific requirements, permanently sealed cases, ultra-violet filtering Plexiglas, and conservation mounting.

The Pitts promise courteous, individual service, consultation, pickup and delivery when desired, and satisfaction guaranteed.

Send for a free brochure and price list.

U.S. CONSUMER PRODUCT SAFETY COMMISSION

Washington, DC 20207

The U.S. CONSUMER PRODUCT SAFETY COMMISSION, a federal regulatory agency, publishes informative materials on product safety as a service to consumers. This arm of the government was responsible for and has information on the Flammable Fabrics Act and The Federal Hazardous Substances Act.

The Commission is also investigating dyes and pigments for possible toxic effects and is monitoring possible problems in this area.

Any fiber artist, and especially those who make toys or other products aimed towards children, should become familiar with these laws.

Send for more information and a list of publications.

VERMONT BUSINESS FORMS COMPANY

Business Cards Division
RD #4, Box 1690
Montpelier, VT 05602
(802) 229-9579

Mail Order; Established in 1976

VERMONT BUSINESS FORMS COMPANY is an excellent source for creative business cards. The owners of the company, Earl and Carole Emerson, offer custom designed cards/hang tags with matching letterhead and envelopes. They use raised print only, and offer a wide selection of colors, card stocks, and type styles. They also have over 160 stock logo illustrations, many of which are perfect for fiber artists: a lamb, spinning wheels, looms, needle and thread, dolls, quilt blocks, fabric bolts, embroidery, crochet designs, and many others. These are printed free on the cards, or you can design your own logo to be included. The company also offers a free layout service for those who are not sure about their design.

Send 50¢ for complete ordering information, samples of logos and type styles, and samples of business cards.

VOLUME 7 SOFTWARE

408 N. Bradley
Mt. Pleasant, MI 48858
(517) 773-5783

Mail Order; Established in 1983

Bill Stanwick, of VOLUME 7 SOFTWARE, offers the Drawdown computer program for weavers. The program requires an Apple II+ or IIe Computer or Franklin. It features drawdowns of patterns using up to eight harnesses and ten treadles, two thread widths allowing up to 254 warp threads, screen display of the harness threading, tie-up and treadling together with drawdown, full editing capabilities, storage, recall and printing of drawdowns.

Write for a free brochure and current prices.

CHAPTER 3 Fabrics

This chapter contains suppliers of natural cottons, linens, silks, etc. that are suitable for dyeing, handpainting, batik, and other surface design techniques. Also listed are sources for felts, leathers, and other fabrics that can be used in rughooking, rag rug weaving, wearable art, quilting, etc.

AIZOME DESIGN FABRICS

P.O. Box 31743
Seattle, WA 98103
(206) 522-4607

Mail Order; Established in 1982

AIZOME DESIGN FABRICS imports hand-dyed Japanese Yukata 100% cotton fabrics. These washable fabrics are used in the traditional Japanese garment known as the "yukata," similar in style to the well-known kimono.

Individual and wholesale discounts are given; write for details.

Send $2.00 for a price list and fabric swatches.

BAZAAR CLOTH

P.O. Box 7281
Santa Cruz, CA 95061-7281
(408) 425-7239

Manufacturer, Mail Order;
Established in 1978

Charlotte Eggleston, President of BAZAAR CLOTH, imports handwoven, 100% cotton fabrics from Guatemala. These beautiful, brightly colored fabrics are all 36 inches wide, and include many ikat designs, lengthwise stripes, and some solids. These fabrics would be perfect for ethnically-oriented wearable art pieces.

Wholesale prices are given with a ten-yard order for one design, or 25 yards total of different designs. Write for more details.

Send $2.00 for a current brochure and a generous set of samples.

 WHAT IS "MERCERIZED COTTON"?

Dull, twisted cotton yarns or threads are kept at a certain tension and immersed into a caustic soda solution. This changes the form of the fiber and imparts a luster-like quality, the silky sheen on "pearl" cottons and some sewing threads. This solution is then washed out, resulting in cotton that is more lustrous, stronger, and better suited for dyeing. The process is called mercerization, and was discovered by John Mercer, a textile worker and one of England's most brilliant chemists.

BERMAN LEATHERCRAFT, INC.

145 South Street
Boston, MA 02111-2882
(617) 426-0870

Manufacturer, Mail Order;
V/MC/AMEX/DC; Established in 1905

BERMAN LEATHERCRAFT, INC., operated by Robert S. Berman, President, is a family-owned business that has been in operation for a long time (80 years in 1985). They sell many items that can be used in fiberwork, such as leather hides in various types and weights, garment leathers (chamois, sueded pigskin, etc.), snake skins, leather lacings, wool shearlings, calfskin, rabbit skins, etc. Leather scraps are also available. Berman also carries a large number of tools for leatherworking, dyes, solvents, and preservatives. Leather sewing supplies are also available from this source, and include threads, chisels, needles, awls, etc. A beading loom, as well as several types of beads and bells can also be ordered from Berman. Other items include "how-to" books, stamping tools, and kits.

Various discounts are given with a $10.00 minimum order; write for details.

Send $1.00 for a copy of Berman's new 1985 catalog.

CAROL BROWN
NATURAL FIBER FABRICS

Dept. TF
Putney, VT 05346
(802) 387-5875

Mail Order, Retail Shop; V/MC;
Established in 1928

CAROL BROWN offers a large line of natural fiber fabrics, including Irish and Welsh woolens (some handwoven), many 100% cottons, linens, and silks, and occasionally some Jack Lenor Larsen fabrics. Ms. Brown offers a personal mail-order service that focuses on the customer. Custom-made clothing is also available.

Wholesale discounts are given with a minimum order of $100.00.

Send for a current brochure.

CENTRAL SHIPPEE, INC.

46 Star Lake Road
Bloomingdale, NJ 07403
(201) 838-1121

Manufacturer, Mail Order; V/MC;
Established in 1923

If you are used to finding 12 x 12 inch squares of felt in only three or four different colors, you should take a look at the color card from CENTRAL SHIPPEE, INC. Their felts come in six-foot widths, two weights, and are made of 40% wool and 60% viscose rayon. The shades-over 75 in all-include names such as fresh lilac, doll face, sweet cantaloupe, ice mint, Williamsburg blue, seafoam, Northern spruce, silver, camel, curry, copper and claret! These are all beautiful, rich colors. This company also carries other special purpose felts — industrial felts (good for blockprinting use), drapery and upholstery felts, and wallcovering felts. Central Shippee also offers special treatments such as stiffening or flameproofing.

Send for free color cards and ordering information.

CLEARBROOK WOOLEN SHOP

P.O. Box 8
Clearbrook, VA 22624

Mail Order, Retail Shop; V/MC;
Established in 1939

CLEARBROOK WOOLEN SHOP carries all types of fabrics, from silks and cottons to wools and blends. They pride themselves in having many different, unusual fabrics under one roof.

Send for a free brochure.

CLEARLY COUNTRY

Jiggs Waysack
Elko, NV 89801
(702) 744-4360

Mail Order, Retail Shop; Established in 1983

Beckie Paris, owner of CLEARLY COUNTRY, carries 100% cotton fabrics from such manufacturers as VIP, Concord, Springmaid, Yours Truly, etc. She also carries 100% muslin "ecology cloth" in 44/45 inch widths, and 100% cotton denims, 60 inches wide. Other fabrics are also available.

A 10% professional discount is given; inquire on your letterhead. A 5% student or 4-H Club discount is also given by sending teacher's or leader's signature.

Send $2.00 and a long SASE for a set of swatches and a price list.

CLOTHWORKS

132 Powell Street
Vancouver, BC
Canada V6A 1G1
(604) 669-0127

Manufacturer, Mail Order, Retail
Shop; Established in 1980

CLOTHWORKS designs and prints natural fabrics and blends for interior and fashion designers. They also supply a wide range of cotton yardage for printing, as well as plain cotton aprons and travel bags.

Various discounts are given; write for details.

Send for a free brochure and price list.

COHASSET COLONIALS

944X Ship Street
Cohasset, MA 02025
(617) 383-0110

Mail Order, V/MC

In addition to offering reproduction furniture kits, COHASSET COLONIALS also sells fabrics by the yard which include over 24 samples of cottons and linens, each typical of Colonial American designs.

Send for more information on ordering fabrics.

COMMONWEALTH FELT COMPANY

211 Congress Street
Boston, MA 02110
(617) 423-3445

Manufacturer, Mail Order;
Established in 1910's

COMMONWEALTH FELT COMPANY supplies Perfection brand felts in both wools and synthetics, and Stik-EE-Felt adhesive-backed felts.

Discounts are given with a minimum order of $50.00.

Send for a free catalog; a color swatch card is $2.00.

W. CUSHING & COMPANY

Kennebunkport, ME 04046-0351
(207) 967-3711

Manufacturer, Mail Order

Besides being a long-time manufacturer of Cushing dyes, W. CUSHING & COMPANY also carries fabrics and accessories used in hooking rugs: plain burlaps, rug binding tapes, monks cloth, and a full line of wool fabrics suitable for hooked rugs.

Send for a price list which includes swatch prices.

Cotton blossom. Photo courtesy The National Cotton Council of America

DICK BLICK

Box 1267
Galesburg, IL 61401

DICK BLICK is another one of those suppliers who carry a little bit of everything. As far as fabrics are concerned, the company does carry a line of canvases that will be of interest to the fiber artist. The unprimed 100% cotton duck comes in three weights and widths (36 inches, 52 inches, and 60 inches). These fabrics are available both by the yard and by the roll. Primed cotton canvas also comes in three widths: 52 inches, 53 inches, and 72 inches. Dick Blick also has both unprimed and primed 100% linens in 52-inch and 84-inch widths.

Quantity prices are available; check catalog for details.

Send for a free catalog.

DORR FABRICS

P.O. Box 88
Guild, NH 03754-0088
(603) 863-1197

Mail Order, Retail Shop; V/MC;
Established in 1965

DORR FABRICS, also known as The Dorr Mill Store, claims to be the only source for 100% wool fabrics used for rug hooking or braiding that has a nice range of colors in stock at all times. They offer these fabrics by the yard or in single strips. Available in over 34 shades, the fabrics are 57 inches side, moth-proofed, and excellent for dyeing. The company also offers a complete line of rug hooking supplies and equipment.

Various discounts are given; write for information.

Send for a current brochure which lists fabric swatch prices.

THE FELTERS COMPANY

22 West Street
Millbury, MA 01527
(617) 865-4401

Manufacturer, Mail Order;
Established in 1909

THE FELTERS COMPANY offers Craft 100 acrylic felts in 25 shades and Craft 2001 wool felts in 37 shades. Both are in 72-inch widths.

Discounts are given with a minimum order of $50.00.

Send for a free price list.

GOHN BROTHERS

Box 111
Middlebury, IN 46540
(219) 825-2400

Mail Order, Retail Shop;
Established in 1900

GOHN BROTHERS has been a clothing and general merchandise supplier to the Amish people since 1900. In addition to their simple, serviceable clothing items, they also carry a line of "yard goods" which includes 100% cotton cheesecloth, terry toweling, outing flannel, flannelette diaper cloth, batiste, denim, VIP Quilting Prints, cloth of gold percale, Fiesta Amish percale, and many other natural fabrics and blends. The prices seem to be fairly reasonable, too. They also offer a line of "dress materials" which also includes 100% cottons: organdy, lawn, huck toweling, muslin, unbleached drill, duck cloth, chambray, etc. They also have 100% cotton bed and quilt sheetings in 90-inch widths. All of these fabrics are white, and should be suitable for dyeing.

Send 25¢ for a current price list.

GUTCHEON PATCHWORKS, INC.

P.O. Box 57, Prince Street Station
New York, NY 10012
(212) 505-0305

Manufacturer, Mail Order, Retail Shop; V/MC; Established in 1975

GUTCHEON PATCHWORKS, INC. is owned and operated by the husband-wife team of Beth and Jeffrey Gutcheon, well-known quilters and authors. They supply the American Classic line of 100% cotton prints and plain, polished coordinated solid fabrics. They claim to have the best line of plain colors in cotton available anywhere. Also offered are a number of books on quilting. Custom work, as well as seminars and classes, are available.

A 25% discount is given to working craftspeople; write for more information.

Send $2.00 for a price list and fabric swatches.

KAGEDO

1000 Lenora Street
Seattle, WA 98121
(206) 467-9077

Mail Order; V/MC

KAGEDO offers bales of antique silk kimonos. These can be decorated and used as-is, or cut into fabric pieces for use in other projects. Since the kimonos come in bales, the minimum order is fairly high. This would be a good time to divide among several friends.

Various discounts are given with a minimum order of $5,000.00.

Send for ordering information and slides or samples of fabrics.

THE KITE SITE

3101 M Street, N.W.
Georgetown, DC 20007
(202) 965-4230

Mail Order; V/MC/AMEX

THE KITE SITE carries many kite-making supplies that will also be of interest to the fiber artist. Rip-Stop Nylons (or parachute fabrics), probably the most durable fabrics available, are offered in two weights. This fabric is 41 inches wide, and comes in nine colors. This company also carries the popular polyester film by DuPont known as Mylar. It is transparent, extremely lightweight, and is very strong. Mylar cannot be sewn; it tends to "run" when punctured. Tape is the best means of fastening it. The Mylar is available in five colors. The Kite Site is also a source for those structural items that you sometimes need when making banners, space sails, kites, etc.: hardwood dowels, aluminum tubing, Fiberglass rod, tubular Graphlex, tubular Fiberglass, bamboo, rattan, polycarbonate tubing, and vinyl tubing. Other supplies, such as tapes, ribbons, and books are available.

Send for a current price list.

KOSIMA SILK COMPANY

RR #4, Box 783
Bloomfield, IN 47424
(812) 825-7519

Mail Order; V/MC; Established in 1982

KOSIMA SILK COMANY, operated by Kathleen Kempter, President, offers excellent quality silk fabrics at competitive prices. The silks have been imported directly from China, and include silk habotais in two weights (36 inches wide), silk satin in black and white (36 inches wide), and silk crepe de chine in two weights (36 inches wide). Ms. Kempter says that she is interested in expanding her selection of silk textiles to further meet the needs of individual craftspeople, and welcomes your interest and comments.

Various discounts are given; check price list for details.

Send for a price list and specific samples.

LAS MANOS

Box 515
Lower Labe, CA 95457
(707) 994-0461

Manufacturer, Mail Order, Retail
Shop; Established in 1975

LAS MANOS can supply handwoven cottons from Guatemala, as well as other items.

Various discounts are given; write for details.

Send $2.00 for samples and a current price list.

A. R. LAWRENCE & ASSOCIATES

Asian Textiles Division
P.O. Box 4096
Fullerton, CA 92634
(714) 525-7069

Mail Order; Established in 1970

A. R. LAWRENCE & ASSOCIATES offers 100% silk fabrics such as crepe de chines, pongees, taffetas, habotais, Fuji broadcloths, and shantungs. They also provide Indian tussahs and cotton greige goods.

Wholesale discounts are given "as appropriate"; write for details.

Send for samples of specific fabrics and prices — no catalog is available.

PERLIAN PRODUCTS, INC.

P.O. Box 3
Terryville, CT 06786-0003
(203) 583-5292

Mail Order; Established in 1981

PERLIAN PRODUCTS, INC. offers cloth strips which can be used for knitting, crocheting, weaving, braiding, etc. The strips come in various widths, lengths, colors, fibers, etc., and are different with each shipment.

Various discounts are given; check price list for information.

Send $1.00 for samples and a price list (refundable with coupon in brochure).

SERICA IMPORTS

P.O. Box 711
Cambridge, MA 02139
(617) 547-3163

Mail Order; Established in 1982

SERICA IMPORTS can supply high quality European silks from France and Italy. They have ribbon chiffons, jacquard weaves, georgettes, crepe de chines, and taffetas in both prints and solid colors.

Quantity discounts are available with a minimum order of ten yards.

Send $3.00 for a current price list and samples.

SEW WHAT FABRICS

2431 Eastern Avenue, S.E.
Grand Rapids, MI 49507
(616) 245-0834

Mail Order, Retail Shop; V/MC;
Established in 1979

SEW WHAT FABRICS offers a line of natural fiber fabrics and yarns.

A price list and complete set of swatches is available for $10.00 (applicable to your first order).

M. SIEGEL COMPANY, INC.

120 Pond Street
Ashland, MA 01721
(617) 881-5200

Mail Order, Retail Shop;
Established in 1918

M. SIEGEL COMPANY, INC. is a family-operated business that specializes in leathers and leathermaking supplies. They offer various luxury leathers such as deerskin, deersuede, elk, goatskin, calfskin, lambskin, and several types of suedes. Also available are a large number of tools and other supplies used to work with leather. Dyes, paints, and waxes are also offered.

Send $2.00 for a current catalog.

SPECIAL SERVICES SHELTERED WORKSHOP

One Blue Street
Romney, WV 26757
(304) 822-7062

Manufacturer, Mail Order, Retail Shop; Established in 1981

SPECIAL SERVICES SHELTERED WORKSHOP is a private, non-profit organization that provides work adjustment training, evaluation, job placement, and extended employment for the handicapped. They offer strips of fabrics wound into balls which can be used for weaving rugs, placemats, etc. The Workshop also offers custom work and tours of their facilities.

Discounts are given with a minumum order of $25.00 on balls of fabric.

Send for a free brochure.

SUREWAY TRADING ENTERPRISES

826 Pine Avenue, Suite 212
Niagara Falls, NY 14301
(716) 282-4887

Mail Order; Established in 1980

SUREWAY TRADING ENTERPRISES sells pure silk fabrics, scarves, yarns and threads. They even claim to "have the largest collection of silk fabrics and scarves" available. Also offered are other accessories used for painting on silk (French dyes).

Wholesale discounts are given with a minimum order of $100.00.

Send for a free catalog.

TESTFABRICS, INC.

P.O. Drawer O
Middlesex, NJ 08846
(201) 469-6446

Manufacturer, Mail Order; V/MC; Established in 1952

TESTFABRICS, INC. is a well-known supplier of fabrics which are scoured and prepared for dyeing, printing, painting, etc. With over 60 different types of fabrics, this company also probably has the largest selection of dyeable fabrics. These fabrics include 100% cotton print cloths, sheetings, poplins, broadcloths, terry cloths, flannels, ducks, sateens, lawns, batiste, Supercale, twills, velveteen, tubular T-shirt cottons, cotton knits, etc. Other types of fabrics include viscose satins, taffetas, challis, linens in various widths, silks (nine different types), wools, etc. Also offered are placemats, napkins, huck towels, aprons, tablecloths, and scarves which are ready to be dyed.

Many quantity discounts are given; check price list for details.

Send for a free price list; fabric sample books are $8.00, or $6.50 with a fabric order. You can trust this company — all of the fabric used in my fiber work in college came from here!

THAI SILKS

252 State Street
Los Altos, CA 94022
(415) 948-8611

Mail Order, Retail Shop; V/MC;
Established in 1964

THAI SILKS offers a selection of over 1,000 different silk fabrics, both prints and solids. These include jacquard crepe de chines, dress and blouse weight silks, shantung, raw silks from India and China, crepe back silk satin, silk brocades, pongees, organza, silk broadcloths, and many, many more. Also available are ready-made scarves, blouses, etc. suitable for handpainting or batik. Upholstery and drapery weight silks are also available.

Wholesale and other discounts are given; check price list for details.

Send 35¢ for a current brochure; includes prices of various samples.

 FIREPROOFING SOLUTION FOR FABRICS OR YARNS

7 oz. borax
3 oz. boric acid
2 qts. hot water

1. Dissolve boric acid by making a paste with a little water.
   Add the borax and remaining water and stir until clear.

2. Dip, spray, or sprinkle fabric or yarn with solution.

   Test on a small sample.

VANETTA FABRICS CORP.

1440 Broadway
New York, NY 10018
(212) 840-8295

Manufacturer, Mail Order;
Established in 1923

VANETTA FABRICS CORPORATION carries Vanvel 100% cotton velveteen fabric in 45-inch widths which is already prepared for batik, handpainting, dyeing, etc. The fabrics are available in both white or off-white shades, and can also be used for clothing or home furnishings. Vanetta says that they are the only source for this special fabric, and that they will grant "30 days net" terms to all. Current price of the fabric is $5.90 per yard.

All prices are wholesale.

No catalog is available; either call or write to place your order or check on prices.

THE VERMONT COUNTRY STORE

Weston, VT 05161
(802) 824-3186

Mail Order, Retail Store; V/MC;
Established in 1945

THE VERMONT COUNTRY STORE catalog features many useful items, including old-fashioned cotton yard goods. Some of these are cotton flannels, diaper cloths, combed cotton sateens, cotton floursack towels, calicoes, cheesecloths, plisse, Turkish toweling, Osnaburg cloth, batiste, and many others. The catalog is a delight to look through — just like a visit to an old general store.

Discounts are given on whole bolts of fabric; write for details.

Send for a current catalog.

VETERAN LEATHER
COMPANY

204 25th Street
Brooklyn, NY 11232
(212) 768-0300

Manufacturer, Mail Order, Retail
Shop; V/MC; Established in 1949

VETERAN LEATHER COMPANY carries a complete line of leather lacings, including suede lacings, latigo lacings, rawhide thongs, round lacings, calf and goat lacings.

Discounts are given with a minimum order of $25.00.

Send $2.00 for a current catalog (applicable to first order).

CHAPTER 4

Dyes
Surface Design Suppliers
and Equipment

Surface design, as defined by The Surface Design Association, is "the coloring/patterning of fabric and fiber with dyes, pigments, or manipulation." The area of surface design, then, can cover such diverse techniques as batik, tie-dye, handpainting, dyeing (natural and synthetic), silkscreen, xerography on fabric, blueprinting, block printing, marbling, Japanese paste-resist methods, color discharge (bleaching), airbrush on fabrics, rubberstamping, stenciling, and many others.

Chapter Four lists sources for many different types and brands of synthetic dyes, natural dye plants and extracts, mordants and other dye assistants, beeswax, tjantings, thousands of rubber stamps, textile inks, untreated fabrics suitable for dyeing, marbling supplies, materials for paste-resists, fabric pigments, wood blocks, squeegees, screens, and other screen printing supplies, and many more — everything you will need for your surface design projects.

ALJO MANUFACTURING COMPANY

450 Greenwich Street
New York, NY 10013
(212) 966-4046 or
(212) 226-2878

Manufacturer, Mail Order, Retail Shop; Established in 1917

ALJO carries direct dyes for cotton and rayon, acid dyes for silk and wool, basic alcohol/water dyes used in hand painting on silk, fiber reactive cold process dyes, and disperse type acetate-nylon dyes. They also handle other supplies for dyeing such as pure beeswax, hydrosulphite, washing soda, urea, thickener, and tjanting tools. NOTE: These dyes are aniline dyes, and when used improperly can be hazardous to your health. All dyes are packaged in ½ ounce, four-ounce, eight-ounce, and one-pound sizes, and come in a wide range of colors. Technical questions are answered cordially, and advice and referrals are given as needed.

Quantity discounts are given with a ten pound minimum (per color) order.

Price lists and information are free.

 WHAT IS "CUTCH"?

Cutch, also known as catechu, is an extract from the heartwood of an East Indian Acacia plant.

ALL NIGHT MEDIA, INC.

P.O. Box 227
Forest Knolls, CA 94933
(415) 488-4963

Manufacturer, Mail Order;
Established in 1975

ALL NIGHT MEDIA, INC. carries over 300 rubber stamps, all made from original art designs. Many humorous animal designs are available, as are fantasy stamps, star, clouds, and moon stamps, food and music stamps, romance, communications, monster stamps, and a line of personalized rubber stamps with name or message included. Accessories include mahogany cases to hold your stamp collection, a booklet called "101 Ways to Stamp Your Art Out," colored papers and brush-tip markers, roll-on inks in ten colors, and inkpads. Custom made stamps are available, as are gift certificates.

A catalog is $2.00 (refundable on first order).

ANTEC, INC.

721 Bergman Avenue
Louisville, KY 40203
(502) 636-5176

Mail Order, Retail Shop;
Established in 1969

ANTEC, INC. is a source for chemicals, glassware, waxes, dyes, acids, bases, metal salts, and solvents used in various forms of fiber work. They also offer special chemical mixtures to your specifications.

Quantity discounts are available.

No catalog is available at this time; write with specific requests.

APPLE ROOM

P.O. Box 26881
Los Angeles, CA 90026
(213) 484-6380

Mail Order; Established in 1969

APPLE ROOM carries Ciba Vat Dyes in 12 colors and in four and eight-ounce bottles, and Inko Dyes in 14 colors in four-ounce bottles. They also handle other supplies for surface design such as tjantings, brushes, waxes, untreated cotton fabrics, caustic soda and sodium hydrosulphite.

Send a large SASE for a free brochure with color samples.

BASIC CRAFTS COMPANY

1201 Broadway
New York, NY 10001
(212) 679-3516

BASIC CRAFTS COMPANY, a division of School Products, Inc., offers a basic kit for marbling on paper (can also be used on fabrics), and individual marbling supplies — coloring agents, caragheen moss, gum tragacanth, prepared ox-gall, alum, and others.

Send for the Basic Crafts Company Bookbinding Catalog.

BATIK & WEAVING SUPPLIER

102 Massachusetts Avenue
Arlington, MA 02174
(617) 646-4453

Retail, Mail Order; V/MC;
Established in 1977

BATIK & WEAVING SUPPLIER handles a full line of supplies for both dyeing and weaving. For dyeing, they carry Deka Series "L" Textile Dyes, Deka Permanent Color dyes for direct application to fabric, Cushing All-Fiber Dyes, Procion Dyes, sodium alginate, urea, washing soda, salt, Princefix dyes for painting on silks and wools, gutta resists, natural dyestuffs (madder, logwood, cochineal, brazilwood, indigo, etc.), as well as the mordants needed for these. They also offer fabrics, waxes, various brushes and tjantings, and protective gear to be worn while using these dyes.

Individual discounts are given by ordering a minimum amount over a six-month period. Write for details.

Send 50¢ for a current catalog, which also includes detailed instructions for using the various dyes that the company carries.

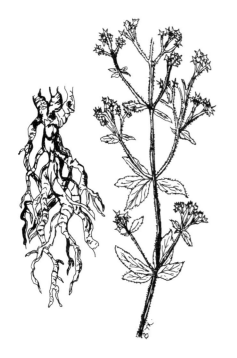

Madder root and plant

BECK'S WARP 'N WEAVE & NEEDLECRAFTS

2815 34th Street
Lubbock, TX 79410
(806) 799-0151

Mail Order, Retail Shop; V/MC;
Established in 1976

BECK'S carries a variety of supplies used in surface design: tjantings, beeswax, microcrystalline wax, unsized fabrics, Cibacron F fiber reactive dyes, Kiton Acid dyes, thickener mix, washing soda and spectralite. Beck's natural dyes include brazilwood chips, cochineal, madder root, natural indigo, alkanet root, and others. Mordants such as copper, chrome, tin, alum and iron are also offered.

Quantity discounts are given; check catalog for details.

Send $1.00 for a current catalog (also includes lots of weaving and other fiber supplies).

BIZZARO RUBBER STAMPS

P.O. Box 126, Annex Station
Providence, RI 02901
(401) 521-1305

Manufacturer, Mail Order; V/MC;
Established in 1969

BIZZARO RUBBER STAMPS is owned by a husband and wife team, the Speisers, whose mail order company was a leading force behind the birth of the "mail art" movement in this country about fifteen years ago. With over 450 creative rubber stamp images (airplanes to zebras) and over 60 different subjects to choose from, there is something to please everyone. Fiber artists will especially love the quilt block design stamps, and the bunnies and the farm animals stamp sets. Bizzaro's designs rely heavily on reproduction designs from the 20's and 30's, but they also have many contemporary stamps. The Bizzaro Catalog also includes over eight pages of accessories, including Deka Permanent Fabric Paints and Deka-Iron on Transfer Paints for fabrics. Other supplies include inks, storage bottles, cleaners and thinners, markers and brushes, erasers and carving knives for making your own stamps, and embossing powder for making metallic images. Various books on rubber stamping are also available.

Wholesale prices are given to qualified buyers with a $100.00 minimum order. Write for more information. A 10% discount is given to schools and other groups with a $30.00 minimum order.

The Bizzaro Catalog is only $1.00, and worth every penny! (Besides, it's refundable with the first order).

Books offered by Bizzaro Rubber Stamps

DICK BLICK

P.O. Box 1267
Galesburg, IL 61401
1-(800) 447-8192

Manufacturer, Mail Order, V/MC

DICK BLICK, an all-around art and craft supplier, also offers a line of supplies for surface design techniques. These include marbling supplies (carragheen moss and preservative, ox-gall, alum, gum tragacanth, etc.), Putnam fiber-reactive cold-water dyes, thickener mix, tjantings, wax melter kits, beeswax, Magik Batik, unbleached muslin, Deka Permanent Fabric Paints and Iron-On Transfer Paints, Dylon Fabric Paints, Versatex Textile Paints, and others.

Send for a current catalog.

BRAND X RUBBER STAMP COMPANY

P.O. Box 6052
Newburyport, MA 01950

Manufacturer, Mail Order;
Established in 1983

Almost all of the BRAND X images are drawn by the owner or friends. These include a flock of tiny sheep, walking fruits and vegetables, pigs dressed in clothes, conversation clouds, and more. They also carry various inks.

Quantity discounts are available; write for more information.

Send $1.00 for a current catalog.

CERULEAN BLUE, LTD.

P.O. Box 21168
Seattle, WA 98111
(206) 625-9647

Mail Order, Retail Shop; V/MC;
Established in 1971

CERULEAN BLUE is probably the most popular supplier for textile and fiber artists. And it's really no wonder — they have the most comprehensive catalog of fiber supplies available anywhere. Their inventory includes Procion M-Series Fiber-Reactive dyes, sodium carbonate, Ciba Vat Dyes, sodium hydroxide, sodium hydrosulfite, Deka Series "L" dyes, resists (beeswax, microcrystalline wax, paraffin, Japanese Nori paste, cassava paste, resist bien), tools for batik, individual ingredients for paste resists, katazome (Japanese stencil dyeing) supplies, brushes, bound resist supplies (for tie-dye, shibori and plangi), starter kits, synthrapol, Inkodyes, disperse dyes for synthetics, Ciba Kiton acid dyes and Cibalon Premetallized dyes, chemicals for printing and painting, fabrics (cottons, linens, silks), glauber's salt, natural dyes (indigo, alkanet, brazilwood chips, cochineal, cutch, henna, madder, weld, etc.), mordants, supplies for discharge-bleaching, workroom and safety equipment, photo printing supplies, and books. Expert technical advice is also offered on all products.

An in-depth educational catalog is $3.25 — includes health and safety tips, periodic "Blue-News" updates with new products, price changes, gallery information, etc.

 WHAT IS COCHINEAL"?

Cochineal is a red dyestuff consisting of the dried, pulverized bodies of certain female scale insects (Dactylopius coccus), cactus-eating insects native to tropical and subtropical America.

The insects are carefully brushed from the cactus into bags and then killed by immersion in hot water or by exposure to steam or heat. The bodies are then dried further and pulverized.

It takes 70,000 cochineal bugs to make one pound of cochineal dye!

CLOTHWORKS

132 Powell Street
Vancouver, BC
Canada V6A 1G1
(604) 669-0127

Manufacturer, Mail Order, Retail
Shop; Established in 1980

Besides being a source for cotton fabrics, CLOTHWORKS also manufactures several textile dyes of their own. The Palomar Dyes/Alpha Series can be used for handpainting and silkscreen. These are brilliant hot water dyes, excellent for wools, nylons and silks. The Polyfab Textile Dye can also be used for silkscreen and handpainting as well as airbrush work. These dyes are water based and heat cured, and can be used on cottons, linens, silks, and synthetics. They are available in 11 different colors.

Various discounts are given; write for information.

Send for a free brochure and price list.

COLOR CRAFT, LTD.

P.O. Box 936
Avon, CT 06001
(203) 282-0020

Manufacturer, Mail Order; V/MC;
Established in 1980

COLOR CRAFT, LTD. manufactures Createx dyes and pigments for fabrics and other materials. The Createx Poster/Fabric Colors are non-toxic, water-based, heat-set pigments that can be used on all fibers — even papers, reeds and cane. Uses for these can include handpainting, silkscreening, stamping, stenciling, airbrushing, warp painting, batik, paper pulp colorant, etc. These are available in 16 colors, and can be mixed. The Createx Liquid Fiber Reactive Dyes can be used on silk, wool, cotton, rayon, nylon, leather, hemp, and other natural fibers. These dyes are washfast, lightfast, and are safer to use than some powders. It is recommended that these dyes be steam set, but ironing, baking, hot-air drying, or air curing can also be used. Color Craft also supplies two types of resists — one to be used with immersion dye baths, and the other to be used with handpainting. Both can be removed by washing. Additives needed for the liquid dyes are also available from this source: urea, Kelgin XL, baking soda, soda ash, water softeners, Fiber Prep SW (a special detergent for degumming silks and removing oils, waxes, dirts, etc. from fibers), TSP, citric acid, etc. The company also carries three types of pigments: Transparent, Opaque Metallic, and Opaque Hi-Lite Colors. Other supplies are also available.

School and group discounts are given with a minimum order of $15.00.

Send for a free catalog and price list.

COUNTRY HERBS

Maple Street
Stockbridge, MA 01262
(413) 298-3054

Manufacturer, Mail Order, Retail
Shop; V/MC; Established in 1977

COUNTRY HERBS carries a wide variety of mordants and natural dyes and several books on natural plant dyeing. In addition to these, they also stock other assorted fiber supplies, such as Romney fleece, spinning tools, wool yarns, etc. The company also has a large inventory of ingredients for potpourris and many herbs, but they say that their specialty is dye plants and dried dye botanicals.

School and group discounts are given; write for details.

The Country Herbs catalog is free; send a SASE for fleece samples and a list of available plant varieties.

CREEK WATER WOOL
WORKS

P.O. Box 716
Salem, OR 97308
(503) 585-3302

Mail Order; V/MC; Established in
1979

In addition to a large number of weaving and spinning supplies, CREEK WATER WOOL WORKS also offers a complete line of natural dyes and mordants. These include exotic wood dyes by Heidi Drudik (require no mordant), fustic, logwood, osage orange, brazilwood, cutch, quebracho, sumac, madder, indigo (natural and synthetic), henna, cochineal, cocabola shavings and black walnut hulls. Mordants include copper, chrome, iron, alum, tin, cream of tartar and others. Thickeners, sizings, and dye assistants are also offered.

Bulk discounts are given on all dyes and mordants. Check catalog for prices.

Send for a free catalog.

W. CUSHING & COMPANY

P.O. Box 351 (North Street)
Kennebunkport, ME 04046
(207) 967-3711

Manufacturer, Mail Order, Retail
Shop; Established in 1879

W. CUSHING & COMPANY manufactures the ordinary type Cushing's Perfection Dyes in 83 shades for use on cottons, silks, and wools, and the all-fiber type dyes in 38 shades. They even package and privately label some of their dyes for use by the Navajo Indians in their rug weavings. Cushing also designs and sells patterns and supplies for rug hooking.

Various discounts are given; write for information.

Send $1.00 for a brochure and Dye Color Card (refundable with $10.00 minimum order).

DECORATIVE PAPERS

P.O. Box 281
Eastford, CT 06242
(203) 974-1185

Manufacturer, Mail Order;
Established in 1981

Faith Harrison, owner of DECORATIVE PAPERS, works in traditional marbled papers. She is also a source for marbling supplies, all of which can be used on fabric. These include: stoneground water-based inks in 14 colors, alum, ox-gall, carrageenan, rakes, wood troughs with skim boards, marbling kits, and a book titled *The Process of Marbling* by Kantrowitz and Spencer. And if you are interested in buying marbled paper for use in other projects, Faith offers a sample book of her marbled papers, all of which are for sale.

Some discounts are given; write for details.

Send for a free list of marbling supplies; a marbled paper sample book is $4.50.

EARTH GUILD

One Tingle Alley
Asheville, NC 28801
(704) 255-7818

Manufacturer, Mail Order, Retail
Shop; V/MC; Established in 1970

EARTH GUILD carries a large number of fiber supplies, including many used in surface design techniques. These include Procion-MX dyes in 16 shades, washing soda, urea, sodium alginate, batik waxes, tjantings, Deka Series L Dyes in 19 colors and Deka Permanent Fabric Paints in 14 colors. Earth Guild also sells a wide variety of natural dyes and mordants. Some of these include alkanet root, brazilwood chips, cutch extract, henna powder, cochineal, alum, cream of tartar, copperas, tin and others.

Quantity discounts are given; check catalog for details.

Send $1.00 for a complete catalog.

ELBOW GREASE

P.O. Box 25056
Richmond, VA 23260

Manufacturer, Mail Order;
Established in 1982

The ELBOW GREASE catalog of rubber stamps contains over 75 designs. ALL of the stamps are unique, and include such images as a "Man With No Dream But a Great Haircut" stamp, a Joan Crawford stamp, a Bette Midler stamp, and a three-dimensional raindrop stamp. The company also carries a set of wonderful "Rubber Architecture" stamps which could be used to make a great "town and city" quilt.

Quantity discounts are given to individuals with a minimum order of $150.00.

The Elbow Grease "Rubber Harvest" Catalog is $1.00, and is applied to your first order.

ELEGANT IMPRESSIONS

P.O. Box 2449
Livermore, CA 94550

ELEGANT IMPRESSIONS features polymer stamps on clear acrylic bases, designed by such fiber artists as Wilcke Smith, Jean Ray Laury, Charlotte Patera, Robbie Fanning, and others. The stamp catalog includes over 600 designs, instructions, and hints for stamping on textiles.

Send $3.00 for a current copy.

 ICI SAFETY PRECAUTIONS

While Procion dyes and the chemicals associated with their use are not highly toxic, they are industrial chemicals and should be handled with care. As a general practice, chemical products should not be allowed to get into the eyes, but if they should by accident, wash the eyes thoroughly with clean water and then obtain medical treatment.

Prolonged or repeated contact with the skin should be avoided. Wear rubber gloves and use implements to stir solutions and dyebaths.

Obviously, chemicals should not be taken internally, and the use of food, drink, and smoking materials should be prohibited where chemicals are employed.

The utensils used for dyeing should not be used for other domestic purposes.

Avoid the inhalation of dusts by working in well ventilated areas and careful handling of powders.

Reactive dyes, of which Procion dyes are one type, are reactive chemicals, and occasional cases of respiratory allergy have occurred among persons who have inhaled dust under industrial conditions over a prolonged period of time. Procion dyes are treated so as to minimize the formation of dust. Inhalation of this dust should be avoided. If dyes are handled in circumstances where particles may become airborne, a suitable dust respirator should be worn.

Safety tips from the FabDec catalog

FABDEC

3553 Old Post Road
San Angelo, TX 76904
(915) 944-1031

Mail Order; V/MC; Established in 1967

FABDEC was founded in 1967 by the late Meda Parker Johnston, co-author of *Design on Fabrics*. Her daughter, Dickie Ferro, took over the business in 1973, and has taken a personal interest in her customers' success as dyers and fiber artists. The FabDec catalog includes such supplies as a Procion Fiber Reactive Dye and Chemicals Kit, Procion "M" and "H" Series Dye Colors, sodium alginate, urea, washing soda, jars, tjantings, natural beeswax, brushes, fabrics and paper for dyeing. The book, *Design on Fabrics,* is also available from this company.

A discount is given on bulk purchases; check catalog for details.

Send $1.00 for a current catalog, which also includes detailed instructions and formulas for using Procion dyes in various ways. Instructions are also given for making an improvised steamer for fabrics.

FAIRFAX RUBBER STAMP COMPANY

P.O. Box 127
Fairfax, CA 94930
(415) 456-8767

Mail Order; Established in 1976

FAIRFAX has a somewhat limited number of rubber stamp images to choose from, compared to some of the other companies. However, it would be worth the money for the catalog just to see the set of stamps which feature Egyptian images. Another interesting set includes beautiful orchids, roses, and hibiscus stamps. Fairfax also has a set of "Animal ABC's," and a border set made of trellis design stamps which could be very striking used on fabric.

The Fairfax catalog is $2.00.

FLYNNS

P.O. Box 11304
San Francisco, CA 94101
(415) 621-5968

Manufacturer, Mail Order; V/MC;
Established in 1980

FLYNNS carries their own brand of cotton dyes (fiber reactive), which can also be used for dyeing rayon and linens. These dyes are offered in 50 shades, and are packed in two ounce bags or one, five, and 25-pound drums. Other supplies available include soda ash, fabric softener, water softener, fixative, color remover and thickener mix. Individual ingredients for making thickeners are also offered. Flynns also supplies a Color Easy All-Purpose Hot Water Dye, which dyes nylon, wool, silk, cotton, linen and rayon in three easy steps. Deka Permanent Fabric Paints and Deka Print Silkscreen Inks are also available.

Quantity discounts are offered; check catalog for details.

A price list is free; color charts of dyes and paints are also available upon request.

FUNNY BUSINESS, INC.

2129 Second Avenue
Seattle, WA 98121
(206) 623-7842

Manufacturer, Mail Order; V/MC;
Established in 1979

FUNNY BUSINESS, INC. carries over 250 rubber stamps in their new catalog. Some of the designs include animals, dinosaurs and birds, as well as a nice variety of fantasy designs. The usual group of "Editorial" stamps is offered, as are markers and ink pads. Some of the more unusual designs that the company carries are based on Oriental designs, and should be of interest to the fiber artist.

Wholesale discounts are given to qualified buyers; write for information. Schools and other groups are given a 20% discount on their first order of $100.00, and subsequent orders of $50.00 (wholesale prices).

A catalog is $2.00, and is applicable to the first order.

GOOD IMPRESSIONS RUBBER STAMPS

1122 Avery Street
Parkersburg, WV 26101
(304) 422-1147

Manufacturer, Mail Order;
Established in 1982

Dale Michels of GOOD IMPRESSIONS says that his home-based business was founded on a "love of the Victorian aesthetic," and that "rubber stamps are his way of sharing his love of Victoriana with anyone." His catalog, which is a good source of decorative Victorian rubber stamps, contains designs such as old buildings, Victorian borders, silhouette stamps, alphabet stamps in several different styles, and many other delightful examples of Victoriana. Helpful hints for using the stamps are included.

Discounts are given to other groups with a minimum order of 20 stamps.

Dale's catalog is $2.00, and is applied to the first order. If you love Victorian images (as I do), you'll want a copy of this wonderful catalog.

G & K CRAFT INDUSTRIES, INC.

P.O. Box 14
Somerset, MA 02726
(616) 676-3838

Wholesale only: Established in 1980

G & K is the wholesale division of PRO Chemical and Dye, Inc., and deals only with retail outlets upon receipt of their state tax number and Federal I.D. number. They offer prompt and efficient service, provide technical assistance when needed, and carry all dyes and supplies for the surface design of fabric, including the fabrics and tools required. G & K claims to be "an excellent source for retail outlets."

Interested retail store owners must send proper identification before a price list and further information will be distributed.

The original centennial celebration quilt by Susan Johnson

 THE STORY OF GRAMMA'S GRAPHICS, INC.

Five years ago, seeking a special 100th birthday gift for her grandmother, Sue Johnson combined her quilting abilities with the old art of blueprinting. The resulting "centennial quilt," made from squares picturing family members and homes from different generations, caused an immediate sensation among her friends and neighbors who also wanted to preserve their family photos in the same way.

The process of printing a photographic negative on fabric, while simple, requires ingredients not commonly available in convenient quantities. To make the quilt, Sue had to purchase ten pounds of each ingredient, even though she only needed 2½ ounces. Realizing that there might be a need for someone to supply smaller quantities of the chemicals, Sue began the mail order distribution of her "Sun Print Kits." With the support and encouragement of her grandmother, Sue's business, Gramma's Graphics, Inc. was born.

GRAMMA'S GRAPHICS, INC.

20-FSB Birling Gap
Fairport, NY 14450
(716) 223-4309

Mail Order; Established in 1980

GRAMMA'S GRAPHICS, owned by Susan Johnson, supplies kits for cyanotype, or blueprinting on fabric. The process is very simple: images are made by contact printing photo negatives on fabric treated with a light sensitive solution. Exposure to the sun, or any source of ultraviolet light, and washing in tap water produces a print in the characteristic colors of blueprints. The prints are permanent and can be washed or dry cleaned. The unconditionally guaranteed Sun Print Kit contains directions plus enough solution to print twenty 9" x 12" squares, or two yards of fabric.

Various discounts are given; write for information.

Send $1.00 and a long SASE for a current brochure and price list.

GRAPHIC CHEMICAL AND INK, CO.

P.O. Box 27
Villa Park, IL 60181
(312) 832-6004

Manufacturer, Mail Order, Retail Shop

GRAPHIC CHEMICAL AND INK, CO. is said to be the world's largest source for printmaking supplies. Although they are primarily an ink manufacturer, the company also carries a large number of other supplies which should interest the surface designer or fiber artist. These include felt blankets, copper, zinc and plastic plates, linoleum blocks, wood blocks, carving tools, water and oil-based inks, a full line of intaglio supplies, Speedball Textile Inks, Naz-Dar Textile Inks, silk-screen frames, photo silk-screen supplies, Ulano films, screen fabrics, safety supplies, miscellaneous supplies, and a complete line of books on all phases of printmaking.

Quantity prices are given on many items; check catalog for prices.

Send for a current catalog.

GREAT ATLANTIC STAMPWORKS

P.O. Box 172
Woods Hole, MA 02543

Mail Order, Established in 1981

GREAT ATLANTIC STAMPWORKS is owned and operated by Caki Herrity and Becky Mountford. Caki says that they started the business to satisfy their greedy desire for stamps, stamps, and more stamps! They live in a small oceanside town on Cape Cod that is known for its internationally famous oceanographic and marine biological institutions, where they both have full-time jobs. Caki goes on to say that they love stamps, but alas, they can't make their living from them. To cater to the local community, they expanded their design line to include various marine life stamps. But because of the tremendous response that they have received from fiber artists, they are adding more textile art-oriented designs such as borders, quilt blocks, Oriental symbols, etc. The current catalog includes such designs as fans, lots of shells, fish, sheep, armadillos, fruit, flowers, Christmas designs, and hundreds more. Alphabet and number sets are also offered, as are stamp pads and markers.

A 20% discount is given with a minimum order of $50.00; schools are offered the same discount with a minimum order of $30.00.

Send $1.50 for a catalog of all designs, or send for a free brochure.

GUMBO GRAPHICS

P.O. Box 606
Midland, MI 48640
(517) 631-9111

Manufacturer, Mail Order, Retail Shop; Established in 1963

David Wiles of GUMBO GRAPHICS collects original artwork from artists all over the world for use on his rubber stamps, and says that he "enjoys talking with high spirited people who create works of art." Artists interested in submitting drawings for consideration should contact David. His catalog contains over 1,500 different images, including humorous stamps, bugs and birds, beasts, animals, dragons, dream images, borders, women, children, lettering stamps, etc. Custom stamps can be ordered, along with stamps from photos, or any images with half-tones. Gumbo also carries the usual accessories, such as stamp pads and inks. Fast service is promised with a two week delivery time.

A 20% discount is given with a $60.00 minimum order.

The Gumbo catalog is $4.00, with a coupon for 10% off enclosed for use with your first order.

HERO ARTS RUBBER STAMPS

P.O. Box 5234
Berkeley, CA 94705
(415) 654-2080

Manufacturer, Mail Order;
Established in 1974

HERO ARTS covers a wide range of designs from cartoons to classics, most of which are from original art designs. Specific images include stamps of bears, cats, music (including a singing mouse), birds, nature stamps, flowers, frogs, travel, "Alice in Stampland," hearts, unicorns and dragons, bookplate designs, Christmas, various messages, and an ornamental alphabet. Gift sets, accessories, and personalized and custom stamps are also available.

A 10% discount is given with a $100.00 minimum order.

Send $2.00 for a delightful catalog; $1.00 is refunded with order.

ILLINOIS BRONZE PAINT COMPANY

300 E. Main Street
Lake Zurich, IL 60047

Manufacturer, Mail Order;
Established in 1980

ILLINOIS BRONZE PAINT COMPANY is a supplier for the Country Colors Fabric Painting Dyes, Country Colors Accent Acrylics, stencils, brushes, kits, etc.

School and group discounts are given with a $200.00 minimum order. Retailers should write for more information.

Send for a current brochure.

IMPRINTS GRAPHIC STUDIO, INC.

225G Cannery Row
Monterey, CA 93940
(408) 373-1565

Manufacturer, Mail Order; V/MC;
Established in 1978

IMPRINTS GRAPHIC STUDIO, INC. guarantees that their Graphistamp images are originals that you will not find reproduced in any other catalog. Imprints' nature series includes designs of a polar bear and cub, a feather, a sand dollar, an eagle, ferns, anemones, trees, a group of penguins, a panda, a sheep, duck and bunny, and many other wonderful, refreshingly-unique stamps. Accessories include stamp pads (metallic and rainbow), marker sets, and collectors boxes.

A 15% discount is given with a $100.00 order.

The catalog is $2.00. If you use rubber stamps in your fiber work, this catalog should be in your collection!

INDIANA BOTANIC GARDENS

P.O. Box 5
Hammond, Indiana 46325
(219) 931-2480

Mail Order, Retail Shop; V/MC;
Established in 1910

The INDIANA BOTANIC GARDENS are the nation's oldest and largest supplier of herbs and herbal products. They carry a large number of botanicals that can be used as natural dyes, including henna, logwood, tumeric, annatoo, butternut, alder, walnut hulls, goldthread, yellow dock, etc.

Send 50¢ for a current catalog.

INKADINKADO, INC.

102 South Street
Boston, MA 02111
(617) 426-3458

Manufacturer, Mail Order; V/MC;
Established in 1981

INKADINKADO, INC. carries almost 1,000 rubber stamps in all. The "Flim Flam Collection" carries unique stamps based on designs from old printers' cuts used to illustrate newspapers. In the regular catalog, you will find the usual images of birds, frogs, lions, pandas, whales, and unicorns. The company also has many unique designs that cannot be found anywhere else.

Wholesale discounts are given; write for information.

Send $3.00 for both the Inkadinkado Catalog and the Flim Flam supplement.

IVY CRAFTS IMPORTS

5410 Annapolis Rd.
Bladensburg, MD 20710
(301) 779-7079

Manufacturer, Mail Order; V/MC;
Established in 1978

IVY CRAFTS IMPORTS is one of the few companies which supply the Sennelier French Colors for painting on silk. In addition to the Tinfix and Super Tinfix Colors, they also carry Tincoton Colors which can be used on cotton, linen and vegetable fibers. Other dyes which the company offers include Tinsilk Colors, Batik Tintout Colors, Polydyes, and Pearlized Texticolor Dyes. A complete line of kits and sets, resists, applicators, fabrics, and steamers are also available through Ivy Imports. The book *Painting on Silk* by Pierre Bruandet is available, as is a booklet, *The Grapevine,* which gives general instructions for using the products.

Various discounts are given to schools, groups, and individuals. Write for details.

Send for a free catalog.

DEKA IRON-ON TRANSFER PAINTS FOR FABRICS can be rubberstamped on to any non-absorbent paper and then ironed on to synthetic fabrics (with up to 40% natural fibers) when dry.

— From the Bizzaro Rubber Stamp catalog

KASURI DYEWORKS

1959 Shattuck Avenue
Berkeley, CA 94704
(415) 841-4509

Mail Order, Retail Shop;
V/MC/AMEX; Established in
1975

KASURI DYEWORKS tries to encourage the preservation of Japanese folk-art traditions by featuring authentic articles from Japan. They offer many items used in Japanese fabric design, including dyestuffs (indigo powder, shibuki, nuka, miyako dyes, etc.), Kasuri supplies, fabrics, basic supplies for paste resist methods, Shibori supplies, Katazome supplies, and Tsutsugaki/Yuken supplies. A number of books, recipes and patterns are also available. Tours and demonstrations of Japanese crafts, fabrics and culture are also offered.

Discounts are given with a $200.00 minimum order.

Send $5.00 for a current catalog (sent in a handmade paper folder, and includes many other ready-made items from Japan).

LUMINOS PHOTO CORPORATION

25 Wolffe Street
Yonkers, NY 10705
(914) 965-4800

Manufacturer; V/MC/AMEX;
Established in 1949

LUMINOS PHOTO CORPORATION manufacturers Photo Linen. This is expensive stuff (approximately $450.00 for a 50 inch x 30 foot roll) but can be used in exciting ways for special photographic effects.

No discounts are given to individuals, and the minimum order is $100.00.

Send for a free brochure and price list.

MAGGET & SON

Rt. 2, Box 58
Courtland, VA 23837
(804) 653-2136

Mail Order, Retail Shop;
Established in 1983

Maggie, owner of MAGGET & SON, offers a line of rubber stamps which include famous faces, trees, houses, a computer, animals, word stamps, 17 quilt block stamps (including a favorite "little house" stamp), a small sheep face and stencil stamps. Maggie says that she uses her rubber stamps in her fiber work and is interested in what others do.

A 20% discount is given on orders over $50.00; all unmounted stamps are 50% off. A coupon is included in each order for $1.00 off on the next order.

A catalog is $2.00 and includes an unmounted sample stamp and two $1.00 off coupons.

NATURE IMPRESSIONS

1007 Leneve Place
El Cerrito, CA 94530
(415) 527-9622

Manufacturer, Mail Order;
Established in 1975

NATURE IMPRESSIONS offers a broad line of nature-image rubber stamps which are deeply etched, making them especially suitable for stamping on fabric. Custom stamps are also available.

Educational discounts are given; write for details.

Send $1.85 for a catalog, and periodic newsletter updates.

---

100 PROOF PRESS

P.O. Box 34F
Eaton, NY 13334
(315) 684-3547

Mail Order; Established in 1980

100 PROOF PRESS offers rubber stamps (both mounted and unmounted) with images of cupids, flowers, trees, people, llamas, sheep, goats, camels, decorative borders, alphabets, holiday stamps, and many more.

Send $1.00 for a catalog (refundable with first order).

PAASCHE AIRBRUSH COMPANY

7440 W. Lawrence Avenue
Harwood Heights, IL 60656
(312) 867-9191

Manufacturer, Mail Order;
Established in 1904

PAASCHE AIRBRUSH COMPANY supplies airbrushes and airbrush kits in various sizes, Paasche Opaque Airbrush Colors (to be used on papers), and a Textile Emulsion Additive which can be added to the colors for use on fabrics. Air compressors, books, and other accessories are also available.

Discounts are given only to qualified retailers; write for information.

Send for a free catalog. Write for the name of the nearest mail-order dealer.

PHOTOGRAPHER'S FORMULARY

P.O. Box 5105
Missoula, MT 59806
(406) 543-4534

Manufacturer, Mail Order;
V/MC/AMEX; Established in
1977

PHOTOGRAPHER'S FORMULARY states that no order is too small for them. They carry all photographic chemicals and supplies (over 400 in all) and labware such as thermometers, graduated cylinders, beakers, and storage bottles. Of interest to surface designers is the fact that the company sells kits for alternative printing processes, such as palladium printing, kallitype printing, brownprinting, blueprinting, and others. Weavers and dyers will be amazed at the number of chemicals that this company carries that will be useful to them as well.

No discounts are given to individuals.

Send for a free catalog.

 WHAT IS "FUSTIC"?

Fustic is the wood from a tropical American tree of the mulberry family that yields a yellow dye.

POLYPRODUCTS CORPORATION

P.O. Box 42
Roseville, MI 48066
(313) 774-2500

Manufacturer, Mail Order; V/MC;
Established in 1970

POLYPRODUCTS CORPORATION manufacturers Magik Batik Resist, a type of resist product in a squirt bottle that hardens when subjected to a hot dye bath. Upon cooling, the resist reverts back into liquid form, and is completely soluble in cold water.

Send for a free brochure.

PRO CHEMICAL & DYE, INC.

P.O. Box 14
Somerset, MA 02726
(617) 676-3838

Mail Order; Established in 1972

PRO CHEMICAL & DYE, INC. is said to be the primary supply source for anyone who works in surface design and other fiber arts. They offer a large number of dyes, including the Procion MX Cold Water reactive dye in 29 shades, Cibacron F reactive dyes, Liquid Reactive Dyes, Procion H Dyes, Ciba Kiton Level Acid dyes, PRO Washfast Acid dyes, PROsperse Disperse Dyes, PROfab Textile Inks and concentrates. A full line of chemicals and auxiliaries used in fabric dyeing are also available. Some of these include acetic acid, ammonium sulfate, glauber salt, metaphos (the pure form of "Calgon"), muriatic acid, print paste mixes, synthrapol SP, PRO thickeners, urea, wool assistant SBS, and more. Other supplies include waxes, workroom equipment, tjantings for batik, 3M-Brand dust respirators, and 100% cotton fabrics suitable for dyeing. PRO offers special services, including general technical assistance, color matching, laboratory bulk dyeing, fastness testing, lectures, seminars, and private consultation.

Bulk discounts are given; check price list for details. Retailers should see entry "G & K Craft Industries, Ltd."

Send for a free catalog, price list and shade card.

PUTNAM COLOR & DYE CORPORATION

P.O. Box 1267
Galesburg, IL 61401
(309) 342-9779, ext. 259

Manufacturer, Mail Order

PUTNAM offers colorfast cold water dyes in 15 colors. These dyes are a combination of fiber-reactive dyes and fixatives, all in one package. Putnam Dyes can be used on cotton, linen, wool, silk and viscose rayons. This company also offers a line of batik and screen printing materials, such as tjantings, stretcher frames, waxes, thickeners, printing screens, squeegees and unbleached muslin.

Send for a current brochure and price list.

PYLAM PRODUCTS COMPANY, INC.

1001 Stewart Avenue
Garden City, NY 11530
(516) 222-1750

Manufacturer, Mail Order;
Established in 1918

PYLAM PRODUCTS offers a complete line of commercially available dyes from all over the world. Hundreds of dyes are listed in their catalog, although you almost need to be a chemist to figure out which ones they are!

The minimum order for any dye is one pound, and the minimum invoice is $50.00 (probably worth the trouble if you need a lot of dye).

Send for a current catalog.

 WHAT IS "QUEBRACHO"?

Quebracho is a hardwood tree from the sumac family found most often in Chili and Argentina. The tannin-rich extract from the dense wood of the tree is often used in tanning leather and in natural dyeing.

QUARTER MOON RUBBER STAMPS

P.O. Box 2089
Santa Clara, CA 95055
(408) 984-2765

Manufacturer, Mail Order; V/MC;
Established in 1983

QUARTER MOON RUBBER STAMPS, owned by Donnie Evert, offers many original stamp designs plus over 400 other designs suitable for printing on fabric. Some of the images include cats, rabbits, bears, sheep, borders, people, ethnic designs, alphabets, and many others. Stamp pads and inks are also offered.

Wholesale prices are given on some stamps with a $100.00 opening order and a $50.00 reorder.

And $1.50 for a complete catalog.

RANGER PRODUCTS COMPANY, INC.

15 Park Road
Tinton Falls, NJ 07724
(201) 389-3535

Manufacturer, Mail Order;
Established in 1929

RANGER PRODUCTS, INC. manufactures a large line of inks, including inks for stenciling on wood, paper, plastic, or fabric, non-toxic ink pads in 37 different colors and metallics, and an ink that can be stamped on both natural and synthetic fabrics.

School or group discounts are given with a minimum order of $150.00.

Send for a free brochure.

ROCKLAND COLLOID CORPORATION

302 Piermont Avenue
Piermont, NY 10968
(914) 359-5559

Manufacturer, Mail Order; V/MC;
Established in 1970

ROCKLAND COLLOID CORP. claims to be the only supplier of photographic emulsion and fabric sensitizers. These can be used to make photo-silkscreens or to produce photographic images directly on fabric. The directions seem fairly easy, and there are not a lot of chemicals to mix.

Quantity discounts are given with orders over $200.00.

Write for a free brochure and price list.

RUBBER STAMPS OF AMERICA

Box 67
Saxtons River, VT 05154
(802) 869-2622

Manufacturer, Mail Order, Retail Shop; V/MC; Established in 1979

RUBBER STAMPS OF AMERICA has over 600 images in their new catalog, and are coming up with new ones every day. Of special interest to fiber artists/stampers is a set of 20 quilt block stamps and lots of nature and animal images, including several stamps of fiber-producing animals, such as sheep, llamas, camels, etc. Custom stamps are also available from camera-ready, black and white artwork.

A 10% discount is given to schools and other groups.

Send $1.50 for a catalog, which also includes several free brochures.

Bridal Wreath
Joseph's Coat
Devil's Claws
Milky Way

RUBBERSTAMPEDE

P.O. Box 1105
Berkeley, CA 94701
(415) 843-8910

Manufacturer, Mail Order; V/MC;
Established in 1977

RUBBERSTAMPEDE offers a wonderful catalog filled with a unique line of rubber stamps. These include cats, bears, rabbits, sheep, dragons, florals, quilt blocks, a penguin party, word stamps, and many more. Also available are books, art pens, storage systems, ink pads and inks.

A 10% discount is given to schools, groups, etc. with a minimum order of $100.00. Free stamps are included in individual orders over $30.00.

Send for a free catalog — It's worth it just to see the "Penguin In Cognito" stamp!

RUMPLESTILSKEINS

12018 Queens Place
Huntsville, AL 35803
(205) 883-9034

Mail Order, Retail Hours by appointment; Established in 1981

RUMPLESTILSKEINS carries a wide assortment of natural dyes including alkanet root, brazilwood extract and chips, cochineal, cutch extract, fustic extract, synthetic indigo, logwood chips, madder root, osage orange, yarrow, kamala powder, marigold, and bloodroot. Mordants and other supplies include alum, copper, chrome, iron, tin, oxalic acid, washing soda, tartaric acid, spectrolite, etc. The company also offers Procion and Ciba-Kiton synthetic dyes.

Quantity discounts are given; write for information.

A current price list is free.

RUPERT, GIBBON &
SPIDER

718 College Street
Healdsburg, CA 95448
(707) 433-9577

Manufacturer, Mail Order; V/MC;
Established in 1971

RUPERT, GIBBON & SPIDER carries a large line of Deka products, including Deka Permanent Color Paints, Dekaprint water-base ink for silkscreen, Deka Series L Dyes, Deka Printing Pastes for rubber stamping, linoleum or wood block printing, and Deka Iron-On Transfer Paints. They also supply the French Princefix paints for silks and wools, along with related items such as resists, fixatives, antifusants, brushes, waxes, and books. The company also carries empty felt markers which may be filled with the Princefix dyes for writing or drawing on silk. Fifteen different types of silk fabrics are also offered.

A 20% discount is given on minimum orders of $60.00.

Send for a free catalog.

SAVOIR-FAIRE

P.O. Box 2021
Sausalito, CA 94966
(415) 332-4660

Manufacturer, Mail Order;
Established in 1980

SAVOIR-FAIRE is one of the few distributors of the French dyes used for silk painting. They offer the entire line of Tinfix, Super Tinfix, Tincoton 2, Texticolor, and Tinsilk dyes from the Sennelier Company in France. Other supplies are available, such as regular and colored gutta resists, aqua-gutta resists, silkscreen gutta, and gutta thinners. Savoir-Faire also offers an easy-to-use "Silkit" to help you get started, along with other supplies such as brushes, stretcher frames, and steam ovens to set the dyes. The book *Painting on Silk* is also available from this source.

Quantity discounts are given: 10% off on orders of $100.00-$250.00; 20% off on orders of $251.00-$500.00, etc.

Send $3.00 for a current catalog, which includes color charts of the various dyes.

SCREEN PROCESS SUPPLIES
MANUFACTURING
COMPANY

1199 East 12th Street
Oakland, CA 94606
(415) 451-1048

Manufacturer, Mail Order; V/MC;
Established in 1930's

SCREEN PROCESS SUPPLIES MANUFACTURING COMPANY manufactures a large assortment of screen printing supplies, including "Inko" dyes, which can be used for silkscreening, batik, tie-dyeing, fabric painting, or block printing onto cottons, linens or rayons. The line of supplies available includes silkscreen printing sets, silks and other fabrics for making your own screens, squeegees, drying racks, stencil films, knife sets, resists and blockouts, solvents, supplies for photo stenciling, various inks, Inkodyes in 14 shades, Inkodye Resists, beeswax, cotton fabrics, tjantings, Inko silk dyes in eight colors, Inko-Tex for printing in 16 colors, books, storage containers, and more.

Bulk discounts are given on many items.

An Inko Silkscreen Printing Manual/Catalog is $9.50, and contains detailed information on using all materials, dye sample cards, and much more. An Inkodye Instruction Booklet is 70¢. A general price list is free.

SHERMAN'S

9317 Guadalupe Trail, N.W.
Alameda, NM 87114
(505) 898-2559

Mail Order, Retail Shop;
Established in 1960

SHERMAN'S is a source for chemicals of all types, as well as whole cochineal bugs, and pure powdered indigo extract. Some of the chemicals available include aluminum potassium sulfate (alum), copper sulfate powder, ferrous sulfate, hematoxylin (pure logwood powder), oxalic acid, potassium bitartrate (cream of tartar), chrome, sodium borate (borax), sodium carbonate, hydrosulfite, lye, Glauber's salt, and tin. Sherman's also carries laboratory equipment and supplies. All orders are shipped prepaid U.P.S. with an invoice enclosed.

Quantity discounts are given; write for information.

Send for a free price list.

 NOTE:

Always use proper safety precautions when working with dyes, chemicals, mordants, waxes, etc. Several of the companies listed in this chapter carry safety equipment along with their other supplies. Users of these materials are strongly encouraged to inquire into and learn about recommended safety measures.

SIPHON ART PRODUCTS

74 Hamilton Drive
Ignacio, CA 94947
(415) 883-9006

Manufacturer, Mail Order;
Established in 1972

SIPHON ART PRODUCTS are the manufacturers of Versatex textile paints and airbrush inks, and Dorland's wax medium and textile wax resists. Versatex pigments come in 22 shades, and are permanent and washable when ironed or heat treated.

Various discounts are given; see price list.

Send for a free brochure.

STAMPWORKS RUBBER STAMPS

10006 Linden
Overland Park, KS 66207
(913) 642-7040

Mail Order; Established in 1979

Carol Zastoupil, owner of STAMPWORKS, offers many images which should be of interest to weavers and other fiber artists. These include spinning wheels, looms, spindles, shuttles, various sheep, a camel, cones, hanks and balls of yarn, a bobbin winder, swift and many more. A very unique and useful stamp is also available for stamping your name and address on to slide mounts. Custom stamps are also offered.

Send $2.00 for a current catalog, which also includes tips for rubber stamping on fabric.

 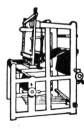

Rubber stamps from Stampworks.

STRAW INTO GOLD, INC.

3006 San Pablo Avenue
Berkeley, CA 94702
(415) 548-5241

Mail Order, Retail Shop; V/MC;
Established in 1971

Alkanet

STRAW INTO GOLD carries the range of Spectrum synthetic dyes, including fiber-reactive dyes for cottons, silks, rayons, and linens (Cibacron F) and reactive dyes for wools and silks (Spectralan). Kiton Wool Dyes (acid-type leveling dyes) are also available. Also offered are a large number of natural dyes and mordants, including extracts of brazilwood, fustic, osage orange, sumac and quebracho, and others such as logwood sawdust, cochineal, madder root, cutch chunks, henna powder, indigo paste (synthetic) and indigo patties (natural). Mordants include alum, tin, iron, and cream of tartar. Pébéo French products for fabric painting are also available: Setacolor (26 shades), Setaskrib (12 shades), and Orient Express paint-on dyes for silk or wool (20 shades). Gutta percha resists are available in silver, gold, black and colorless. Various additives used in dyeing are also available. Straw Into Gold also carries a large number of rubber stamps, most of which feature fiber designs (sheep, looms, etc.).

Send a SASE for a current catalog and price list.

SUREWAY TRADING ENTERPRISES

826 Pine Avenue, Suite 212
Niagara Falls, NY 14301
(716) 282-4887

Mail Order; Established in 1980

SUREWAY TRADING ENTERPRISES can supply all materials needed for handpainting on silks — French dyes, fabrics, books, brushes, etc.

Wholesale discounts are given with a minimum order of $100.00.

Send for a free catalog.

THE WOOLMARK

322 Fifth Street
Eureka, CA 95501
(707) 442-9272

Mail Order, Retail Shop;
Established in 1975

Besides offering a very large number of other fiber supplies, THE WOOLMARK also handles a number of natural dyes, mordants, and dye assistants. These include: logwood extract, madder, cochineal, indigo, brazilwood, henna, cream of tartar, alum, iron, copper, chrome, tin, synthrapol, spectralite, washing soda, thickener mix, sodium alginate, Glauber's salt, levellers, synthetic beeswax and urea.

Some quantity discounts are given; check price list for details.

Write for a free price list.

CHAPTER 5

Yarns and Fibers
Weaving and Spinning Equipment
Knitting and Crochet
Other Basic Fiber Art Supplies

This chapter contains everything that you could ever want or need for your fiber projects. These suppliers offer raw fibers for spinning, looms and spinning wheels, knitting and crochet supplies, tatting and lace-making supplies and equipment, rug making supplies, and hundreds of yarns for weaving, knitting, or crocheting, including many handspun and dyed yarns.

ABERDEEN YARN COMPANY, INC.

27 East 31st Street
New York, NY 10016
(212) 889-8525

Mail Order; Retail Shop;
Established in 1961

ABERDEEN sells all varieties of yarns in all fibers and blends below wholesale cost to craft shops nationwide. They are jobbers who handle stock lots and mill overruns and can offer deeply discounted prices. Aberdeen is a wholesale supplier only, but will sell retail to individuals who visit their showroom.

A wholesale price list and samples will be sent to qualified buyers; write for more information.

ANDEAN YARNS, INC.

54 Industrial Way
Wilmington, MA 01887
(617) 657-7680

Manufacturer; Mail Order;
Established in 1981

An alpaca

ANDEAN YARNS, INC. claims to offer the "best alpaca available at the best price." Andean Yarns, imported directly from Peru, include seven lines of beautiful 100% alpaca yarns in three different weights. These are available in natural shades and blends, vegetable dyed shades, and other shades. Also available are 100% mercerized Pima Cottons from Peru in nine shades and plant dyed Peruvian Worsted Wools in 12 shades. The company also offers a line of sweater patterns and brochures.

Although Andean Yarns does not sell directly to the public, they will be happy to give you the name of their nearest mail order dealer.*

Interested retailers with a tax resale number should contact Doug Crawford, President of Andean Yarns, for wholesale information. *Author's Note — Several companies listed in this book offer these yarns by mail. Check Index for page numbers.

ANDES LLAMAS RANCH

P.O. Box 300
Athena, OR 97813
(503) 566-2448

Ranch; Established in 1975

If you have ever wanted your own fiber-producing llama, this is one place to buy one! The Andes Llama Ranch offers distinctive llama breeding stock, each one bred for good size and quality wool. The Ranch also publishes *Llama World, The Magazine for Llama Health and Husbandry.*

Send 25¢ for a current brochure.

ARCHER

Box 80023
St. Paul, MN 55108
(612) 227-3448

Manufacturer; Mail Order; Retail
hours by appointment;
Established in 1977

Marcie Archer O'Connor, owner of ARCHER, offers a beautiful selection of carded heathered wool batts for spinning or feltmaking. These beautiful New Zealand Romney wools are carded and dyed into a combination of 342 shades. Ms. O'Connor also sells handspun heathered yarns, available in three different weights and 342 shades. She teaches classes at her studio on "Color and Spinning," and is available to teach classes and seminars to guilds and other groups. Custom wool carding is also offered.

Send $4.00 for brochure and generous, colorful samples.

THE ARMEN CORPORATION

P.O. Box 8348
Asheville, NC 28814
(704) 667-9902

Distributor; Established in 1977

THE ARMEN CORPORATION is the distributor for Chat Botté Yarns and pattern books and Marjorie Ivey patterns. The company does not sell directly to the public. Interested retailers may write for wholesale information and prices.

A complete catalog with samples is $20.00.

THE ARTISAN'S
ACCOMPLICE

201 E. Lancaster Avenue
Wayne, PA 19087
(215) 688-6658

Mail Order, Retail Shop; V/MC;
Established in 1976

THE ARTISAN'S ACCOMPLICE, owned by Carole and R. Mark Hainsfurther, is a complete weaving supply store. They are dealers for Leclerc, Glimakra, Beka, Harrisville, and Schacht looms. Also available are Ashford and Louet spinning wheels, drop spindles, Clemes and Clemes Machine Carders, wool top, rovings and fleece. Yarns are offered from such companies as Tahki, Harrisville Designs, and Manos del Uraguay, as well as a special 100% wool 2-ply mill-end yarn at 25¢ per ounce. The company also offers a large selection of tools, books, and basketry supplies. A number of classes are also offered.

Quantity discounts are given on orders over $50.00.

Send $1.00 for general information and mill-end yarn samples.

THE PHRASE, "YOU ARE WHAT YOU EAT," HAS never been more true than in the case of the silkworm. Cultured, or "tame" silkworms, after eating the delicate leaves of the mulberry tree, produce white silks. Wild, or Tussah, silkworms eat coarser leaves such as oaks, which contain tannins. The tannins color the silk a beige or brown shade, which also can vary from a dark grey to a yellow.

AURORA SILK

5806 N. Vancouver Avenue
Portland, OR 97217
(503) 683-2359

Manufacturer, Mail Order, Retail
hours by appointment;
Established in 1970

Cheryl Kolander-Williams, owner of AURORA SILK, offers a selection of over 39 types of beautiful, imported silk yarns, including white silks, lustrous, textured, and Tussah (wild) silks in many different sizes. All of the yarns can be hand-dyed with natural dyes in any of 44 stock colors, or custom dyed to your specifications. Cheryl has also written the only book available on silk for the contemporary textile artist. The book, *A Silk Worker's Notebook,* (currently $50.00 ppd) contains 140-pages of information on the story of silk, the silk fiber, reeled and spun silk, silk yarns, handspinning, fabrics (including tipped-in swatches), care of silks, and much more. Ms. Kolander-Williams also gives workshops on silk dyeing, and offers a custom dyeing service for silk fabrics.

Quantity and wholesale discounts are given; check catalog for details.

Send $9.00 for a generous set of silk yarn samples, price list and book information.

AUTUMN HOUSE FARM

R.D. #1, Box 105
Rochester Mills, PA 15771
(412) 286-9596

Manufacturer; Mail Order, Retail
hours by appointment;
Established in 1979

AUTUMN HOUSE FARM, owned by Harriet Converse Knop, has the largest colored sheep flock in Pennsylvania. They have developed their own breed of sheep called "Karashire", which has a unique variegated fleece on one animal. Their wool ranges from a medium to long grade (suitable for knitting and weaving), and a coarse grade for warp, carpets, or tapestry. Other fleece are available from Romney, Border Leicester, Rambouillet, Cheviot and Corriedale sheep. Additional fibers available include combed flax, cotton, and mohair. The Farm carries spinning and weaving equipment and accessories from Louet, Beka, Ashford, Clemes and Clemes, and Camelot, and custom-made tools. Handspun woolen yarns are available.

Discounts are given on volume orders of fleece. Wholesale prices are given to retailers on handspun yarns. Write for more information.

Send $1.00 for a current catalog. Wool samples (specify type) are $1.00.

 THE ANCIENT EGYPTIAN CULTURES MADE
linens so shear that they could be drawn through a finger ring.

— Courtesy of the Wool Education Center, Denver, CO

AVL LOOMS

601 Orange Street
Chico, CA 95926
(916) 893-4915

Manufacturer; Mail Order; V/MC;
Established in 1976

AVL (Ahrens & Violette Looms) specially designs and hand-builds looms for professional handweavers. The AVL Basic Modular Loom is available in 40, 48, and 60 inch weaving widths, with four to 12 harnesses and six to 14 treadles. The Modular Looms allow you to start out simply and add options later such as the dobby head, flyshuttle beater, automatic cloth storage roller, computer, etc. AVL Production Dobby Looms are also available in widths of 40, 48, and 60 inches. It features 16 harnesses and an automatic cloth storage system that allows warps of up to 100 yards or more. Optional weaving equipment, production warping equipment, and computer software is also available for use with the looms. Other services include class referrals and marketing consultation for fiber artists.

School or organizational discounts are given; write for price quotes.

Send $1.00 for a complete catalog of AVL products.

AYOTTES' DESIGNERY

P.O. Box 287-Maple Street
Center Sandwich, NH 03227
(603) 284-6915

Manufacturer; Mail Order, Retail
Shop; Established in 1958

Robert and Roberta Ayotte, of AYOTTES' DESIGNERY, carry a wide variety of weaving and spinning supplies. All items in the Leclerc catalog are stocked in the Ayottes' warehouse, ready for shipment. They also carry over 1,000 types and brands of yarns and weaving books. The Ayottes' also offer membership in their Yarn Club, with a $5.00 membership fee. For this fee, you will receive yarn samples for as long as you purchase $25.00 worth of yarn each year. They also publish a handweaving course titled *Handweaving with Robert and Roberta*.

Various discounts are given; write for more information.

Send $1.00 for a loom catalog and brochure.

SUSAN BATES, INC.

212 Middlesex Avenue
Chester, CT 06412
(203) 526-5381

Manufacturer; Mail Order;
Established in 1873

SUSAN BATES, INC. is a complete art-needlework supply source. The company distributes Anchor 100% cotton embroidery flosses in over 300 beautiful, vibrant colors, and Anchor Tapestry Wools from Scotland in over 265 shades. A wide assortment of knitting yarns, including wools, cottons, synthetics, alpacas, and blends are available under such labels as Susan Bates, Patons, and Jaeger. The company also carries a full line of knitting needles, crochet hooks, afghan hooks, embroidery and sewing supplies, needlepoint canvases, and much more.

Susan Bates, Inc. only sells to designers and retail outlets who can meet the credit criteria. Write for full details.

Send $3.00 for a catalog of knitting and crochet supplies.

BATIK & WEAVING SUPPLIER

102 Massachusetts Avenue
Arlington, MA 02174
(617) 646-4453

Mail Order, Retail Shop; V/MC;
Established in 1977

The BATIK & WEAVING SUPPLIER carries looms and other weaving supplies from Harrisville Designs, Willow Tree, Schacht, Leclerc and Norwood. Spinning fibers include combed flax, camel hair, Tussah silks, cottons, domestic and New Zealand fleece, and others. A full line of yarns are also available from Tahki, Bernat, Berroco, Henry's Attic, Borgs, and more. Spinning wheels from Ashford and Louet are offered. Knitting and crochet supplies include wooden knitting needles and crochet hooks, Penny Straker Knitting Patterns and pattern books. They also carry a variety of natural and synthetic dyes and other supplies for surface design. Books on weaving, spinning, knitting, and dyeing are also available. Fiber classes and workshops are offered during the year.

Discounts are given by ordering a minimum amount over a six-month period. Write for details.

Send 50¢ for a current catalog.

ARACHNE, A SPINNER IN ANCIENT GREECE, challenged the goddess Athena to a spinning contest and eventually won. Athena could not permit such rudeness from a mortal woman, so she changed Arachne into a spider, condemned to spin for eternity. Hence the name for spiders — arachnid.

— From *Spin Span Spun,* by Bette Hochberg.

BEAR TRAP FIBERS

Rt. 2, Box 110A
Ashland, WI 54806
(715) 682-9010

Mail Order; Established in 1982

BEAR TRAP FIBERS can supply colored wool fleece, angora rabbit fur (black, white, chinchilla, buff), and angora goat fibers for handspinning. They also have the above animals for sale, and offer tours of their farm.

Send for more information on specific fibers and prices.

BECK'S WARP 'N WEAVE & NEEDLECRAFTS

2815 34th Street
Lubbock, TX 79410
(806) 799-0151

Mail Order, Retail Shop; V/MC;
Established in 1976

BECK'S supplies a full range of materials for weaving, spinning, dyeing, and other fiber arts. Looms are available by Leclerc, Schacht, Beka and Harrisville Designs. Ashford spinning wheels are also available. Fibers for spinning include domestic wool top, New Zealand fawn top, abaca, and New Zealand Romney raw white fleece. Beck's also stocks a variety of natural and synthetic dyes, supplies for fabric design, tatting, basketry, knitting, crochet, and other types of needlework. Yarns and threads are available from such companies as Harrisville Designs, Unger, NZ Handspun, Bernat, Balger, DMC, and others, along with some mill ends. A large number of books are also offered.

A variety of good discounts are offered by Beck's. Check catalog for more information.

Send $1.00 for a current catalog.

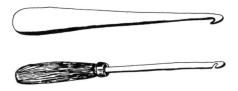

Two types of reed hooks

BEGGARS' LACE

3036 East 6th Avenue
Denver, CO 80206
(303) 388-LACE

Mail Order, Retail Shop;
V/MC/AMEX; Established in
1978

BEGGARS' LACE specializes in and carries a large line of supplies and patterns for bobbin lace, tatting, and other types of lacemaking. Over fifteen different types of lace bobbins are offered, as are other bobbin lace supplies such as pillows, pins, prickers, etc. A large number of patterns and books are also available. Beggars' Lace also carries tatting shuttles (ten different styles), tools, and kits. Threads for lacemaking are offered, and include all DMC threads, pearl cottons, Cebelia 3-Cord Threads, Cordonnet 6-Cord Threads, tatting cottons in 42 colors, linen and silk threads. In addition to these, a large number of historical, reference, and identification books on lace are available, as are clothing patterns from Folkwear, Fashion Blueprints, Patterns of History, Past Pattern Replicas, and more. Classes are also offered at the retail location.

Quantity discounts are available; write for more information.

Send $1.00 for a current catalog.

BEKA, INC.

1648 Grand Avenue
St. Paul, MN 55105
(612) 222-7005

Manufacturer; Mail Order;
Established in 1973

BEKA, INC. manufactures several looms, portable and non-portable. Beka's rigid heddle looms come in weaving widths of eight to 44 inches. These also have ratchet tensioning systems which control warp tension. An inkle loom, weaving frame, and other accessories are also available. Beka also manufactures an eight-harness jack-type floor loom in 36, 48, or 60-inch weaving widths. The entire line of Simpkin's 100% Perendale wool yarns from New Zealand are imported by Beka, and are available in 2-ply Sportsweight, 3-ply Double Knit and Worsted weights.

Institutional discounts are given with an order of six or more looms.

Send $1.00 for a brochure and yarn samples.

JEANNE BENJAMIN

Box 754
West Brookfield, MA 01585
(413) 436-5980

Manufacturer; Mail Order;
Established in 1979

JEANNE BENJAMIN carries over 130 shades of 100% wool fabric swatches and backgrounds to be used in rug hooking. She also offers a custom dyeing service, help with color planning, and classes.

Discounts are given to teachers only.

Send 50¢ for a catalog. Swatch sample prices vary; check with catalog for current prices.

STANLEY BERROCO

Elmdale Road
Uxbridge, MA 01569
(617) 278-2527

Manufacturer; Established in
1905

STANLEY BERROCO carries a wide variety of specialty yarns for weaving, knitting and crocheting, including wools, synthetics, and blends. The company also publishes knitting and crocheting instruction leaflets.

Berroco only sells by mail order to retail establishments. Qualified businesses should write for more information and a wholesale price list. Others may write for the address of the nearest mail order dealer.

A current catalog is $10.00.

BLACK SHEEP STUDIO

P.O. Box 158
Athens, OH 45701
(614) 592-4077

Mail Order; Retail Shop; V/MC;
Established in 1982

Sig-Britt Sandh, owner of BLACK SHEEP STUDIO, offers the entire line of Schacht and Glimakra floor, table and tapestry looms, and Louet and Ashford spinning wheels. Natural dyes and mordants, synthetic dyes, and batik and silk painting supplies are also available. Wool, cotton, alpaca, silk and cashmere spinning fibers, as well as yarns from Tahki, Lopi, Borgs, Harrisville, Scheepjeswol and Schaffhauser are also offered by this company. The latest books on spinning, weaving, dyeing, knitting, crocheting and basketry are also listed in Black Sheep Studio's in-depth catalog. Classes and weekend workshops on a variety of fiber subjects are given.

Quarterly specials on equipment and supplies are offered — worth watching for!

Send $1.00 for a current catalog.

A boat shuttle

**BLACK SHEEP WEAVING
AND CRAFT SUPPLY**

530 S.W. 4th Street
Corvallis, OR 97333
(503) 752-0739

Manufacturer; Mail Order, Retail
Shop; V/MC; Established in 1968

BLACK SHEEP WEAVING AND CRAFT SUPPLY carries Leclerc and Harrisville looms, Candide, Condon and Harrisville yarns, spinning wheels, fleeces, and handspun yarns. The company also offers a wool carding service, and carded wool batts.

Quantity discounts are given to individuals, and a 10% discount is given to schools/guilds/groups, etc. Handspun yarns are also available at wholesale prices; write for details.

Send for a current catalog and price list.

ANNY BLATT

24770 Crestview Court
Farmington Hills, MI 48018
(313) 474-2942

Manufacturer; Mail Order

ANNY BLATT carries a very large line of beautiful yarns in an extensive color range. These include 100% alpacas, angoras, wools, Egyptian cottons, mohairs, silks, and even 100% genuine beaver, and blends of feathers/cotton, mohair/silk, angora/wool, mohair/wool, and many other metallics and natural/synthetic fiber blends. Anny Blatt also offers a selection of knitting patterns and project books.

Interested retailers may inquire about wholesale prices. The initial minimum order is $300.00. Others should write for the address of the nearest mail order dealer.

A complete yarn sample book with updates is $50.00.

DICK BLICK COMPANY

Box 1267
Galesburg, IL 61401
(309) 343-6181

Manufacturer; Mail Order, Retail Shop; V/MC; Established in 1911

DICK BLICK offers a large number of weaving supplies, including a Craft Weaving Loom, Erica Two-Harness Rigid Heddle Loom, Maya 15-inch Backstrap Loom, Inkle Loom, Todd Loom, Peacock Two-harness Loom and cardboard looms. Yarns include the entire line of Trait-Tex yarns, cotton mop yarns, Maysville Rug Filler yarns, carpet warp, Aunt Lydia's rug yarns, and more. Yarn assortment boxes are also offered.

Send for a current, free catalog.

BLUENOSE WOOLS

114 Henderson Street
Chapel Hill, NC 27514
(919) 967-8800

Mail Order, Retail Shop; Established in 1977

BLUENOSE WOOLS, owned by Louanne Watley, carries a wide variety of looms and weaving accessories by such suppliers as Glimakra, Schacht, Harrisville, Dorset, Toika, and spinning wheels by Louet and Ashford. Fleece from South America and New Zealand is available in the grease, greasy-carded, clean-combed, and dyed. Yarns are too numerous to mention, but include 1, 2, and 3-ply virgin wools in heathers, solids, and tweeds in cones and skeins from New England and Canada, and cottons, linens, silks and specialty yarns from Europe and the U.S. Ms. Watley also carries a wide assortment of buttons: handmade, antique, one-of-a-kind, wooden, bone, mother-of-pearl, porcelain, pewter, nut, etc. Knitting and clothing patterns are also available, as are books on weaving, spinning, dyeing, and knitting. Beginning lessons in knitting, weaving, and spinning are also given.

Various discounts are given; write for details.

Send for a general listing of supplies available.

BONNIE'S BUNNY BARN

38431 Darnel Court
Fremont, CA 94536
(415) 793-6261

Manufacturer; Mail Order; Established in 1980

BONNIE'S BUNNY BARN supplies hand-plucked, handspun Angora rabbit yarns in natural colors. Lectures are also available on angora spinning with "traveling bunny and wheel."

Write for current prices and ordering information.

BRADSHAW
MANUFACTURING
COMPANY

P.O. Box 5645
West Columbia, SC 29171
(803) 794-1151

Manufacturer; Mail Order; V/MC;
Established in 1930

BRADSHAW manufactures custom-made loom reeds in either carbon or stainless steel, from two to 30 dents-per-inch (d.p.i.) and four to six-inches outside height, in regular or metric dimensions. Bradshaw states that their company is special because they "are willing to do custom work for a single order."

A 10% discount is given on an order of four or more reeds.

Send for a free price list.

BRAID-AID

466 Washington Street
Pembroke, MA 02359
(617) 826-6091

Manufacturer; Mail Order, Retail
Shop; V/MC; Established in 1947

BRAID-AID, considered by many to be the leading authority on rug braiding in the country, offers a complete line of rug braiding and hooking supplies. Their catalog includes a large number of 100% wool fabrics by the yard and by the pound, Braid-Aids (automatically folds strips while braiding), cotton threads, Fraser, Rigby and Bliss cloth and strip cutters, pattern books, rug kits, rug hooks, dyes, hooking frames, supplies for shirret, and more. Braid-Aid also carries supplies for quilting, spinning and weaving.

Wholesale prices are given to stores on items manufactured by Braid-Aid. Other discounts are given to schools, professionals, teachers, etc. Write for further information.

Send $2.00 for a complete catalog.

BROWN SHEEP COMPANY,
INC.

Rt. 1
Mitchell, NE 69357
(308) 635-2198

Manufacturer; Mail Order;
Established in 1980

BROWN SHEEP COMPANY, INC., a small, independent, family-oriented business, is owned by Robert G. and Harlan Brown. In December of 1979, they began purchasing and installing spinning equipment. The company now owns their own dye house. Their yarns are 100% wools and wool/mohair blends in several weights and over 35 different colors. The "Top of the Lamb #2" yarns are suitable for knitting machine use. The Browns say that their yarns are very versatile, and have been very popular for handknitting, crocheting, machine knitting and weaving. Natural white and gray wool top is also available for handspinners.

Wholesale prices are given to prospective retail outlets with no minimum purchase; professional knitters and weavers can purchase at these prices with a minimum initial purchase of 50 pounds of yarn.

Send $2.50 for a price list and samples of all yarns.

HELEN BROWN-THE FIBER SHOP, INC.

Box 22694
Rochester, NY 14692-2694
(716) 334-4281

Mail Order, Retail Shop;
Established in 1972

HELEN BROWN, owner of THE FIBER SHOP, INC., carries a large number of yarns, including those from LaMieux, Harrisville, Fawcett, Patons, Heirloom, Jaeger, Tahki, Crystal Palace, and others. She is also a dealer for Harrisville, Kyra and Glimakra looms, Superba, Brother, Bulky-8 and Bond knitting machines. Spinning wheels are also available from Louet, Kiwi, Ashford, Clemes, Saxon and Normandy Reproductions. The Fiber Shop also offers a large number of other supplies: roving, rug wools, silks, metallics, ribbons, dyes, batik and papermaking supplies, and more.

Some discounts are given; write for details.

A catalog is not available at this time; write for specific prices.

CABIN CREEK LOOMERY

1319-250th N.E.
Redmond, WA 98053
(206) 883-1899

Manufacturer; Mail Order;
Established in 1984

CABIN CREEK LOOMERY is a family business which furnishes "old Swedish style" handbuilt looms by Gunnar Lindberg. Gunnar's daughter, Edna Reichert, says "Gunnar has taught us well so that we can carry on when he retires. He's only 85!" The looms come in two weaving sizes, 46 and 60-inches. The basic looms are counterbalance or countermarch (or both), convert in minutes, and are available in four to 10-harnesses. Extra harnesses may be purchased as needed. Each loom purchase includes an adjustable bench with storage tray and many other accessories, including "easy to follow" assembly instructions.

School discounts are given; write for details.

A well-illustrated color brochure and price list is $1.00.

THE CAMEL

761 8th Street
Arcata, CA 95521
(707) 822-4269

Mail Order, Retail Shop, V/MC;
Established in 1971

THE CAMEL offers a variety of supplies for fiber work. These include yarns from Condon, Brown Sheep Company, Harrisville Designs, Conshohocken Cottons, Tahki, Crystal Palace, etc. They also stock several types of synthetic dyes (Tinfix, Versatex, Kiton, Cushing, etc.), and natural dye extracts. Spinning wheels are available from Louet and Ashford, and looms from Louet and Harrisville. Domestic Romney fleece is also available, in addition to other assorted weaving, basketry, spinning supplies and books. Classes in Basketry, Needlepoint, Tatting, Crochet, etc. are offered.

Quantity discounts are given; write for more information.

A catalog is not available at this time; write for specific prices.

CEDARHURST WOOLS

Cedarhurst Ranch
Britt, MN 55710
(218) 258-3968

Manufacturer; Mail Order, Retail Shop; Established in 1980

Jean Jasinsky of CEDARHURST WOOLS, raises only black sheep which are prized for their natural black, brown, gray and silver wools. Yarns in four natural shades are available, as are other weaving supplies. Jean's retail shop displays many "Critter to Craft" items such as 100% wool blankets, vests, sweaters, etc. Cedarhurst Ranch sponsors several interesting annual events, such as a "Shearing and Sharing Potluck" in March, an "Annual Open Gate" in May to visit new, baby lambs, and an "Old Fashioned Fall Festival" in October.

Send a SASE for a free brochure.

CHESTER FARMS

Rt. 1, Box 275
Raphine, VA 24472
(804) 377-6633

Manufacturer; Mail Order, Retail
Shop; Established in 1946

CHESTER FARMS is the only sheep farm-to-wool mill operation in the United States. The family-owned farm raises American Columbia, Black Karakul and Columbia/Karakul cross sheep. From these they produce 100% "mule-spun" wool yarns in 1, 2, and 3-plys, and in 17 colors. Tours of the farm can also be arranged.

Discounts are given on "misweight" yarns. Write for details.

Send $1.00 for samples and a current price list.

CHULE'S

2044 Redondela Drive
San Pedro, CA 90732
(213) 831-3850

Manufacturer; Mail Order, Retail
Shop

CHULE'S carries only high quality wool yarns that are known for their softness.

Some discounts are given; write for more information.

Send for a current price list and ordering information.

CITY SPINNING

6817-147th Court, N.E.
Redmond, WA 98052
(206) 883-6562

Manufacturer; Mail Order;
Established in 1979

CITY SPINNING Handspuns are created by fiber artist Chris Ann Shurtleff from only the finest natural fibers and fleece. From start to finish, each process is done by hand. Chris's yarns have been featured in *Yarn Market News,* and include cottons, goat, mohair, silks, yak, wools, wool blends, camel/silk blends, and others. Chris also provides custom dyeing of her yarns.

Retail shops and professional weavers/knitters who are buying to make items for resale can buy at wholesale prices with a $40.00 minimum order. Individuals get a 10% discount with orders over $50.00.

Send a SASE for a free price list; prices of sample cards will be listed on order form.

Handspun yarns at City Spinning

CLEMES & CLEMES, INC.

650 San Pablo Avenue
Pinole, CA 94564
(415) 724-2036

Manufacturer; Mail Order, Retail
Shop; Established in 1971

CLEMES & CLEMES, INC. only sells spinning supplies that they manufacture themselves. These items include a castle or upright spinning wheel, a Clemes Kit Wheel, wool carders, child's hand carders, cotton carders, flickers, threading hooks, drum carders, oils, drop spindles in several styles, cotton spindles, Niddy-Noddy, Lazy Kate, warping board, a distaff kit for the Ashford wheel, shuttles, electric bobbin winders and spinners. Fibers for handspinning include New Zealand wools, long-stapled ginned cotton, roving tops, flax, and acrylic and polyester fibers in roving form for those who are allergic to wools.

Wholesale price lists are available to retailers when requested on letterhead with a business card. Discounts are given to schools and instructors on quantity orders.

Send for a free catalog; fiber samples are $1.50.

COGSWELL HANDICRAFTS

77 Tatham Hill Road
West Springfield, MA 01089

Manufacturer; Mail Order

Celia Cogswell, owner of COGSWELL HANDICRAFTS, manufactures and sells polished brass reed hooks.

Quantity discounts are given; write for details.

Send for current prices and ordering information.

COMMUNTIY CRAFT COTTAGE, LTD.

7577 Elmbridge Way
Richmond, B.C.
Canada V6X 2Z8
(604) 278-0313

COMMUNITY CRAFT COTTAGE, LTD. owned by Nancy Vivian, offers unique yarns for weaving, knitting and crocheting from Canada. Also available are imported specialty wools, cottons and silks from Europe, England, Ireland, and the U.S. Ms. Vivian is also a dealer for Leclerc looms.

Discounts are given with a minimum order of $150.00.

Send $1.00 for a current, detailed catalog.

CONES UNLIMITED, INC.

445 East 80th Street, Suite 3
New York, NY 10021
(212) 535-3875

Mail Order; Established in 1981

CONES UNLIMITED, INC. carries a wide variety of knitting yarns and supplies. The yarns, available in 14 different types and 373 shades, come on one-pound and ½ pound cones or tubes. These yarns include mercerized cottons, Parisian cottons, Australian wools, worsteds, Velveens, etc. Cones Unltd., Inc. also carries knitting machines, parts and accessories by Studio, Brother, Passap, and Superba. A full line of knitting and pattern books are also available from this source.

CUI offers an exclusive Designer Yarn Club for $7.00 per year; write for membership details and benefits.

Send $6.75 for a current catalog, which includes samples of all yarns, booklist, information on knitting machines, etc. ($5.00 of this is applicable to your first order of $25.00 or more).

COSMOS RABBIT COMPANY

P.O. Box 1002
Silverdale, WA 98383
(206) 692-1330

Manufacturer; Mail Order;
Established in 1974

COSMOS RABBIT FACTORY supplies angora rabbits, wools, yarns, and garments. Spinning wheels by Wilson Woodworks and Country Craftsman are available, as are lessons in angora spinning and management. A publication called "Handbook of Angoras" is available at $10.00 per year. The owner of Cosmos Rabbit Factory is also available for special workshops and lectures.

Send $5.00 for current price list and samples.

COTTON CLOUDS

P.O. Box 604
Safford, AZ 85548
(602) 428-7000

Mail Order, Retail hours by appointment; V/MC; Established in 1979

COTTON CLOUDS is an all-around source for 100% cottons: yarns, fibers, fabrics, etc. Cotton Clouds 100% cotton yarns include Aurora Cloud yarns, In-a-Mist cotton yarns, Cloudburst II cotton chenilles, cotton rug warps, Baby Perly Perles mercerized cotton yarns, and Aurora Earth yarns in over 60 colors. Cotton Clouds also carries the Roberta Electronic Spinner from Australia, and the Bond knitting machine. A wide variety of 100% cotton fibers are available, and all come with fiber information and spinning instructions. These include Pima cottons, Acala cottons from California, sliver cotton, brown cottons, and punis (cotton rolags from India). A Cotton Cloud Combo, a sample pack of all of the different types of cotton fibers, is also offered. Other supplies include cotton seeds (to grow your own), a "Learn to Spin Cotton" kit, a Charkha Spinning Wheel (designed for spinning cotton in India and used by Gandhi), cotton carders, bamboo knitting needles, walnut crochet hooks, a large number of books, Spectrum Dyes, and Precut Calico Clouds fabric strips for rugmaking or weaving.

Wholesale discounts are available with a minimum order of $200.00 and $100.00 reorders. Schools will receive Educational Packets along with their orders.

Send $2.00 for a current catalog and samples; this will entitle you to receive all future mailings. This catalog is professionally designed and a joy to read; I recommend it!

COUPEVILLE SPINNING AND WEAVING SHOP, INC.

P.O. Box 555
Coupeville, WA 98239
(206) 678-4447

Mail Order, Retail Shop; V/MC;
Estalished in 1974

COUPEVILLE SPINNING AND WEAVING SHOP, INC. offers a variety of fiber supplies, including looms by Harrisville Designs, Schacht, Beka, Louet and Jefferson, and spinning wheels from Louet, Ashford, and Clemes. Yarns are available from Harrisville Designs, Old Mill, Oregon Worsted, Lily, Aurora Earth, Scott's, Tahki, Chat Botte, E'Lite, Berroco, Condon, Paton, Berger du Nord, Brown Sheep Company, Indiecita Alpaca, Lane Borgosesia, and many others. Other supplies include a large number of books, buttons, shuttles, Aero Knitting needles, Ciba Dyes, etc. Classes in various fiber arts are offered.

Quantity discounts are given.

Send for a free newsletter and mail order information.

CRAFTS UNLIMITED/ WEAVER'S WEB

23 Langdon Street
Montpelier, VT 05602
(802) 229-5803

Mail Order, Retail Shop; V/MC;
Established in 1980

CRAFTS UNLIMITED/WEAVER'S WEB carries supplies such as Leclerc looms, Asheville spinning wheels, and yarns by Harrisville, Brunswick, Phildar, Unger, Tahki, Candide, Pinguoin, and Vermont Wools. Classes are also offered in many craft areas.

Occasional discounts are given to individuals and schools/groups.

Although this company does not have a catalog available at this time, they say that they will mail anything! Write with inquiries.

A GOOD TEST YOU CAN MAKE TO SEE IF YOU have quality synthetic yarn is to pull fibers from the yarn; if they are long (two to three inches) with a little crimp, and spring back from the pull, the yarn will be good. If the fibers pull out readily and are short, this can be a yarn made of acrylic waste and will pill when washed.

— A tip from Charles and Mary Lue Brinker, owners of Mary Lue's Yarn Shop.

CREEK WATER WOOL WORKS

P.O. Box 716
Salem, OR 97308
(503) 585-3302

Mail Order; V/MC; Established in 1979

CREEK WATER WOOL WORKS supplies a wide variety of spinning fibers, including Oregon Romney and Romney cross raw wools, Oregon Mohair, French angora, Oregon llama, alpaca, camel hairs and down, silks, wool top, batts and sliver, cottons, flax and qiviut (in limited supply). Louet, Ashford, Restoration Arts, Peacock, Pioneer, Fox, and Obadiah Tharp spinning wheels and accessories are available from this company. Other supplies include Fricke drum carders, Charkha spinning wheels, Meck wool picker and yarn blockers, Louet looms, knitting frames, a large variety of dyes, and other assorted supplies and materials. The company also offers a repair service for antique spinning wheels.

Some quantity discounts are given; check catalog for details.

Send for a free catalog.

CROSS CREEK FIBERS

Highway 30E
Decatur, TN 37322
(615) 334-5963

Mail Order, Retail Shop;
Established in 1979

CROSS CREEK FIBERS, owned by Emily Dewhirst, is housed in a restored cabin which dates back to the 1800's. Ms. Dewhirst also raises Russian Black Sheep which she has cross-bred with Black Columbias. She sells the fleece from these sheep, which has a staple length of four to nine-inches. The fleece are very clean and very unusual. Emily is also a dealer for Leclerc products, and Harrisville Designs yarns. Also available are very reasonable odd-lot yarns, weaving books, and more. Classes are offered in weaving, in which antique looms from 1775 (as well as newer models) are used.

Discounts are given to professionals who are producing work for resale.

Send $1.00 for a current catalog (applicable to first order).

CURTIS FIBERS

Star Rt. Box 15
Ritzville, WA 99169
(509) 659-1913

Mail Order, Retail hours by
appointment; V/MC; Established
in 1984

CURTIS FIBERS carries a good selection of hard-to-find spinning fibers and various yarns. Ready-to-spin fibers include mohair sliver, cultivated silk, Tussah silk, white and brown alpaca sliver, camel down sliver, cashmere down (fawn) and cashmere sliver (ecru). Wools include scoured, carded New Zealand roving in eight shades, raw fleece from seven breeds, raw colored fleece in six colors, greasy carded fleece, and dyed carded wool in 13 colors. Other fibers include pima cotton, water-retted flax, bleached flax and ramie. Also available is a Spinning Fibers Sample Kit and a "Learn to Spin Cotton" kit. Yarns from Curtis Fibers include linens, silks, cottons, and novelties. Suppliers include Oregon Worsted, Brown Sheep, Condon, Ironstone Warehouse, Wilde, etc. Mill ends are also available.

Discounts are given with a minimum order of $100.00.

Send for a free catalog. Yarn samples cost: $1.00-Curtis Fibers Yarn samples; $1.00-Curtis Fibers Spinning samples; $2.50-Brown Sheep samples; $1.00-Oregon Worsted samples.

W. CUSHING AND COMPANY

Kennebunkport, ME 04046-0351
(207) 967-3711

Manufacturer; Mail Order

Some companies go out of their way to supply materials for certain crafts. W. CUSHING AND COMPANY is one of these. Besides manufacturing their well-known line of Perfection Dyes, Cushing also carries a complete line of supplies and equipment for rug hooking. Equipment includes two types of frames, hoops, strip cutters, scissors, transfer pencils, four types of rug hooks, and much more.

Send for a current price list.

CUSTOM HANDWEAVERS

Allied Arts Guild
Arbor Road at Creek Drive
Menlo Park, CA 94025
(415) 325-0626

Manufacturer; Mail Order, Retail
Shop; Established in 1960's

CUSTOM HANDWEAVERS-Allied Arts Guild offers all Leclerc and Schacht products, and some Navajo weaving and spinning supplies. Yarns are available in linens, silks, wools, and acrylics. They also import Swiss handspun wools for the U.S. and Canada. Various classes are offered in weaving, spinning, Navajo weaving, etc.

Send for a frec catalog.

CUSTOM HANDWEAVING BY NANCY

P.O. Box 477
Redondo Beach, CA 90277-0477
(213) 316-0910

Mail Order; Established in 1979

CUSTOM HANDWEAVING BY NANCY carries a large variety of yarns which include Douppioni silks, Tussah silks, Tram silks, white spun silks imported from England, 100% cashmeres, wool/cashmere blends, 100% camel hair yarns, cotton flake yarns, 100% brushed mohair yarns, large loop mohair/wool blends, 100% silk noils, silk tweeds, 100% wool flake yarns from Ireland, and many others. Nancy also handles hospital-quality cleaned sheepskin in random sized pieces. These can be cut into strips and woven into jackets, rugs, vests, etc.

Quantity discounts are given with a $200.00 minimum order.

Send $4.00 for samples and price list.

DAVIDSON'S OLD MILL YARN

109 Elizabeth Street
Eaton Rapids, MI 48827
(517) 663-2711

Mail Order, Retail Shop; V/MC;
Established in 1921

DAVIDSON'S extensive line of 100% wool yarns includes dyed Rug Wools in 43 shades, Giant yarns in 15 shades, Colorov and Double Colorov New Zealand yarns in 62 shades, and others. Natural White Yarns include Tapestry, Navajo warp, Upholstery Warp, 3-ply Rug Yarns, 2 and 4-ply Worsteds, etc. Novelty Ecru yarns include mohair/wool/nylon blends in Mohair Brush, Curl and Loop yarns. Yarns from other suppliers are also offered, and include those from American Thread, Berroco, Borgs, Brunswick, Chat Botte, Fawcett, Ironstone, Lily, Jaeger, CUM, Plymouth, Reynolds, Robison-Anton, and others. Cottons, wools, silks, camel hair, alpaca, flax, mohair, ramie, goat hair, yak, angora, and other fibers are available for spinning. A line of supplies for spinning are also available, and include products from Leclerc, Clemes and Clemes, Ashford, Country Craftsman, Lendrum, etc. Looms are offered from Leclerc and Schacht. A large list of books are also included in Davidson's catalog.

Various quantity prices are given; check price list for details.

Send $3.00 for samples of all Old Mill yarns, price sheets and general information on other yarns.

DAWN ENTERPRISES

P.O. Box 1006
Cucamonga, CA 91730
(714) 982-8176

Mail Order; Established in 1982

DAWN ENTERPRISES supplies New Zealand clean, carded fleece in white and natural colors, from Perendale/Romney and Purebred Lincoln sheep. These fleece are ready to spin with no additional preparation time needed. The company also promises fast, friendly service.

Some discounts are given; see price list.

Send $1.00 for a current price list and samples of all wools.

DEATON FARMS' ANGORA

9095 Paddock Road
Eaton, OH 45320
(513) 456-5630

Manufacturer; Mail Order;
Established in 1981

Diane Deaton of DEATON FARMS' ANGORA, raises angora rabbits for the special fibers that they provide. She has white angora rabbit wool available. She also is interested in doing custom spinning, as well as teaching workshops on the angora rabbit.

Send $3.00 for Diane's basic catalog and angora sample.

(By the way, this is no ordinary catalog. It contains extensive information on angora rabbit wool, angora fiber chemistry, spinning angora wool, dyeing the wool, designing angora yarns, and instructions for a French angora beret. Well worth $3.00!)

Angora baby bunny and angora rabbit from Deaton Farms

DELAINE WORSTED MILLS

Box 951
Gastonia, NC 28052
(704) 865-2300

Manufacturer; Mail Order; V/MC;
Established in 1899

DELAINE WORSTED MILLS manufactures Acridel, Delsoft, Del-Lite machine knitting yarns and ply twisters and wool winders. They can also supply hand knitting yarns on cones, and have 60 shades of all yarns in stock for immediate shipment.

Send for a free brochure.

THE DIGNAM HOUSE

P.O. Box 1226
Lake Oswego, OR 97034
(503) 620-4590

Mail Order; Established in 1984

THE DIGNAM HOUSE offers a complete line of quality yarns especially for machine knitters. They handle yarns from such manufacturers as Schaffhauser, Scheepjeswol, Andean Yarns, Plymouth, Scott's Woolen Mill, Nomis, E'Lite, Bernat, Brown Sheep Company, Chester Farms, and more. All of the yarns are offered at savings of 10% to 30% off the suggested retail price. While most of the yarn samples are compiled with the machine knitter in mind, Dignam House can also offer the hand knitter top quality yarns at the same savings.

Quantity discounts are given with a minimum order of 25 pounds.

Send $3.00 for a complete catalog and yarn samples; specify if you wish a list of hand knitting yarns, also.

DRAGONFLY STUDIO

P.O. Box 482
Lafayette, CO 80026
(303) 665-9504

Mail Order, Retail Shop; V/MC;
Established in 1982

Sandie, of DRAGONFLY STUDIO, calls herself a "Quality Craft Gallery in your Mailbox." She sells handmade fiber objects, beads, yarns, and other materials from her studio. Specifically, Dragonfly Studio handles Andean Yarns imported from Peru. These yarns come in 3-ply alpacas in 12 natural shades, three tweeds, and 16 dyed shades. Andean Plant Dyed Wools (single ply) are available in 12 shades. Sandie also sells Toika looms and spinning wheels, New Zealand fleece, Clemes spinning wheels and equipment, and quality mill ends.

Professional discounts are given with a minimum order of $100.00.

Send a SASE for a price list and yarn samples.

DREAM WEAVER

2980 Grandview Avenue, N.E.
Atlanta, GA 30305
(404) 237-4588

Mail Order, Retail Shop; V/MC;
Established in 1979

DREAM WEAVER carries a large variety of natural fibers and equipment. Suppliers represented include Harrisville Designs, Beka, Norwood, Glimakra, Louet, Schacht, Borg, Scheepjeswol, DMC, Lily, Henry's Attic, Tahki, Ultex, Scott's, Reynolds, Bernat, and many others. The company also handles a lot of books, dyes, buttons, fleece, and basketry supplies.

A 20% discount is offered to schools and non-profit groups. Individuals or shop owners may also qualify for a 20% discount with a resale tax number and a $200.00 minimum order.

Write for more information.

M. DURSIN & SONS, INC.

P.O. Box 909
Woonsocket, RI 02895
(401) 767-0700

Mail Order

M. DURSIN & SONS, INC. is a source for natural and dyed wool tops in three different grades (54s, 64s, and 56s-superwash), a 58s grade in dyed wool only; and a wool/alpaca blend (50/50). Wool tops can be custom dyed, with a 100 pound minimum per shade. The current price for this service is $2.14/pound.

Discounts are offered on quantity orders; write for details.

DYEWORKS

2750 Nicollet Square
Minneapolis, MN 55408
(612) 870-7728

Manufacturer; Mail Order, V/MC;
Established in 1980

DYEWORKS supplies silk, wool, and mohair yarns, all hand-dyed with natural dyes (or available undyed), silk soap, natural dyes and mordants. They offer studio tours, and custom dyeing of the customer's yarns.

Wholesale discounts are given to qualified buyers with a minimum order of $200.00. Write for further information.

Price lists and sample cards are $6.00 for silks, and $4.00 for wools. Price lists are not sent without samples.

EAGLE AGRICULTURAL PRODUCTS

Rt. 4, Box 4B
Huntsville, AR 72740
(501) 738-2203

Manufacturer; Mail Order;
Established in 1983

Kathy Turner, owner of EAGLE AGRICULTURAL PRODUCTS, has grown her own cotton for four years on her farm. It was only in 1983 that she had a crop large enough to sell to others. Kathy plants and picks her cottons by hand. All crops are organically grown, without chemical fertilizers, herbicides, or pesticides. Ms. Turner can provide undyed natural colored cottons (white, green, and brown). She also has white and colored Rambouillet/Romney fleece for sale.

Send for a current price list.

EARTH GUILD

One Tingle Alley
Asheville, NC 28801
(704) 255-7818

Manufacturer; Mail Order, Retail Shop; V/MC; Established in 1970

EARTH GUILD carries a full line of fiber art supplies, which include Brother Knitting Machines, various dyes, spinning fibers (wools, mohair, camel, silk, flax, ramie, and cotton), Glimakra and Clemes hand carders, as well as Ashford and Country Craftsman spinning wheels. Weaving supplies and accessories include shuttles, Beka looms, cardweaving cards, warping mills, bobbin winders, and swifts. Most Earth Guild yarns are composed of 100% cottons with some blends. Rug making supplies are also offered.

Quantity discounts are offered on many items; check catalog for details.

Send $1.00 for a current catalog.

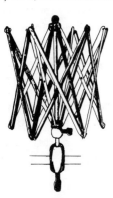

A table model umbrella swift

EATON YARNS

c/o Craft Skellar
Marymount College-North Hall
Tarrytown, NY 10591
(914) 631-1550

EATON YARNS supplies Toika looms and weaving accessories, yarns imported from Finland, looped mohair, Shetland wool and 100% wool yarns, cottons and cotton chenilles, Poppana cut fabrics, tow linens and more. Workshops are also offered.

Wholesale discounts are given to qualified buyers; write for further information.

Send $1.00 for a yarn sample card and price list, or $5.00 for a set of six sample cards.

EWE & ME

P.O. Box 1563
Myrtle Creek, OR 97457-0140
(503) 863-4146

Manufacturer; Mail Order;
Established in 1982

Barbara Gulewich of EWE & ME provides 100% wool roving and batts from Romney and Lincoln sheep, grown on her Oregon farm. Wool and angora rabbit blends are also available in rovings and batts. Felting and quilting batts are available from a slightly lower quality wool, at a lower price. Barbara also has a custom washing and carding service for your fibers, and can custom blend fibers or colors. Ewe & Me is also a dealer for Louet spinning and weaving equipment.

Various discounts apply; write for details.

Send 50¢ for a current price list.

FAIRMOUNT FARM

Thomas Road
Rindge, NH 03461

Manufacturer; Mail Order

Georgia Wolterbeek, of FAIRMOUNT FARM, can provide whole wool fleece in many colors and shadings, lengths and textures, purebred and crossbred. All fleece are carefully skirted.

Send a SASE for samples and information sheet.

FALLBROOK HOUSE

R.D. #2, Box 17
Troy, PA 16947
(717) 297-2498

Mail Order; Established in 1973

Jean R. Case, owner of FALLBROOK HOUSE, offers a very extensive line of silk fibers which include Italian silk rovings from combed Bombyx mori, combed Tussah, carded Bombyx mori and Tussah, Bombyx Mori Mawata silk caps, Tussah Mawata silk caps, thrown raw silk waste, seven types of China silk fibers, silk and wool top blends, and three types of raw cocoons. She also offers printed materials on the silk fiber. Ms. Case has also produced a slide show on Sericulture (legend and related information) which is available for rental to guilds, schools, etc. And, in case you're wondering, Jean has also raised silkworms!

A 10% discount is given to guilds, museums, schools, etc. with a minimum order of $60.00.

Send $15.00 for a copy of Jean's "Silk Portfolio" — includes extensive information on 28 silk fiber forms, complete procedures for reeling, making mawata, degumming, etc. Also included are directions for drawing, spinning, blending, natural and synthetic dyeing, and care of the silks. Generous spinning samples of the 19 fiber forms available at this time are also included.

FREDERICK J. FAWCETT, INC.

320 Derby Street
Salem, MA 01970
(617) 741-1306

Manufacturer; Mail Order, Retail
Shop; Established in 1881

A silkworm and moth

FREDERICK J. FAWCETT, INC. is *the* source for linen. They carry linen yarns and cords for weaving, macrame, embroidery, and lacemaking, 100% linen evenweave and twill fabrics in 51, 54, and 59-inch widths, Linwool (linen/worsted blend), and Bouclin (linen boucle). Fawcett is also a source for cottons: perle cotton, warp cotton, and fine cottons (gassed and mercerized). Included in their extensive inventory are Leclerc looms and accessories, Superba Knitting Machines, and hackled and dressed flax fibers for spinning.

Various discounts are given; check catalog for details.

Send for a free catalog; an order sheet is enclosed for ordering sample cards.

FIBERCRAFTS BY MARY FRANCES

3009 Vermont, N.E.
Albuquerque, NM 87110
(505) 294-7252

Manufacturer; Mail Order, Retail hours by appointment; Established in 1979

FIBERCRAFTS is a source for space-dyed roving for spinners, space-dyed brushed mohair, and space-dyed silk yarns. Also available are handspun yarns and Louet products.

Some discounts are given to qualified businesses; write for information.

Send a SASE for a price list and Louet brochure.

FIBER DIRECTIONS/
COLOR CONNECTIONS, LTD.

P.O. Box 2143
Corrales, NM 87048
(505) 898-7345

Manufacturer; Mail Order, Retail Shop; V/MC; Established in 1983

Coralie Jones and Trudy Maxwell, owners of FIBER DIRECTIONS/ COLOR CONNECTIONS, LTD. offer a very wide variety of supplies for the fiber arts. They offer Forté Fibers wool yarns, "Earth Colors" hand-dyed yarns in two weights of singles and two weights of 2-ply wools, cotton, rayon, and linen yarns, spinning equipment, Louet spinning wheels and drum carders, a wide range of spinning fibers including fleece from New Mexico and Colorado, Navajo looms and tools, basketry and papermaking materials, pre-metallized dyes for wool, silk and mohair, Chlorantine Direct Dyes for cellulose fibers, Procion F Reactive Dyes, natural dyes and mordants, and a number of books. Coralie and Trudy also offer classes in various fiber arts for children and adults, and custom dye wools, cottons, rayon, silk, etc. Ms. Jones also does Navajo, Rio Grande, and Chimayo Textile Restorations.

Send $2.00 for current catalog (applicable to first order); $2.00 for dye samples; $1.50 for paper pulp samples.

THE FIBER STUDIO

Foster Hill Road
Henniker, NH 03242
(603) 428-7830

Mail Order, Retail Shop;
Established in 1973

THE FIBER STUDIO, owned by Pamela Grob, carries weaving and spinning equipment and accessories from Beka, Schacht, Tools of the Trade, Leclerc, Ashford, and Louet. Spinning fibers include domestic and imported wool, yak, and silk tops, cashmere, flax, and polyester top. New Zealand fleece are available from Romney, Perendale and Border Leicester sheep. Yarns are available, including rug wools, alpacas, mohairs, novelties, silks, Shetland wools, England wool fancies, silk/wool blends, mill-ends, and many others. The Fiber Studio is also a dealer for Studio and Bond Knitting Machines. They offer natural dyes, and a line of unusual handmade buttons.

Many discounts are given; check catalog for information.

Send $2.00 for a current catalog.

FIBRE CRAFTS

38 Center Street
Clinton, NJ 08809
(201) 735-4469

Mail Order, Retail Shop;
Established in 1971

Kerry Adams, owner of FIBRE CRAFTS, offers a large assortment of yarns from Borgs, Maypole, Harrisville Designs, Manos, LaMieux, Henry's Attic, Crown Colony, Maysville, and others. She is an exclusive dealer for all Leclerc looms and accessories, and also carries equipment by Glimakra, Tools of the Trade, Ashford, Louet, Clemes and Clemes, etc. Raw fibers include wools, cashmere, llama, alpaca, flax roving, ramie roving, noils and cotton. Fibre Crafts also carries a wide variety of books on spinning, weaving, dyeing, etc., and offers a wide range of classes.

Quantity discounts are given with a minimum order of $100.00.

Send for a free brochure and price list.

FIRESIDE FIBERS

705 Cook Street
Ketchikan, AK 99901
(907) 225-2983

Mail Order, Retail hours by
appointment; Established in 1979

FIRESIDE FIBERS supplies looms by Glimakra, Schacht, and Rasmussen, and spinning wheels by Ashford and Louet. Yarns are available from Henry's Attic, Cotton Clouds, Wilde, Beka/Simkins, Ironstone Warehouse, and Brown Sheep Company. Fleece are also available in raw form, scoured or dyed. Spinning and weaving classes, as well as custom weaving are offered.

Discounts are given with a minumum order of $100.00.

Send $1.00 for a current catalog (applied to first order).

Loom and Bookmobile from Fireside Looms and Weaving

FIRESIDE LOOMS AND WEAVING

91600 West Fork Road
Deadwood, OR 97430
(503) 964-3771

Manufacturer; Mail Order;
Established in 1972

The owners of FIRESIDE LOOMS AND WEAVING, Gary and Rachel Sweatt, offer handcrafted jack-type looms in 40 and 54-inch weaving widths, with either four or eight harnesses. The looms are built of solid oak, cherry, or walnut, and feature dovetail and mortise and tenon construction. Coupled with the weight of an exceptionally heavy loom frame, these looms can handle the most demanding materials. Each loom is also hand-sanded and rubbed with oil to preserve the natural wooden character. Gary and Rachel say that they stand behind their equipment, and give prompt attention to inquiries. Accessories and additional equipment are available.

Educational discounts are given; write for information.

An illustrated brochure and price list is available for $1.00.

FLORIDA FIBER CO-OP

630 May Street
Jacksonville, FL 32204
(904) 354-6661

Mail Order, Retail Shop; V/MC;
Established in 1981

FLORIDA FIBER CO-OP is an all-purpose fiber supply store that carries a little of everything. Spinning fibers include raw wools, rovings, dyed and carded fleece, camel hair roving, hackled and dressed flax line, and others. Spinning wheels and accessories from Leclerc and Ashford, and looms from Harrisville Designs, Tools of the Trade and Schacht are available. Other offerings include Cushing dyes, Folkwear Patterns, and fiber books. Shetland wool yarns from Harrisville Designs, as well as 100% cottons, cotton blends, mohair/wool blends, cotton/silk blends, silk/wool blends, 100% silks, mohairs and linen, as well as many others, can be ordered.

Co-op members automatically receive a 10% discount on all orders. Other discounts are also given. Write for membership information.

Send $2.00 for a complete package of yarn samples, loom and spinning wheel brochures, book list, etc.

JANE MCGOWN FLYNN, INC.

85 Lakeshore Drive
Box 301
Sterling Junction, MA 01565
(617) 365-7278

Manufacturer; Mail Order;
Established in 1980

JANE MCGOWN FLYNN, INC. carries a number of supplies for rug hooking: frames, cutters, swatches, background hooks, dye books, pamphlets, and hooked rug designs stamped on burlap. Jane also conducts a Correspondence Course for training to teach, and directs three teacher workshops and one rug school.

Educational discounts are given; write for information.

Send $5.00 for a current catalog.

FORT CRAILO YARN COMPANY

2 Green Street
Rensselaer, NY 12144
(518) 465-2371

Manufacturer; Mail Order, Retail Shop; V/MC; Established in 1968

FORT CRAILO YARN COMPANY manufactures several types of virgin wool yarns and cotton yarns. Crailo Rya Wool Yarns are available in 31 shades, Crailo Lite-Spun Wools in 28 shades. Crailo Worsted Wools are available in 28 shades. Crailo-Spun Wool yarns come in 30 shades, while Crailo Combed Cottons are available in 2, 3, 4, 5, and 6-ply and 19 shades.

A 5% discount is given on orders of 50 to 99 pounds. A 10% discount is given on orders of 100 pounds and over.

Send $2.00 for wool yarn samples and 80¢ for cotton samples.

FORTÉ FIBERS

P.O. Box 818
Palisade, CO 81526
(303) 464-7397

Manufacturer; Mail Order;
Established in 1978

FORTÉ FIBERS is a source for beautiful Softspun 100% wool yarns in various sizes and weights, Intrigue 100% wool yarns, and luxury yarns in alpaca, cashmere, camel, etc. Forté also carries a line of beautiful, exotic spinning fibers such as white wool sliver top, dyed and blended wool top, mohair sliver top, dehaired Iranian cashmere in three colors, dehaired Mongolian camel hair (also called "camel down"), dehaired Chinese brown cashmere, silk top in white mulberry and Tussah, alpaca tops in natural colors, Chinese camel down sliver, cashmere slivers in Chinese brown, Persian ecru, and Persian off-white natural.

Retail stores and professional studios selling finished goods made from Forté products can order at wholesale prices. Send for wholesale price list and ordering requirements. A 10% discount is given to schools/guilds, etc.

Send $6.50 for a generous package of spinning fibers and yarn samples (applicable to your first order).

FRANKENMUTH WOOLEN MILL

570 S. Main
Frankenmuth, MI 48734
(517) 652-8121

Manufacturer; Mail Order, Retail
Shop; V/MC; Established in 1894

FRANKENMUTH WOOLEN MILL makes 100% virgin wool batts, and custom hand-tied woolen comforters. In addition to this, they also offer custom wool work. The Mill will wash, scour, pick and card your raw wool into batting or roving. For a slightly higher cost, they will card goat, mohair, alpaca, or other fibers.

Some discounts are given; write for full details.

Write for a free brochure.

HARRY M. FRASER COMPANY

(R & R Machine Co., Inc.)
192 Hartford Road
Manchester, CT 06040
(203) 649-2304

Manufacturer; Mail Order, Retail
Shop; Established in 1950

HARRY M. FRASER COMPANY manufactures and sells a large line of equipment and supplies for rugmaking. These include cloth cutting machines and Fraser cutter heads for cutting fabric strips in various sizes. Fraser also carries such accessories as hooks, rug punch needles, Rush 'n Punch needles, books and manuals on rug hooking, frames and hoops, burlap and monks cloth, wools and wool blends by the pound, rug padding, Cushing dyes, shirret kits, patterns, and more.

Send for a current brochure and price list.

FREELAND BROOK SHEEP AND WOOLS

Russell Road
Blandford, MA 01008
(413) 848-2031

Mail Order, Retail hours by
appointment

Tricia Bergland of FREELAND BROOK SHEEP AND WOOLS sells black and white fleece from registered Border Leicester sheep, Leicester cross sheep, and colored fleece from Lincoln and Lincoln cross sheep.

Discounts are given with a minimum order of 30 pounds of wool.

Send $1.00 for a price list and sample cards.

FRICKE ENTERPRISES

8702 State Road 92
Granite Falls, WA 98252
(206) 691-7590

Manufacturer; Mail Order;
Established in 1973

FRICKE ENTERPRISES manufactures bench wool carders in nine different models. They also offer a "Knuckle-Saving-Batt-Picker."

Send a SASE for a current brochure and price list.

GALLERY ONE

3500 Central, S.E.
Albuquerque, NM 87106
(505) 268-7449

Mail Order, Retail Shop; V/MC;
Established in 1972

GALLERY ONE offers looms, books, accessories, classes and seminars in weaving. They also serve as a showplace for high quality crafts.

Educational discounts are given; write for details.

No catalog is available at this time; write for specific information.

HELEN GANT-THE STUDIO
OF HANDWEAVING

713 E. Willowbrook Drive
Burlington, NC 27215
(919) 226-3330

Manufacturer; Mail Order, Retail
hours by appointment; V/MC;
Established in 1975

HELEN GANT opened her business in 1975 for the same reason that a lot of people do it — she could not find supplies close to her home. Now, her business continues because she carries only first quality yarns — no outlet yarns or mill-ends. Her yarns come from such companies as Henry's Attic, Frederick Fawcett, Galler, J. Marks, Melrose Farms, etc. Ms. Gant also carries the entire line of Schacht, Louet, and Ashford looms and spinning wheels.

Send $1.00 for a current catalog.

GLASS HOUSE FIBER
IMPORTS

P.O. Box 105
Westminster Station, VT 05159
(802) 463-4315

Mail Order; Established in 1977

GLASS HOUSE FIBER IMPORTS carries imported "oddments" such as brushed Italian yarn, KB wools from Scotland, roughspun English wools, and Shetland wools from Scotland. These yarns come in beautiful colors, with such names as jasmine, ivy, iris, blueberry, lupine, etc. The Shetland wool from Scotland is also said to be an excellent yarn for use in knitting machines. Same day shipment is promised on most orders.

Discounts are available; write for information.

Samples of all yarns and a price list is available for $2.00.

THE GLEANERS YARN BARN

P.O. Box 1191
Canton, GA 30114
(404) 479-5083

Mail Order, Retail Shop;
Established in 1974

THE GLEANERS YARN BARN offers a line of first quality mill-end yarns with no labels.

Quantity discounts are given with a minimum order of $200.00.

Send $2.00 for prices and mailing of samples for one year.

GLIMAKRA LOOMS AND YARNS, INC.

P.O. Box 16157
Rocky River, OH 44116
(216) 333-7595
and
P.O. Box 1271 (Western Division)
Sonoma, CA 95476
(717) 938-8229

Mail Order; Established in 1974

GLIMAKRA LOOMS AND YARNS, INC. carries the entire line of traditional Swedish looms and weaving accessories made by the largest manufacturer of looms in the world. The Glimakra floor looms include both "Standard" and "Ideal" model, countermarch looms in various sizes. Counterbalance looms, as well as jack action looms, are also available. Other looms include the Regina Tapestry loom, the Sara tapestry weaving frame, the Victoria table loom, a Flemish weaving frame and belt looms. Glimakra Damask Looms, with a 60-inch weaving width, are also available with various features. Other weaving equipment, as well as a line of books, are supplied. Borgs Yarns from Sweden are also distributed by these companies, and include many wools, cottons, linens, and cottolins (50% cotton/50% linen).

Send $10.00 for a complete sample set of all yarns, and $2.50 for a loom catalog.

GLIMAKRA WEAVING STUDIO

1741 Allston Way
Berkeley, CA 94703
(415) 549-0326

Mail Order; Retail hours by appointment; Established in 1969

GLIMAKRA WEAVING STUDIO, owned by Maj-Britt Mobrand-Robinson, also handles the entire line of Glimakra looms and weaving accessories, as listed in the entry above. Various weaving classes in both traditional and contemporary techniques are offered by Ms. Mobrand-Robinson's Studio.

A 10% discount is given on yarns only with a minimum order of $100.00.

Send $1.00 for a complete Glimakra loom catalog and price list.

THE GOLDEN FLEECE

190 Sacramento Street
Auburn, CA 95603
(916) 885-8118

Mail Order, Retail Shop; V/MC; Established in 1982

THE GOLDEN FLEECE currently carries yarns from 32 different companies. Looms are available from Beka, Schacht, Norwood, Glimakra, Toika, Varpapuu, and Harrisville Designs. Fibers include silk, cotton, mohair, angora, cashmere, yak, and many wools. A large variety of dyes, both natural and synthetic, are also available. Beginning, Intermediate, and Scandinavian weaving classes, as well as creative knitting and crochet classes, are offered.

Send for a current price list.

GOLDEN THREADS WEAVING AND KNITTING STUDIO

120 Main Street, East
Humble, TX 77338
(713) 446-8766

Mail Order, Retail Shop; V/MC/AMEX; Established in 1979

GOLDEN THREADS WEAVING AND KNITTING STUDIO carries a variety of weaving and knitting supplies, including yarns from Unger, Henry's Attic, Knitting Fever, Pingouin, Susan Bates, Tahki, Crystal Place, Anny Blatt, Reynolds, DMC, Merino, Pasa, Blumenthal, Hibiscus, and others. Brother Knitting Machines, as well as looms and spinning equipment are also offered from Harrisville Designs, Beka, Schacht, and Louet.

Quantity discounts are given on yarns. Write for information.

A catalog is not available at this time; write or call for specific prices or other information.

GRANDOR INDUSTRIES, LTD.

4031 Knobhill Drive
Sherman Oaks, CA 91403
(818) 213-5855

Mail order; Established in 1975

GRANDOR is a wholesale supplier for yarns imported from Great Britain in wool, mohair, linen (roving), yak, cotton, and silks. They can also provide domestic chenille yarns and Sunbeam Knitting Yarns. McMorran Yarn Balances are also available from Grandor.

Wholesale discounts are given to qualified retailers and production establishments. Write for information. Others can write for the name of the nearest store or mail order dealer that handles their products.

A complete set of sample cards and a price list is $3.25.

 WHAT IS "ANGORA"?

The angora fiber comes from the angora rabbit. Literally covered with fur, these rabbits produce about sixteen ounces of wool per year. The rabbits believed to have originated in the area of Ankara, Turkey, along with the angora cat, and the angora goat (which produces mohair). Originally regarded as an idol by the Babylonians, angoras were also the pets of sultans and the royal French court of the Middle Ages. Angora is a unique natural fiber, possessing useful characteristics not found in any other fiber. Surprisingly, angora is eight times warmer than sheep's wool. This means that, ounce for ounce, angora has eight times the insulating capacity of sheep's wool. Angora is also one of the softest fibers, and is not irritating like many wools.

— From SunRise Farm brochure

GREAT PLAINS FLEECE

P.O. Box 34068
Omaha, NE 68134
(402) 571-1573

Mail Order; Established in 1976

GREAT PLAINS FLEECE carries a nice assortment of fibers, including U.S. raw wools from Rambouillet, Targhee, black and gray sheep; U.S. prepared wools in medium and low tops, New Zealand wools in gray and black, cleaned and carded, alpaca and camel tops, and Australian colored raw wools from Border Leicester and Merino sheep. The spinning wheels marketed by the company are all manufactured by Ashford. Several books of interest to spinners are also offered.

Wholesale discounts are given to qualified businesses; write for prices.

Send 50¢ for a current price list. Samples are also 50¢.

GREAT SCOT

5606 Mohican Road
Bethesda, MD 20816
(301) 229-3632

Mail Order; Established in 1983

GREAT SCOT has invented and markets the Great Scot Argyler, a new device that makes it possible to hand knit argyle patterns without bobbins. The company also carries patterns for adult and children's sizes, and imports Shetland yarns in kits.

Send $2.00 for a brochure and yarn samples.

PATRICK GREEN CARDERS, LTD.

48793 Chilliwack Lake Road
Sardis, B.C.
CANADA V2R 2P1
(604) 858-6020

Manufacturer; Mail Order;
Established in 1974

PATRICK GREEN CARDERS, LTD. manufactures wool pickers and drum carding equipment for spinners and weavers. Paula Simmons, spinner, weaver, author, and lecturer, is currently working with the company as a technical advisor and consultant. Patrick Green Carders is now supplying the new improved "Paula's Picker," a wool picker that is based on the cradle wool picker detailed in Ms. Simmons' book "The Handspinner's Guide to Selling," published in 1979. Paula's Picker is a continuous process machine that passes the wool from the front to the rear, where it can drop into a box or container. The picker will tease, clean and/or blend your wool prior to carding, and will pick six to ten-pounds of wool per hour. The standard picker is constructed of mahogany, but is also available in Eastern maple. Patrick Green also offers a 16-inch Cottage Industry Carding Machine (power-driven). This machine was developed to fill the gap between the table-top drum carders and the larger mill machinery. It can handle long staple wools from two inches and up, including mohair. This carder will produce eight to ten pounds an hour in batt form, or six to eight pounds an hour of rovings. Drum carders are also available from this source in three grades. Other accessories and supplies are available, such as industrial fetling combs, swifts, doffer sticks, flickers, fetling brushes, carding cloth fillet, and replacement drive belts.

Send for a free brochure and price list on all equipment.

NOTE: Due to the potentially dangerous nature of the Paula's Picker, Patrick Green Carders, Ltd. has added a positive lock on the swinging cradle to protect children and unauthorized people from playing with the machine and causing possible injury. The author strongly recommends that the user of this device take all requisite safety precautions and follow operating instructions, in order to minimize the risk of accident or injury. Also, the author and publisher take no responsibility whatsoever for any such injuries as might occur during the use of this machine.

Paula Simmons with "Paula's Picker"
Patrick Green Cottage Industry Carder

GREEN MOUNTAIN SPINNERY

Box 54
Putney, VT 05346
(802) 387-4528

Manufacturer; Mail Order, Retail Shop; V/MC; Established in 1981

GREEN MOUNTAIN SPINNERY, a worker-owned cooperative, is also the smallest spinnery in the United States. They supply New England wool yarns put up on cones for machine knitters or weavers. The yarns, available in 17 shades, include ten "Colonial Colors." The Spinnery also offers natural white and grey carded fleece. Vermont Designer Kits and Knitting Patterns include pullovers, vests, hats, socks, cardigans, etc. Production tours of the Spinnery are also given on the first and third Friday of each month for a 50¢ charge.

Discounts are given to schools/guilds, etc. with a $50.00 minimum order.

Send $1.50 for a price list and samples of all yarns.

MYAL GRIFFIN-NATIVE AND EXOTIC FIBERS

R.D. #1, Box 5404
Grove City, PA 16127
(814) 786-9776

Manufacturer; Mail Order;
Established in 1980

MYAL GRIFFIN handspins over 200 pounds of yarn per year, and specializes in yarns of wool and exotic fibers such as alpaca, camel, cashmere, mohair and silk. Custom handspun yarns are available, as are coned yarns for weaving. Rainbow Mills Handspun and hand-dyed silk yarns are also offered.

Wholesale discounts are given to designers and retail shops with a minimum order of $100.00. Write for further information.

Send a SASE for a current brochure and price list.

HALCYON

12 School Street
Bath, ME 04530
(207) 442-7909

Mail Order, Retail Shop;
Established in 1972

HALCYON offers a unique mail order presentation service — their complete "Yarn Store in a Box." A suitcase-type box comes packed with over 42 yarn sample sheets which also give suggestions on usage, sett, compatible yarns, stitches and rows per inch for knitters, other tips, etc. The yarns are exclusively manufactured for Halcyon by many well known yarn companies. A small sampling of the yarns offered include "Rustic" 100% wools, warps (wools, linens), "Kitten" yarn by Reynolds, Farm Meadow Tweeds and Heathers, Astro-Glow Metallics, Pomfret Sport Wools by Brunswick, Luxury Yarns (cashmeres, silks, camel), Homestead 100% cottons in 51 shades, Featherlight Merino, Gemstone Silks, Victorian wools, 4-ply 100% Wool Rug Yarns in 50 shades, Linens, carpet warps, Pearl Cottons in 66 shades, Scottish tapestry wools, Oregon Worsted wools, Halcyon Rug Wools in "Desert Blush," "Desert Sunset," and "Maine Coast" shades, Victorian brushed mohair in 36 shades, and many, many more! Fibers for spinning include wool tops, rovings, Harrisville Dyed and Carded Fleece, cashmere, camel down tops, cottons, flax, ramie, alpacas, Tussah and cultivated silk tops, carded silk noils, angora rabbit/lambswool blend, and others. To round out their extensive selection of supplies, Halcyon has also included brochures on Schacht Spindle, Louet, Loomcraft, and Leclerc spinning and weaving equipment, tools and accessories. Other supplies are also available, including a list of over 200 books.

Many different quantity discounts are available; check catalog for prices.

Now — the price for all this wonderful information: The "Yarn Store in a Box" plus periodic newsletter updates, new sample sheets, and new catalogs, is $23.00. (A $10.00 credit is applied after the first $50.00 in orders). Halcyon takes your order by phone (toll free), it is processed instantly and usually shipped within 24 hours. Invoices are sent with the order.

MARTHA HALL

46 Main Street
Yarmouth, ME 04096
(207) 846-9334

Mail Order, Retail Shop;
V/MC/AMEX; Established in
1972

MARTHA HALL carries looms by Harrisville, Leclerc, Schacht, Norwood, Beka, Northfield, and Glimakra. Spinning wheels are furnished by Louet, Ashford, Wee Peggy, and Pipy. Yarns include wools, silks, alpacas, cottons, cottolins, linens, rayons, cashmeres, camel hairs, and more.

Discounts are given to individuals and groups; write for information.

Send $2.00 for a catalog (refundable with first order).

HANDWEAVER

340 Coventry Road
Virginia Beach, VA 23462
(804) 497-1461

Manufacturer; Mail Order, Retail
Shop; V/MC; Established in 1976

HANDWEAVER manufactures a tapestry loom, and carries other looms by Leclerc, Herald, and Harrisville. They carry many supplies for tapestry weaving, such as yarns, wools, perle cottons, bobbins, and warp from France. They also offer classes and workshops in tapestry weaving.

Write for more information.

HARMONY FARM

Rt. 1, Box 175A
Ware Shoals, SC 29692
(803) 861-2991

Mail Order, Retail Shop;
Established in 1980

HARMONY FARM offers fleece from Romney and Lincoln sheep, both white and colored. Carded wool batts, as well as vegetal dyed fleece, are also available. The company also supplies mohair fibers, handspun yarns, and looms from Harrisville and Tools of the Trade.

Send $1.00 plus a large SASE for a sample card and prices.

HARRISVILLE DESIGNS, INC.

Main Street
Harrisville, NH 03450
(603) 827-3334

Harrisville is a village nestled in the Monadnock Highlands of southwestern New Hampshire. It is recognized as the only nineteenth century textile village that survives in its original form in the entire country. The people at HARRISVILLE DESIGNS, INC. are dedicated to preserving the tradition of craftsmanship that was established in earlier times. As weavers themselves, they strive to make the finest handweaving yarns and equipment possible. Harrisville products include a line of handweaving looms and accessories, 100% wool Cable Yarns, Shetland Style 2-ply yarns, 100% wool Designer Yarns, Homespun Yarns, Natural Yarns, and much more.

As Harrisville Design products are not sold directly to individuals, please contact them for the name of the dealer closest to you. They do, however, offer classes and workshops in the fall, spring, and summer; write for a descriptive brochure.

Interested dealers may receive a catalog by sending $4.00.

Yarns and accessories; Ashford spinning wheel

Model A Four Harness loom

Harrisville Designs loom shed with shuttle

HEIRLOOM

P.O. Box 239
Rochelle, IL 61068-0239
(800) 435-2938

Manufacturer; Mail Order; V/MC;
Established in 1916

HEIRLOOM supplies worsted spun yarns on one pound cones suitable for machine knitting, weaving, hand knitting, and crochet. Most of the yarns are synthetics or synthetic blends, although several 100% pure virgin wool yarns are offered. All of the yarns are available in many solid and heathered shades.

Quantity (over six pounds) discounts are given to all; additional discounts are given to qualified retailers.

Send $2.50 for a folder containing all yarn samples and prices (applied to first order).

HEMLOCK HILL FARM

P.O. Box 148
Sabillasville, MD 21780
(301) 241-3944

Manufacturer; Mail Order, Retail
hours by appointment;
Established in 1974

John and Jean Woodward of HEMLOCK HILL FARM breed registered Romney, Border Leicester, and Black cross sheep for their fleece. They carry looms by Leclerc, Schacht, Harrisville, and spinning wheels by Louet, Ashford, and Leclerc. Yarns include handspun wools, cottons, and silks. They have also designed and are producing their own spinning wheel called the "Hemlock Hill Handspinner" in solid maple hardwood. The Woodwards offer spinning and weaving classes, and promise that they have sheep to pet and free advice when you need it!

Various discounts are given; write for information.

Send a SASE for a brochure.

HENRY'S ATTIC

5 Mercury Avenue
Monroe, NY 10950
(914) 783-3930

Mail Order; Established in 1972

HENRY'S ATTIC, owned by Henry and Samira Galler, supplies a large number of natural fiber textured yarns in silks, cottons, wools, linens, mohairs, cashmere/wool blends, and more. These yarns are very interesting and will add a lot of textural interest to your weavings. Henry's Attic is also known for their service and reliability, and they are usually well-stocked at all times.

Although Henry's Attic does not usually sell directly to the public, they will send names of mail-order dealers on request. Retailers should write for wholesale information.

Send $7.50 for a complete sample set and price list.

HERALD LOOMS

118 Lee Street
Lodi, OH 44254
(216) 948-1080

Manufacturer; Mail Order, Retail
shop; Established in 1954

HERALD LOOMS manufactures jack-type floor looms in weaving widths of 24, 32, 40 and 45-inches, with four or eight harnesses. The looms are available in natural or walnut finishes. Related accessories are also offered. Tours of the manufacturing plant are conducted by appointment only. Future weaving classes are also planned.

Send for a free brochure.

HERITAGE HUT

916 S. Oliver
Wichita, KS 67219
(316) 682-4082

Mail Order, Retail Shop; V/MC;
Established in 1972

HERITAGE HUT carries a wide selection of yarns from such manufacturers as Unger, Pingouin, Berroco, Tahki, Reynolds, Brown Sheep Company, Andean, Lily, and Hibiscus Yarns. They also carry various mill-ends as available.

School/guild discounts are given with a minimum order of $100.00.

Request samples of specific yarns and prices.

HOLLY BIRCH FARM

3576 Ridgeway Road, R.D. #1
Lakehurst, NJ 08733
(201) 657-0565

Mail Order, Retail hours by
appointment

HOLLY BIRCH FARMS carries the full line of Louet products, as well as Ashford spinning wheels, handspun yarns, dyes, accessories, fleece and angora. Classes are also offered in spinning and knitting.

Send $1.00 for a current catalog.

HOME WOOLS

R.D. #2, Box 167D
Dundee, NY 14837
(607) 243-5282

Mail Order, Retail hours by
appointment; Established in 1982

Marty and Perry McGee of HOME WOOLS raise llamas and Jacob sheep, and farm with Percheron draft horses. They sell both the wools and handspun yarns from these animals. They also offer Louet products — spinning wheels, looms and carding equipment. Marty teches weaving and spinning classes on an individual basis, and the farm is open to visitors by appointment.

Send for a current price list.

Marty and Perry McGee collect wool from their llama "Tingo"

HOMEPLACE

1676 S. Lumpkin Street
Athens, GA 30606
(404) 549-0829

Mail Order, Retail Shop;
V/MC/AMEX; Established in
1976

HOMEPLACE is primarily a gift business, but they also carry a variety of weaving and spinning supplies. These include looms by Harrisville, Leclerc, Schacht, Loomcraft, Norwood and Glimakra, along with accessories. They also carry yarns by Lily, Borgs, Harrisville, Leclerc, Berroco, Maysville, and others. Classes are offered in beginning and intermediate weaving.

A 25% discount is given with a $135.00 minimum order. A 5% discount is given on loom sales when payment is made with order.

A catalog is $2.00.

HOMESPUN & HANDWOVEN

330 Avenue D
Snohomish, WA 98290
(206) 568-8101

Mail Order, Retail Shop;
Established in 1980

HOMESPUN & HANDWOVEN carries a diverse line of weaving and spinning supplies, including looms by Beka, Schacht, Rasmussen, Herald, Glimakra, and Harrisville. Yarns are from Merino, Tahki, Berroco, Brown Sheep, Lily, Oregon Worsted, Green Mountain Spinnery, Crystal Palace, and others. Spinning wheels are available from Ashford, Clemes, Poly Wheel, and Wee Peggy. Classes, workshops, and custom work are also offered.

A 10% discount is given on sales of $100.00 or more.

Send for a current catalog. A $5.00 donation will keep you on the mailing list for one year.

HOMESPUN FIBER ARTS

1550 Lewis Center Road
Lewis Center, OH 43035
(614) 548-6189

Manufacturer; Mail Order, Retail Shop; V/MC; Established in 1976

HOMESPUN FIBER ARTS offers looms and equipment from Tools of the Trade, Kyra, Dorset and Schacht, and spinning wheels by Ashford. Yarns are available from Blumenthal (Lily), Novitex, Fawcett, School Products, Manos, Silk City, Candide, Condon, Bates, Pingouin, Tahki, Oregon Worsted, Conshohocken Cottons, and many others. Spinning fibers include wools, flax, alpaca, mohair, and angora. They also carry natural and synthetic dyes, some basketry supplies, books and magazines.

A 10% discount is given with minimum orders of $25.00 with a tax resale number, and to schools.

Write for specific prices; a catalog is not available at this time.

HOOK & NEEDLE GALLERY

8653 Apple Hill Road
Chagrin Falls, OH 44022
(216) 543-9228 or (216) 247-3123

Mail Order, Retail hours by appointment; Established in 1980

The HOOK & NEEDLE GALLERY, owned by Fran Willey and Pat Keyes, provides a large line of rug hooking supplies; Dorr Mills 100% wool fabrics (57 inches wide) by the yard, hand-dyed swatches, Scottish burlap, Cushing dyes, rug binding tapes, Jiffy Frame and hoops, hooks in three sizes, Bliss wool stripping machine, and a Puritan lap frame. The Gallery also offers rug hooking designs and kits, custom designs and color plans, classes and workshops.

Various discounts are given; check catalog for details.

Send $4.00 for a current catalog which includes updated supplements.

HUB MILLS FACTORY STORE

12 Perkins Street
Lowell, MA 01854
(617) 937-0320

Mail Order, Retail Shop; V/MC; Established in 1982

HUB MILLS is a factory outlet store located in the heart of the old mill district of Lowell, Massachusetts. The majority of the yarns are manufactured on the premises, which results in a constant variety of stock available. These yarns include 100% wools in various weights, mohair/wool and nylon blends, silk and Merino wool blends, 100% acrylics, 100% cottons, and more. Hub Mills Factory Store also handles Brother and Passap Knitting Machines, and offers knitting classes. They guarantee personal service and a large selection at all times.

A 10% discount is given with a minimum order of $200.00.

Send $1.00 for yarn samples and a price list.

S & C HUBER
ACCOUTREMENTS

82 Plants Dam Road
East Lyme, CT 06333
(203) 739-0772

Mail Order; Established in 1967

S & C HUBER ACCOUTREMENTS offers a variety of spinning fibers, as well as many other interesting items.

Discounts are given with a minimum order of $100.00.

Send $1.50 for a current catalog.

 ABOUT THE ALPACA ...

The Alpaca is a new world camel of the same family as the coarser-haired llama, virtually extinct guanaco, and the endangered vicuna. It is indigenous strictly to the highlands of the Andes Mountains of Peru and Bolivia (about 85% in Peru), and thrives at altitudes of 13,000 to 15,000 feet. The wool is sheared every two years to insure sufficient fiber length for spinning. Unfortunately, the alpaca is not very prolific. This factor, coupled with the inability of a significant portion of the babies to survive the extremely harsh Andes climate, has lead to the stabilization of the population at around 3,000,000 animals.

— From the Andean Yarns, Inc. catalog.

JANINE HUDSON

Handspun Silk Yarns
334 Bowery 2F
New York, NY 10012
(212) 477-5615

Manufacturer; Mail Order;
Established in 1982

JANINE HUDSON has a line of unique handspun silk yarns, all in beautiful, vibrant hand-dyed colors. She also carries machine spun, hand-dyed silk ribbons, chenilles, cords, and bourettes in the same colors.

Send $1.00 for a price list and samples; a Silk Sampler is also available for $21.00 + $2.00 postage.

HUMBOLDT BAY SHEEP &
WOOL COMPANY

P.O. Box 4392
Arcata, CA 95521
(707) 822-7716

Manufacturer; Mail Order, Retail
Shop; V/MC; Established in 1983

HUMBOLDT BAY SHEEP & WOOL COMPANY sells historical crafts and supplies in a turn-of-the-century setting. They offer Candide knitting yarns in two weights, Romney raw fleece, batts and rovings for spinning, felting or quilting, handspun Romney yarns, cardweaving cards, the McMorran Yarn Balance, rubber stamps, Louet and Ashford spinning wheels, a large number of books, knitting patterns, and many other "sheepish" supplies and accessories. The company also offers a custom wool carding, blending, scouring and picking service.

A current catalog is $1.00. A very interesting newsletter is published for $4.00 per year.

INDIAN VALLEY WOODWORKING

Rt. 1, Box 17, White Oak Road
Bradfordsville, KY 40009
(502) 337-3268

Manufacturer; Mail Order, Retail shop; Established in 1973

INDIAN VALLEY WOODWORKING manufactures a solid black walnut spinning wheel with a 12-inch bobbin that holds up to three pounds of wool. The wheel design allows high speed or production spinning, smooth treadling, and a flyer brake that regulates the draw-in. The ⅞″ orifice accomodates a variety of yarn sizes and textures. Also available are lazy kates and bobbins, and an Indian Valley spinning head that can be attached to an old treadle sewing machine base.

Send a SASE for a free brochure and price sheet.

INTERNATIONAL CREATIONS, INC.

P.O. Box 696
Stony Brook, NY 11790

Mail Order; V/MC; Established in 1963

INTERNATIONAL CREATIONS, INC. is the mail order distributor for Reynolds brand knitting yarns.

Send 50¢ for color cards and a current price list.

INTERTWINE YARN & FIBER SUPPLY

130 East 900 South
Salt Lake City, UT 84111
(801) 363-9305

Mail Order, Retail Shop; V/MC; Established in 1971

INTERTWINE YARN & FIBER SUPPLY carries a variety of supplies for the fiber arts.

Various discounts are given; check catalog for details.

Send $1.00 for a current catalog.

ISLAND HANDSPUN

Rt. 1, Box 798
Vashon Island, WA 98070
(206) 567-4027

Manufacturer; Mail Order; Established in 1978

Suzette Moulin of ISLAND HANDSPUN can provide wool yarns, spun by hand from long staple New Zealand fleece which is especially selected for its softness, warmth, and luster. The beautiful, exciting colors range from natural shades to hand-dyed variegated or solid colors. The dyes are used over white fleece for solid, clear shades, and over grey fleece for muted, heathery tones. All of the yarns, however, retain a special richness because of the natural luster of the New Zealand fleece.

Wholesale prices apply if yarn or finished products are for resale. Write for more information.

Send $1.00 for a price list and wool samples.

JAGGERSPUN

Water Street
Springvale, ME 04083
(207) 324-4455

Manufacturer; Mail Order; V/MC;
Established in 1983

JAGGERSPUN is a new division of Jagger Brothers, Inc., a spinner of fine quality worsted specialty yarns since the 1880's, and supplier to large commercial knitters and weavers. Because of the many requests that they had for smaller quantities of various yarns, JaggerSpun was started. They offer only natural fiber yarns, wool and wool/silk blends, which they sell through mail order and some yarn shops. JaggerSpun's yarn line currently consists of JaggeRagg, Mountain Heather, Zephyr Wool-Silk, Superfine Merino, Highland Heather, Alpine Frost wool/mohair blend, and the Maine Line, appropriate for machine knitting.

Quantity discounts are given; check catalog for details.

Send $4.00 for complete sample cards of all yarns and price list (applied to first order).

J-MADE LOOMS & WEAVING ACCESSORIES

P.O. Box 452
Oregon City, OR 97045
(503) 631-3973

Manufacturer; Mail Order, Retail Shop; V/MC; Established in 1969

J-MADE LOOMS provides a variety of Alaskan birch and maple looms and accessories. The 22 and 30-inch table looms with 4, 8, and 12 harnesses can be converted to floor looms with Conversion Kits. Multi-Harness Floor Looms are available in 45, 60, and 72 inch weaving widths, in a choice of 4, 8, or 12 harnesses. All floor looms include a Worm Gear Brake System. A large line of weaving accessories are also available and include benches, shuttles, bobbins, tapestry beaters, shed sticks, reeds, puleys, niddy noddys, etc.

Wholesale discounts are given to qualified dealers; write for information.

Send $1.50 for a Loom catalog, and $1.00 for an Accessories catalog.

JONES SHEEP FARM

R.R. #2, Box 185
Peabody, KS 66866
(316) 983-2815

Mail Order; Established in 1966

The people at JONES SHEEP FARM aren't kidding when they claim that they have the largest selection of colored wools in the United States. They can provide wool from 26 different breeds of sheep. These include: Corriedale, Romney, Cheviot, Targhee, Karakul, Columbia, Navajo, Spinning Cross, Cotswold, Lincoln, Tunis, Kerry Hills, Hampshire, Southdown, Oxford, Dorset, Suffolk, Border Leicester, Finnsheep, and more! The Farm also sells a "Breeds of Sheep" booklet and black sheep breeding stock. Spinning lessons are given at the Farm each June.

Discounts are given with a minimum order of 50 pounds.

Send $1.00 for a current price list of available wools.

KAMOURASKA YARNS

Route 230, West
St. Pascal, Quebec
CANADA G0L 3Y0
(418) 492-3517

Mail Order; Established in 1925

KAMOURASKA YARNS are made in Quebec, and are an all-Canadian product. The company currently has two yarn collections, the "Tradition" collection, and "Haute Mode" collection. The "Tradition" yarns are blends of 75% virgin wools/20% nylons/5% acrylics, and some 100% virgin wools. The "Haute Mode" collection consists of 60% wools/40% cottons, 60% wools/40% mohairs, and wool/acrylic/polyester blends. All of the yarns are beautiful, and are suitable for knitting.

Write for ordering information.

KESSENICH LOOM & KNIT SHOP, INC.

7463 Harwood Avenue
Wauwatosa, WI 53213
(414) 258-2025

Manufacturer; Mail Order, Retail
Shop; Established in 1952

KESSENICH manufactures and sells Standard Foot Looms built of red oak with 4, 6, or 8 harnesses in weaving widths of 30, 36, 42, and 46 inches. Sectional beams, available at extra cost, are equipped with counter, guide and tension box. Kessenich Standard Hand Operated Looms (4 harness) are available with weaving widths of 30 and 36 inches, and specially built 72 inch widths. The table loom manufactured by Kessenich is a 4-harness, hand operated loom in weaving widths of 20, 14, and 10 inches. Also available are many weaving supplies, accessories and pattern books. The company also carries yarns by Bernat, Berroco, Bucilla, Merino, Pingouin, Plymouth, Reynolds, Tahki, Unger, Maysville, Novitex, etc.

Discounts are given with a minimum order of $100.00.

Send for a free loom brochure and price list.

KINGS VALLEY ANIMAL FAMILY

Rt. 2, Box 62
Monmouth, OR 97361
(503) 929-2100

Manufacturer; Mail Order, Retail
hours by appointment;
Established in 1971

The owners of KINGS VALLEY ANIMAL FAMILY say that their acquaintance with sheep began in 1970 with "Emily," a charming white bummer lamb who lived in their house, ran with their dogs, used the cat's litter box, and slept in a basket beside their bed! They now sell registered breeding stock of colored and white Romney and Romney/Salish sheep and other animals. They also offer carefully skirted, clean fleece in the grease for handspinning from their flock. Farm tours are also offered.

Quantity discounts are given with a minimum fleece order of 50 pounds.

Send a SASE for a general brochure, a flock list or a detailed fleece list with prices. Fleece samples are available for $2.00 (applied to order).

KLOTH BY KATHEE

402 Countyview Drive
Mill Valley, CA 94941
(415) 383-8631

Mail Order; Established in 1982

Kathleen Jermaine, owner of KLOTH BY KATHEE, has been selling mill-end yarns to local shops, weavers, and knitters for about four years. She is now expanding into mail order mill-end wool and wool blend yarns, which come in a wide range of colors and shapes. Although the colors and quantities vary with each shipment, Kathleen says that the yarns are great for weaving clothing, rugs, tapestries, or for knitting. The yarns are available in three weights.

Despite the minimum order policy of 100 pounds, the yarns are priced low, and the samples include some nice contemporary colors.

Send a large SASE for a price list and samples of available yarns.

KNITKING CORPORATION

1128 Crenshaw Blvd.
Los Angeles, CA 90019
(213) 938-2077

Mail Order, Retail Shop; V/MC;
Established in 1934

KNITKING CORPORATION offers a line of supplies for machine knitting, including KnitKing and Genie Knitting Machines, KnitKing yarns, books, and other products. The corporation also publishes *KnitKing Magazine,* the only knitting machine magazine produced in North America. A seminar is offered each year in October for machine knitters.

Quantity discounts are given; write for details.

Send for a free catalog.

KNOTS & TREADLES

101 E. Pittsburgh Street
Delmont, PA 15626
(412) 468-4265

Mail Order, Retail hours by
appointment; V/MC; Established
in 1980

KNOTS & TREADLES, owned by Peggy Cost-Peltz, offers looms by Harrisville Designs, Herald, Leclerc, Tools of the Trade, Beka, and Schacht. Yarns are from Tahki, Reynolds, Phildar, E'lite, Berroco, Unger, plus many odd-lots. Other items include knitting machines, dyes, and over 100 fiber art book titles. Various classes are given in weaving, spinning, etc.

Send a SASE for a free brochure.

THE KNOTTING CHAMBER

3257 S.E. Hawthorne Blvd.
Portland, OR 97214
(503) 232-1043

Mail Order, Retail Shop; V/MC;
Established in 1979

THE KNOTTING CHAMBER is one of the largest yarn stores in the United States. They carry complete lines in about 400 types of knitting and weaving yarns, from about 50 different suppliers. The Knotting Chamber is located in a Victorian house, painted lavender. Sounds like an interesting place to visit! Knitting classes are also given.

A 10% discount is given on orders of $100.00 or more.

Write for specific information; a catalog is not available at this time.

KRAFTWORKS STUDIO

Otto Star Route
Box 117E
Spencer, WV 25276
(304) 927-5936

Manufacturer; Mail Order, Retail
hours by appointment;
Established in 1979

Susan Kraft of KRAFTWORKS STUDIO (how lucky to have a name like that!) raises her own angora goats and handspins the mohair fibers she gets from them. These handspun yarns are available in several stock colors, or can be custom dyed to your specifications. These beautiful yarns come in such colors as terra cotta, dusty rose, teal, blueberry, etc.

Send a SASE for a current price list.

LA LANA WOOLS

Box 2461
Taos, NM 87571
(505) 758-9631

Manufacturer; Mail Order; Retail
Shop; Established in 1978

Luisa Gelente, owner of LA LANA WOOLS, makes and sells her own handspun and plant-dyed yarns of wool, silk, mohair blends, exotic fibers and textures. She also offers carded blends for spinners and felters, custom work, and spinning and dyeing classes.

Various discounts are given to schools and individuals. Write for details.

Send a SASE for general information, which will list prices of various sample cards.

LA PAJAROSA

2010 Pleasant Valley Road
Aptos, CA 95003
(408) 724-2044

Mail Order; Established in 1960

LA PAJAROSA is a supplier of colored wools (beige, silver, black, and white) from Lincoln-Corriedale sheep, with a seven to eight inch staple.

Discounts are given with a minimum order of 20 pounds.

Send $2.00 for sample (applied to first order).

LACIS

2982 Adeline Street
Berkeley, CA 94703
(415) 843-7178

Manufacturer; Mail Order, Retail
Shop; V/MC; Established in 1965

LACIS is a textile arts center specializing in antique lace and textiles, as well as tools, equipment, and services geared to the less-known textile arts such as bobbin lace, Battenberg and Point Lace, tatting, Kumi-Himo (Japanese Braiding), Filet and other lace techniques. Specific supplies include lace threads (cottons, gimps, silks, metallics, nylons, and linens), bobbins (over 20 in all), pillows, bobbin winders, prickers, lace kits, tapes, netting needles and shuttles, specialty fabrics, tatting shuttles, knitting needles, crochet hooks, Tambour lace hooks and kits, smocking supplies, rugmaking supplies, patterns, and much more. Some weaving supplies are also offered, and include the Kliot Bow Loom, the Kliot Tapestry Loom, shuttles, tapestry bobbins and beaters, etc. An enormous number of books on the history of lace, textiles, lace techniques, patterns, needlework, etc. are also offered by Lacis. The company also offers classes, seminars and textile conservation services.

Discounts are given to schools/guilds, etc. Many of the items in the Lacis catalog are also available on a wholesale basis to qualified retailers; write for more information.

Send $1.00 for a very complete catalog.

> WOOL YARNS ALSO VARY IN QUALITY. OFTEN you can judge if a skein is good just by the feel. Poor quality yarns are made from coarser and shorter fibers whereas top quality wool worsted yarns are made from the finest and longest wool fibers. This will also make a difference in the yardage in comparing yarns. Quality yarns should not irritate the skin.
>
> — A tip from Mary Lue's Yarn Shop

LAS MANOS, INC

7131 Midbury Drive in Kramer
Center
Dallas, TX 75230
(214) 739-1940

Mail Order, Retail Shop; V/MC;
Established in 1967

LAS MANOS, INC., owned and operated by Barbara Ryan, tries to stock yarns by small companies or individuals. In addition to these yarns, many of which are handspun, Barbara also carries yarns from such suppliers as Anny Blatt, Hibiscus, Reynolds, and La Lana. Other items offered include fabrics from Guatemala, Cushing dyes, books, etc. Ms. Ryan also offers workshops in fibers, creative clothing, fiber jewelry, rigid heddle weaving, etc.

Quantity discounts are given with a minimum order of $100.00.

Send for a current price list.

LEAFWOOD STUDIO

3007 Leafwood Drive
Marietta, GA 30067
(404) 952-0694

Retail Shop; Established in 1981

Although LEAFWOOD STUDIO does not deal in mail order supplies, they do offer a complete loom and spinning wheel repair service, specializing in antique looms and wheels.

Write for more information.

NILUS LECLERC, INC.

C. P. 69, L'Islet
Quebec, CANADA G0R 2C0
(418) 247-3975

Manufacturer; Mail Order;
Established in 1876

NILUS LECLERC, INC. has been manufacturing looms and weaving equipment for a long time, and has earned a well-deserved reputation for high quality items. They offer a complete line of looms in all sizes, from their 15¾" "Maya" backstrap loom to their 12-harness Dobby loom with flying shuttle beater. Other supplies include spinning wheels, bobbin winders, spindles, carders, benches, tapestry supplies, sectional warp beams, warping mills, reeds, swifts, shuttles, bobbins, and all necessary accessories. Therapeutic looms and "bed patient" loom racks are also available. A custom loom-building service for studios, rehabilitation centers, etc. is also offered. A line of books, including the "Master Weaver" Encyclopedia of Weaving, is available.

Leclerc sells directly to dealers only. Write for the address of your nearest mail order outlet. Interested retail establishments should write for wholesale information.

A Leclerc catalog is 25¢.

LEMCO

P.O. Box 40545
San Francisco, CA 94140

Mail Order; Established in 1974

LEMCO is an all-around craft supplier who also carries a number of fiber supplies. Along with waxed cotton and linen threads, Lemco carries several types of jute, Belgian linen flax, and leather thongs. Synthetic fibers include tubular rayons in 16 shades and various braided cords. Raw fibers include wool, ramie tops, Tussah silks, degassed ramie, ramie noils, and raw jute roving. Other supplies such as beads, rings, and bells are also carried. A number of basketry supplies are also listed in Lemco's catalog.

A 10% discount is given on orders of $50.00 or more.

Send $2.00 for separate "Macrame and Fiber Arts" catalog. For a complete set of supply catalogs, send $10.00.

R. H. LINDSAY COMPANY

393 D Street
Boston, MA 02210
(617) 268-4620

Mail Order; Established in 1936

R. H. LINDSAY COMPANY is a third-generation family-owned business that specializes in wool. They can supply at least five breeds of New Zealand greasy fleece in natural and dyed colors, available for prompt delivery. Scoured and carded Romney/Perendale fleece blends are available in eight natural shades, as well as carded in five shades. They also have Icelandic tops in three shades, and British Isles wools, Jacob, and Irish crossbreeds in greasy fleece form.

Wholesale prices are given to those retailers buying for resale. The minimum order is 10 pounds.

Send $2.50 for current catalog.

LITTLE SHEPHERD

48924 Wear Road
Belleville, MI 48111
(313) 461-6392

LITTLE SHEPHERD offers The Support Spindle, which features a solid brass base, whorl and shaft, stainless steel ball bearings and a safety tip. The spindle will fit in your pocket or purse and goes anywhere.

Dealer inquiries are invited.

Send for a free brochure.

LOOM ROOM

6813 W. 45th, North
Wichita, KS 67205
(316) 722-7862

Mail Order; Established in 1980

LOOM ROOM specializes in and carries only Navajo wool yarns in twelve colors, spun from wool produced on the Navajo Indian Reservation from their sheep.

Send $1.00 for brochure and sample card.

LOOMCRAFT

P.O. Box 65
Littleton, CO 80160
(303) 789-3066

Manufacturer; Mail Order;
Established in 1970

LOOMCRAFT manufactures 4, 6, and 8-harness looms in weaving widths of 30, 40, and 45 inches. These are available in a choice of three hand-rubbed hardwoods: maple, cherry, or walnut. Other options are plain or sectional warp beam rails, additional reeds and heddles, a Double Warp and Back Beam System. Weaving benches are also available.

Send for a free brochure.

THE LOOMS

Shake Rag Street
Mineral Point, WI 53565
(608) 987-2277

Mail Order, Retail Shop; V/MC;
Established in 1965

THE LOOMS specialize in complex weaving equipment and patterns and are dealers for AVL, Leclerc, Harrisville, and Glimakra looms. They have been involved with the AVL Pattern Master textile design computer system, and market it as well as other AVL computer programs. The Looms also carries unusual tools for weavers, as well as a number of books. A number of unique workshops are offered. Among these are Complex Looms, Finn Weave, Overshot, Production Techniques, as well as more basic topics. The Looms is also involved in, and can provide information on, The Annual Conference on the Creation of Complex Weave Structures.

Send for a free catalog and booklist.

LOUET SALES

Box 70
Carleton Place, Ontario
CANADA K7C 3P3

Manufacturer; Mail Order;
Established in 1981

LOUET SALES in Ontario is the North American distributor for all Louet products. These include spinning wheels, skeinwinders, portable and mini spinning wheels, spindles, bobbins, flax spindle, lazy kate, felting supplies, drum and hand carders, convertible table loom, frame loom and warping posts.

Qualified retailers should write for more information. Others may write for a list of Louet dealers in your area.

Send for a free full-color catalog.

LOVE BUNNYS

870 Valley High Avenue
Thousand Oaks, CA 91362
(805) 496-3894

Mail Order; Established in 1983

Susan Isaac of LOVE BUNNYS sells English and French angora rabbit wool (homegrown) and handspun yarns. Custom spinning and dyeing, as well as custom handmade garments in natural fibers are available. Susan also teaches spinning, beginning weaving, and angora rabbit raising.

Some discounts are given; write for information.

No catalog is available at this time; write for specific prices.

MC FARLAND CUSTOM
CARDING

Rt. 3, Box 244
Columbus, WI 53925
(414) 623-3686

Manufacturer; Mail Order, Retail
Shop; Established in 1983

MC FARLAND CUSTOM CARDING offers colored and white Romney raw wools, well skirted. Custom carding services are also available. Other supplies include Kiton dyes, camel hair, Chinese cashmere, mohair, goat hair, silk, cotton, dyed wools, angora, and more. Romney breeding stock is also for sale.

Send for a free brochure. Wool samples are $1.00.

MACOMBER LOOMS

P.O. Box 186 Beech Ridge Road
York, ME 03909
(207) 363-2808

MACOMBER LOOMS is another one of the well-respected loom manufacturing companies. They produce a full line of weaving supplies and equipment, including computer programs for weaving design.

Write for a current catalog.

MAGNUS WOOLS

RFD #1
Barnet, VT 05821

Mail Order; Established in 1980

Marilyn Magnus of MAGNUS WOOLS offers luxurious angora goat hair for sale, either by the pound or by the fleece. Romney sheep are also available from Magnus Wools.

Send for current prices.

MAINE MAID

13 Bow Street
Freeport, ME 04032
(207) 865-9202

Manufacturer; Mail Order, Retail
Shop; V/MC; Established in 1982

MAINE MAID specializes in original knitting patterns and a fine selection of handspun wool yarns. Maine Maid Yarns are available in approximately 40 shades, including heathers, naturals, and tweeds. These are all 2-ply yarns for use with patterns calling for "knitting worsted weight" yarns. Penny Peters handspun yarns are naturally dyed in shades of blue, pink, apricot and lavendar. Maine Maid knitting patterns and kits include a line of sweaters and hats in sizes for adults and children. Also offered are walnut and birch knitting needles and crochet hooks, cherry wood and oak buttons, sheep ornaments, cards, etc. The book, *Fox and Geese and Fences: The Book of Traditional Maine Mittens,* by Robin Hansen, is also available.

Quantity discounts are given; write for details.

Send for a free brochure and price list. A yarn sample card is $1.00 (refundable with first order).

SUSAN H. MANES

R.D. #2
Pompey Hollow Road
Cazenovia, NY 13035
(315) 655-8365

Mail Order

SUSAN H. MANES raises registered angora goats. She sells both fleece and animals.

Wholesale discounts are given with a minimum order of 25 pounds.

Send for a current price list.

THE MANNINGS HANDWEAVING SCHOOL AND SUPPLY CENTER

R.D. #2
East Berlin, PA 17316
(717) 624-2223

Mail Order, Retail Shop; V/MC; Established in 1950

THE MANNINGS HANDWEAVING SCHOOL AND SUPPLY CENTER is a complete center for weaving and spinning supplies and instruction. They stock a large inventory of yarns, cotton and linen threads, carpet warp, and other miscellaneous yarns. They also have rugmaking materials, looms by almost all manufacturers, spinning wheels and accessories, and more. Spinning fibers include alpaca, angora, wools, silks, camel top, roving, flax, cotton, llama, ramie, mohair, yak top, synthetic fibers, and more. Supplies for dyeing include dyestuffs for natural dyeing, mordants, synthetic dyes, etc. Over 250 books are offered, as are supplies for basketry, bobbin lace, and other fiber arts. Year-round weaving classes are offered at the Mannings studio.

Send 50¢ for a complete catalog (a list is enclosed to order sample cards).

MAPLEWOOD ENTERPRISES

P.O. Box 340
Rio Vista, TX 76093

Manufacturer; Mail Order

The company only sells their products wholesale to retail stores. Retailers should write for more information. Others should contact the company for the names of mail order dealers.

THE MARIPOSA TREE, INC.

P.O. Box 336, Stapleton
Staten Island, NY 10304

Mail Order; Established in 1982

THE MARIPOSA TREE, INC., owned by Madalen Bertolini, carries a variety of supplies for spinning and weaving. The entire line of E'Lite yarns comes in 100% wools, 100% cashmere, 100% mohair, 100% silk, and blends. Wool fleece and rovings from New Zealand are available from the following breeds: Border Leicester, Merino, Romney, Corriedale, Borderdale, Coopworth, Drysdale, and half and crossed breeds. The Mariposa Tree also carries a number of raw silk fibers, yarns and pure silk embroidery threads from China. In addition to wools and silks, other exotic fibers such as cashmere, alpaca and mohair are offered. Other equipment includes solid cherry wood tapestry looms and accessories, Ashford and Louet spinning wheels, etc. A wide range of natural dyestuffs and mordants are also available.

Discounts are given to schools and qualified teachers with a minimum order of $50.00.

Send $1.00 for a catalog.

MARY LUE'S YARN SHOP

101 W. Broadway
St. Peter, MN 56082
(507) 931-3702

Manufacturer; Mail Order, Retail
Shop; V/MC/AMEX; Established
in 1867

MARY LUE'S YARN SHOP is a family-owned and operated business that proclaims to be the largest independent retailer of weaving, knitting, and stitchery supplies in the entire Midwest. The shop carries yarns by Reynolds and Brunswick, factory outlet wool weaving yarns, coned yarns for knitting machines, wool tapestry yarns, Lily Carpet Warp and crochet threads, and much more. A variety of Brother Knitting Machines and accessories are available, as is a large number of knitting and needle art accessories and popular needlecraft books. Ashford spinning wheels, Beka rigid heddle and Leclerc looms are also available.

Some discounts are given; write for details.

Send $2.00 for a complete catalog.

MEADOWS VALLEY HANDSPUN

P.O. Box 80
Fruitvale, ID 83620

Mail Order; Established in 1982

MEADOWS VALLEY HANDSPUN carries some of the softest angora rabbit wools and handspun yarns. The yarns are available in two sizes, five colors and white. Meadows Valley also offers custom spun wool, angora or mohair. Spinning classes are held once or twice a year.

Send $1.00 and a SASE for a sample card and price list.

THE MIDDLE KINGDOM GOAT COMPANY

10076 Nishinam Gulch Road
Nevada City, CA 95959
(916) 265-5737

Mail Order; Established in 1975

THE MIDDLE KINGDOM GOAT COMPANY raises their own mohair goats and sells raw mohair fibers and handspun novelty yarns. They also handle the entire line of Louet spinning and weaving supplies. The company offers classes in spinning, as well as custom designed clothing.

Quantity discounts are given; write for more information.

Write for current prices.

MOSTLY HANDSPUN

7410 77th Avenue, S.E.
Snohomish, WA 98290
(206) 568-1274

Manufacturer; Mail Order;
Established in 1981

MOSTLY HANDSPUN offers rainbow wool batts in 22 color combinations, and solid color batts in 23 beautiful coordinating shades. Custom-blended rainbow batts, as well as a custom dyeing and carding service, is also offered by Mostly Handspun.

Wholesale discounts are given with a five-pound minimum order.

Send a large SASE for a color card and current price list.

MOURNING STAR

3075 New Castle Avenue
New Castle, DE 19720
(302) 655-8269

Manufacturer; Mail Order, Retail
Shop; Established in 1979

MOURNING STAR carries a number of spinning and weaving supplies, including looms by Leclerc, Schacht, Norwood, Harrisville Designs, and Beka, and spinning wheels by Louet, Leclerc, Ashford, and Hiram McCracken. Handspun and hand-dyed yarns in 2-ply tweeds and novelty "Bright Star" yarns are also offered. The owner, Jean, has also written a book on dyeing, titled *I'd Rather Dye Laughing*.

Quantity discounts are given with a minimum order of $50.00.

Send for a current newsletter and yarn prices.

LARRY & CLARA MOYLE

R.R. #2, Box 183A
Eagle Bend, MN 56446
(218) 738-4341

Mail Order; Established in 1983

LARRY & CLARA MOYLE say that they "try to make people happy" with their products. They provide white, raw wools from Corriedale Finn, Hampshire, Corriedale Montdale, Columbia Cross and Rambouillet, and black wools from Suffolk-Scottish Blackface Salish sheep. French angora rabbit wools are also available in black, fawn, white and agouti. The Moyle's also conduct shearing tours in the spring where they give lessons on spinning and carding wool.

Send $1.50 for wool samples and prices (refunded with an order of $5.00 or more).

MUDRA

219 West Gurley Street
Prescott, AZ 86301
(602) 778-5947

Mail Order; Retail; Established in 1982

MUDRA carries a large inventory of weaving and spinning supplies. They carry the Louet and Ashford spinning wheels, Mark IV Drum Carders, various spindles, flickers, cotton and wool carders, Clemes and Clemes Drum Carder, skein winders, swifts, ball and cone winders, felting boards, Beka warping reels, and other accessories. Spinning fibers include silks (combed Tussah, carded Bombyx Mori, Tussah mawata caps, Bombyx Mori mawata caps), and rainbow carded batts. Other fibers include combed flax top, ramie, and angora rabbit. Basketry fibers include round reed in various sizes, flat reed, sea grass, pigtail raffia (natural), and Fiber Flex. Yarns are available from such suppliers as Beka, Berroco, CUM, Harrisville, Lily, Ironstone, Oregon Worsted, Scott's, Silk City, Tahki, and others. Looms are all manufactured by Harrisville or Beka. Mudra also handles over 150 book titles.

A 10% discount is given on minimum orders of $100.00.

Send for a free catalog.

THE NAKED LAMB

Rt. 1, Box 1408
Eastsound, WA 98245
(206) 376-4606

Manufacturer; Mail Order, Retail
Shop; V/MC; Established in 1979

THE NAKED LAMB, owned by Sharon Gallentine Wehle, offers handspun wools, silks, and mohairs, spinning equipment, dyes, patterns, handmade buttons, and other supplies. Classes and custom work are available.

Discounts are given with a minimum order of $100.00.

A catalog is not available at this time; write for specific information.

NASCO

901 Janesville Avenue
Fort Atkinson, WI 53538
(414) 563-2446

Manufacturer; Mail Order, Retail Shop; V/MC/AMEX; Established in 1940

NASCO has one of the most comprehensive craft catalogs in the United States. In addition to a huge inventory of basic art and craft supplies, the company also carries a large number of fiber supplies that can be used in fiberwork. These include airbrushes and compressors, all types of printing supplies, beeswax, basketry supplies, macrame cords and supplies, school weaving yarn assortments, Fabri-Print textile paints and cotton embroidery flosses. Nasco also offers a large selection of looms, including waist looms, backstrap looms, tapestry looms, inkle looms, table looms, lap weaving looms, rigid heddle looms, and looms by Leclerc and Peacock. Other fiber supplies include a spinning wheel kit, drop spindle, swifts, bobbins, carders, shuttles, hooks, etc. Dyes are available from Fibrec, Putnam, Dylon and Deka. Supplies are also offered for batik, rugmaking, and various needlearts.

Quantity discounts are given; check prices in catalog.

Send for a free 370-page catalog.

NATTY LOCKS FARM

Rt. 2, Box 9
Moyers, WV 26813
(304) 249-5127

Mail Order; Farm visits by appointment; Established in 1980

NATTY LOCKS FARM, owned by Mary Child, can claim extra clean fleece because all of the sheep wear coats! They supply high lustre, long staple, natural colored fleece and rug wools, and a finer grade fleece from Lincoln and Lincoln crosses.

Discounts are given with a minimum order of $100.00.

Send $1.00 for a current catalog (refundable with first order).

Sheep from Natty Locks Farm

NATURAL FIBER NOOK

R. R. #1, Box 55
Primghar, IA 51245
(712) 757-4675

Mail Order, Retail Shop; Established in 1982

NATURAL FIBER NOOK carries a wide variety of weaving and spinning supplies, including Tools of the Trade table and floor looms, Harrisville kit looms, Louet spinning wheels and looms, Ashford spinning wheels, Bulky 8 Knitting Machines, Fricke Machine Carders, Clemes and Clemes hand carders, Beka rigid heddle looms, Wildwood wooden buttons, and Sight/Feel Weaving Cards. Yarns include those from Harrisville Designs, Brown Sheep Company, Condon, and Schoolhouse. Wool roving, cottons, flax, silk, angora and mohair are offered for spinning. Natural dyes and mordants are also available.

Discounts are given, with a minimum order of $25.00.

Send $1.00 for a current catalog.

NATURES FIBRES

Box 172
Newbury, VT 05051
(802) 866-5684

Mail Order; Established in 1970

NATURES FIBRES promises "personal, fast service" on their high quality silk yarns in natural shades and plant-dyed and natural alpaca yarns.

Yarn is being advertised with 20% off; write for information.

Send $2.00 for a current price list.

NEW ZEALAND IMPORTS

P.O. Box 863687
Plano, TX 75086
(214) 548-1775

Manufacturer; Mail Order, Retail hours by appointment; Established in 1982

NEW ZEALAND IMPORTS offers raw and carded fleece "in the grease" for spinning in five natural colors, and handspun 100% wool yarns for weaving or knitting, either washed or in the grease. Spinning wheels include the "Wee Peggy" and the "Mitzi," both by John Rappard from New Zealand. Wheels by Pipy Craft are also available. Other supplies include a rotary drum carder and hand carders. Private or group classes in knitting and spinning are offered.

Quantity discounts are given on wools; write for details.

Send $2.00 for a current catalog (applied to order) and $1.50 for a wool and yarn sample card.

NEW ZEALAND WOOL COMPANY

P.O. Box 2076
Corvallis, OR 97339
(503) 758-5518

Mail Order; Established in 1979

NEW ZEALAND WOOL COMPANY raises their own fleece on their farm in New Zealand and imports it to the U.S., thus insuring high quality. These fleeces are then sold for handspinning.

Quantity discounts are given; write for more information.

Send $2.00 for a price list and samples.

THE NORRISES OF STORRS

52 Willowbrook Road
Storrs, CT 06268
(203) 429-2986

Manufacturer; Mail Order; Established in 1978

THE NORRISES OF STORRS continue to make looms patterned after the original "Rollo Purrington" loom. The 4-harness Folding Floor Loom is available in weaving widths of 20, 26, or 32 inches. The Folding Table Looms, with an automatic harness release, are available in 14 and 18-inch widths and from four to sixteen harnesses. All looms are individually made from maple and hand signed by the maker. The Norrises also offer free Bed and Breakfast to those who pick up their loom orders at the Studio.

Educational/guild discounts are negotiable; call for details.

Send a SASE for a brochure and price list.

NORTHWARP, LTD.

The Weaving Studio
5531 Arctic Blvd.
Anchorage, AK 99502
(907) 561-1826

Manufacturer; Mail Order, Retail Shop; V/MC; Established in 1972

NORTHWARP, LTD. carries a variety of spinning and weaving equipment from such suppliers as Schacht, Norwood, Glimakra, Louet, Ashford, and Harrisville Designs. Yarns are available from Tahki, Lane Borgosesia, E'Lite, Harrisville, Candide, Berga, Manos, Nomis, Anny Blatt, Ironstone Warehouse, and many more. The company specializes in unusual fibers, and carries wools, silks, cashmere, alpaca, rayons, mohairs, etc. Alaskan Handspun, Hand-dyed Wool Yarns by Jan is also supplied by Northwarp in beautiful, soft variegated shades. Other supplies include the Bond Knitting Frame, dyes, and books.

Discounts are given with a minimum order of $100.00.

Write for specific prices and yarn samples.

NORTHWEST LOOMS

P.O. Box 10369
Bainbridge Island, WA 98110
(206) 385-5489

Manufacturer; Mail Order;
Established in 1967

NORTHWEST LOOMS manufactures the Pioneer Floor Loom, a patented open-top heddle and open reed loom that permits fast, easy warping directly on the loom. The loom uses the continuous thread warp concept, which does away with lengthy pre-calculations. The Pioneer Table Looms fully extended will hold a warp of 84-inches; the Floor models will hold 100-inches. A warping attachment is also available which permits continuous warping of up to nine yards. The looms are built with eight harnesses, but may be ordered with only two or four harnesses. Each loom is also equipped with 12 heddles per inch of loom width.

A 10% discount is given to schools or other groups.

Send for a free brochure and price list.

NYLON NET COMPANY

P.O. Box 592
Memphis, TN 38128
(901) 525-8616

Manufacturer; Mail Order; V/MC

NYLON NET COMPANY carries a variety of cords, twines, braids and ropes in cottons, nylons, and other synthetics. Even though the company mainly sells fishing supplies, it still looks like a good bet for macrame, knotting, netting, etc. materials.

Send for a current catalog and sample set of cords.

OLE OAXACA LOOM EXPORTS

851 Hamilton Avenue
Menlo Park, CA 94025
(415) 322-0109

Manufacturer; Mail Order;
Established in 1976

OLE OAXACA carries wool top and roving, along with yarns by American Harvest and Douglas Heathers, Mexican handspun wools and cottons. Custom spinning and weaving services are also offered.

Professional discounts are given; write for details.

Send $5.00 for a current catalog.

ON THE MOUNTAIN

Rt. 1, Box 76
Shady Valley, TN 37688
(615) 739-5077

Mail Order; Established in 1977

ON THE MOUNTAIN, owned by Todd Eastin, specializes in mohair fibers. These can be ordered in the grease or scoured in three grades, or as roving in two grades.

Discounts are given with a minimum order of 10 pounds.

Send $1.00 for a price list and samples.

ONCE UPON A SHEEP

P.O. Box 613
Amawalk, NY 10501
(914) 962-7261

Mail Order, Retail hours by appointment; Established in 1983

ONCE UPON A SHEEP carries a wide variety of spinning and weaving supplies, including many raw fibers for spinning. These include angoras, camel down, cashmere, white mulberry and Tussah silk tops, Tussah noils, white mohair top, alpaca, water retted flax, ramie, Massam wool top, New Zealand wool sliver, acala and brown cottons, Corriedale and Romney fleece in the grease. Many natural dye extracts are available, including brazilwood, cutch, fustic, logwood powder, osage orange, quebracho, sumac, and cochineal. Other supplies include ball winders, spindles (six types), carders, Louet spinning wheels, skeinwinders, carding tools, felting supplies, and lots of accessories. The company also offers twelve types of yarns in wools, cottons and blends, and a linen thread for both weaving and machine knitting. A large number of books are also available on spinning, dyeing, weaving, knitting, and crochet.

Some discounts are given; write for information.

Send for a free brochure. A yarn color card is $2.00 (refunded on first order).

Once Upon a Sheep

> IN EARLY COLONIAL DAYS, IT WAS ILLEGAL TO kill a sheep for food. The animal was needed too badly to produce fiber and offspring.
>
> — Courtesy of the Wool Education Center, Denver, CO

O'NEILL STOCK RANCH
KARAKUL REGISTRY

Rt. 1, Box 179
Rice, WA 99167
(509) 738-6310

Manufacturer; Mail Order

Julie O'Neill of the O'NEILL STOCK RANCH, raises Karakul sheep in colors which range from black to grey, occasionally grey-brown, cream-beige, or white. Karakul wool is strong — yarns made from it are usually classified as "rug weight" yarns — excellent for blankets, upholstery fabrics, rugs, saddle blankets, etc.

Write for more details and current prices; minimum order is one fleece.

OREGON ROMNEY WOOLS, LTD.

1780 Cleveland Hill Road
Roseburg, OR 97470
(503) 673-7913

Mail Order; Retail hours by appointment; Established in 1980

Skyshine Farm, home of OREGON ROMNEY WOOLS, LTD. is owned and operated by Karen Wilts-Morrison. Karen offers award-winning, high quality Romney wools, wool blends and yarns. Wools include raw, skirted fleece in white and natural colors, and rovings in white, natural colors, and custom dyed colors. Angora/wool rovings and mohair/wool blends are also available. Karen also produces handspun yarns in five weights, as well as wool batts for felting or quilting. Custom services include spinning and custom dyeing or carding of your washed wools.

A 10% discount is given on orders over $100.00. Retailers should write for wholesale information.

Send $1.00 for samples and current prices.

OREGON WORSTED COMPANY

P.O. Box 02098
Portland, OR 97202

Manufacturer; Mail Order

OREGON WORSTED COMPANY offers 100% pure virgin wool yarns in 2-ply Willamette, 3-ply Nehalem, and 4-ply knitting yarns. These are put up on tubes and cones and are available in 52 colors.

Send $1.00 for a color card and current price list.

THE ORIENTAL RUG COMPANY

214 S. Central Avenue
Lima, OH 45802
(419) 225-6731

Manufacturer; Mail Order, Retail Shop; Established in 1923

THE ORIENTAL RUG COMPANY sells three types of looms: the Orco 2-harness loom with 36-inch weaving width, the 2-harness Peacock table loom with 12-inch weaving width, and the Orco 4-harness, six treadle loom with 36-inch width. These looms are shipped fully assembled, warped, and ready to weave. The company also sells a line of spinning and weaving accessories, which includes rug filler, rug yarns, rags, carpet warps, 100% cotton yarns, shuttles, electric bobbin winders, spool racks, heddle frames, reeds and more.

Send 25¢ for a brochure and price list.

ORIGINAL ME, ENTERPRISES

Box 444
Roseburg, OR 97470
(503) 672-8780

Mary Arthur, owner of ORIGINAL ME, ENTERPRISES, offers angora fibers and handspun angora yarns, with some unique blends for weaving.

Send for a current price list.

PASSAP KNITTING MACHINE COMPANY

1275 Bloomfield Avenue
Fairfield, NJ 07006

Importer/Distributor

As PASSAP does not sell directly to individuals, write for the name of the nearest dealer who can provide more information.

Wholesale discounts are given to dealers and schools; write with proof of business.

THE PENDLETON SHOP

P.O. Box 233
Sedona, AZ 86336
(602) 282-3671

Manufacturer; Mail Order, Retail
Shop; Established in 1948

THE PENDLETON SHOP is owned and operated by Mary Pendleton (also owner of the Pendleton Fabric Craft School). The shop carries a full line of weaving and spinning supplies. Looms are available by Pendleton, Schacht, Norwood, Glimakra, Leclerc, Brittany, and others. Spinning fibers include wools, yak, goat, camel, cotton, silk, angora and mohair. Spinning wheels are available from Ashford, Louet, Clemes, etc. A large number of accessories and yarns are also available from this source, as is a line of books on the fiber arts. Ms. Pendleton also edits and publishes *The Looming Arts* for handweavers and spinners. Published five times a year, it includes articles related to weaving, with generous woven samples and detailed directions.

Discounts are given; write for details.

Send $1.00 for current prices and yarn samples.

DEMPSY PERKINS

Rt. 2, Box 505
Ragley, LA 70657
(318) 666-2252

Mail Order; Established in 1980

DEMPSY PERKINS supplies top quality, pure white spinning wools which are skirted, medium grade, high yielding, with a nice crimp. Personal attention is given to each order. An Open House is held each year around sheep shearing time (usually April).

Quantity discounts are given with a five-pound minimum order.

Write for current prices.

PHILLIPS IMPORTS

903 16th Street
Port St. Joe, FL 32456
(904) 229-6841

Mail Order; Established in 1980

PHILLIPS IMPORTS can supply Sunbeam Yarns and knitting patterns from England, and Tivoli Spinners Ltd. yarns and patterns from Ireland. The knitting pattern selection is large — over 350 in all.

Phillips Imports sells wholesale only to qualified retailers; write for more information. Others can write for the name of the nearest shop or mail order dealer.

A current catalog is available for $7.50 (applied to first order).

THE PITMAN

4868 Rhoads Avenue
Santa Barbara, CA 93111
(805) 964-7457

Manufacturer; Mail Order, Retail
hours by appointment;
Established in 1972

Edith Ogella, owner of THE PITMAN, offers a line of handspun yarns of 100% wools, mohair, dog hair, silk, goat, alpaca, camel, cashmere, flax and cotton. Also available are blends of the above fibers, mixed plies and dyed wools. Yarns can also be spun on a custom basis. Ms. Ogella also offers a repair service for spinning wheels and equipment, a consultation service, three levels of spinning lessons and lectures.

A 20% discount is given on orders of $100.00 on a specific type of yarn.

Send $1.50 for samples and a price list.

POSSUM VALLEY FARM WEAVER'S SHOP

Hyndsver Road, Route #2
Martin, TN 38237
(901) 587-3489

Mail Order, Retail hours by appointment; Established in 1979

POSSUM VALLEY FARM WEAVER'S SHOP is housed in a log cabin built in 1844. Jacqueline S. Moore, the owner of the shop, is a weaver, spinner, and quilter who tests all of her products before selling them. She is an exclusive dealer for Leclerc looms and accessories and Superba Knitting Machines and accessories. The shop also carries Ashford and Wee Peggy spinning wheels, Clemes spinning wheels, Australian and New Zealand spinning wools, domestic cotton fibers, and imported mohair/silk yarns. Other yarns are available by Berroco, Chester Farms, Christopher Farms, Condon, Fort Crailo, Harrisville Designs, Henry's Attic, Oregon Worsted, Tahki, Unger, Lily, Fawcett and G. Whitaker Linen. A book list is also available, and a newsletter is in the planning stages. Ms. Moore also gives classes in spinning, weaving, quilting and knitting, and seminars on specific subjects. Restoration work is also available.

No discounts are given; Ms. Moore says that "our prices are competitive."

Write for a current price list.

PROVERBS 31

Box 814346
Dallas, TX 75381-4346

Mail Order; Established in 1976

Mary McGowan-Welp, owner of PROVERBS 31, bases her business on Proverbs 3:9, a verse from the Bible: "Honour the Lord with thy substance, and with the first fruits of all thine increase," so she contributes 12% of her company's income to "the Lord's work." Mary also believes in using only natural materials in her work. She sells many natural fibers, including carded wools, dyed wools, greasy fleece, scoured carded wools, mohair silver top, white mulberry silk top, Tussah silk top, cashmere, camel down, and alpaca. Also available are spinning wheels and looms by Ashford and Louet, along with other weaving and spinning accessories. Ms. McGowan-Welp also offers private and group spinning lessons, felting classes, handspun yarns and felted purses.

Send $1.00 for a current catalog.

PUDDLEDUCK FARM

1607-232 Avenue, N.E.
Redmond, WA 98053
(206) 885-3508

Manufacturer; Mail Order; Established in 1978

PUDDLEDUCK FARM, owned by Ingrid Painter, is a source for natural color handspun yarns, fleece, and breeding stock from the rare Navajo sheep. Since there are very few breeders of this particular sheep in the U.S., they are very special. Ingrid also teaches and gives lectures on sheep breeds and their uses.

Send for a free price list.

Jacob rams from Puddleduck Farm

*Ingrid Painter shears a Jacob
ewe while lamb looks on.
Photo by Annette Ramsour*

RABBIT RENDEZ-VOUS

1253 Valley High Avenue
Thousand Oaks, CA 91362
(805) 497-7641

Mail Order; Established in 1979

Dominique Jewett, owner of RABBIT RENDEZ-VOUS, specializes in English angora rabbit wools. She can provide the plucked, unspun wool in white and other colors. She also gives classes and seminars on angora wool spinning and angora rabbit breeding.

Quantity discounts are given; write for information.

Send $1.00 and a SASE for samples and prices.

RAINBOW SKY RANCH

38359 Shelburn Road
Scio, OR 97374
(503) 394-2475

Manufacturer; Mail Order;
Established in 1978

RAINBOW SKY RANCH is a supplier for silky white Romney fleece, well-skirted and very clean.

Quantity discounts are given with a minimum order of 100 pounds.

Send for a price list and samples.

RASMUSSEN LOOM COMPANY

P.O. Box 15451
Seattle, WA 98115
(206) 524-1368

Manufacturer; Mail Order;
Established in 1971

RASMUSSEN LOOM COMPANY claims to have the best built and best priced 4-harness table loom on the market. The Rasmussen Table Loom, available with both 4 and 8-harnesses, is constructed of Eastern hard maple, and weaves widths up to 25 inches. The loom is compact, easy to store and carry to classes or workshops. Included with the loom are lease sticks, stick shuttle, 12-dent reed, and 300 flat steel heddles with 9/16″ eye.

Discounts are given with the purchase of two or more looms.

Send for a free brochure and price list.

RAYE'S ECLECTIC CRAFT YARNS, INC.

P.O. Box 2356
La Mesa, CA 92041-0640
(619) 460-0721

Mail Order, Retail Shop;
Established in 1972

RAYE'S carries Cotton Caper and Berber yarns, chenilles, rug wools, cotton warp, rovings, basketry supplies, feathers, beads, raffia, and many other fiber supplies.

Discounts are given with a $25.00 minimum order; write for details.

A catalog is $5.00.

REDANIC RABBITRY

7665 Picardy Place
Charleston, SC 29418
(803) 552-6246

Manufacturer; Mail Order;
Established in 1983

REDANIC RABBITRY can supply English and French angora rabbit wools. Custom handmade spinning wheels are also available upon request.

Discounts are given with a minimum order of $50.00.

Send for a current price list.

RESTORATION ARTS

P.O. Box 304
Williamston, MI 48895
(517) 655-2609

Manufacturer; Mail Order;
Established in 1981

Victor Hogg, owner of RESTORATION ARTS, has been involved with historic preservation activities for years, and has made replicas of antiques for museums. He now makes a line of unique spinning wheels which are, he says, "The world's most beautiful!" His Saxony wheel is a reproduction of a Norwegian spinning wheel from the 1800's. This wheel, made from select hardwoods, includes a ⅜" orifice which is located 25½" from the floor. Mr. Hogg's Normandy French-style wheel is a lightweight but sturdy wheel. His line of Peasant wheels (Aries, Britannia, Fleur and Erin), come in four colors and designs. These also have a ⅜" orifice diameter which is 27½" high. Mr. Hogg also offers custom made wheels and repairs of antiques.

Restoration Arts usually sells to dealers only. However, they will mail order to areas with no dealer. Send a SASE for a brochure and dealer list.

REYNOLDS YARNS, INC.

15 Oser Avenue
Hauppauge, NY 11788
(516) 582-9330

Manufacturer; Established in 1954

REYNOLDS YARNS, INC. is the manufacturer of Lopi, Reynelle, Clover, Capri, Las Brisas, Slique, St. Tropez, Orient Express yarns, and many more. They also produce a large line of knitting instruction books.

Although Reynolds does not sell to individuals, they do give discounts to schools/guilds or other groups with a minimum purchase of $500.00. Others should check entry under "International Creations, Inc." for a Reynolds mail order source.

A catalog is available to the trade only for $50.00.

RIO GRANDE WOOL MILL, INC.

P.O. Box B
Tres Piedras, NM 87577
(505) 758-1818

Manufacturer; Mail Order;
Established in 1983

RIO GRANDE WOOL MILL, INC. offers a line of Southwestern yarns for weavers and knitters. The yarns are available in four natural color blends: creamy white, Pearl/Beige, Warm Grey, and Chocolate Grey. The yarns can be spun in 1, 2, or 3-ply and in a variety of weights and twists. They also have strong, high-twist yarns designed for use as warp, and softly spun wool yarns for knitting. The mill also offers custom carding of your wools to your specifications. They also carry carded batts and rovings. Custom spinning is also available.

Quantity discounts are given; check price list for information.

Send $2.00 for prices and samples of yarns and wools.

ROBIN & RUSS HANDWEAVERS

533 North Adams Street
McMinnville, OR 97128
(503) 472-5760

Manufacturer; Mail Order, Retail Shop; Established in 1946

ROBIN & RUSS HANDWEAVERS stock an unbelievable assortment of weaving, spinning, and bobbin lace supplies and equipment. Looms include the Oregon Trail Loom, manufactured by Robin & Russ. They also distribute Norwood, Leclerc, Macomber, and other looms. Carded, dyed wool tops are offered, as well as a large number of yarns and threads in cottons, wools, ramie, linens, silks, metallics, exotics, and many odd-lots. A complete line of supplies for making bobbin lace is available, and includes pillows, bobbins, prickers, patterns, linens, etc. Over 500 books on weaving, spinning, dyeing, lacemaking, etc. are also offered. Quantity discounts are given on books published or distributed by the company.

Send for a free 55-page catalog. For a complete set of yarn samples, (15-25 sheets), send $2.25 + $1.75 postage. You will then receive future samples at no charge (for five years!).

ROMNI WOOLS & FIBRES, LTD.

3779 W. 10th Avenue
Vancouver, BC
CANADA V6R 2G5
(604) 224-7416

Mail Order, Retail Shop; V;
Established in 1974

Even though shipping charges from Canada can be high, I felt justified in listing ROMNI WOOLS & FIBRES, LTD. because of their enormous list of fibers, yarns, and supplies. Spinning fibers include raw wools from many breeds of New Zealand sheep, mohair fleece, acrylic top, alpaca top, angoras, antron fleece and sliver, camel hair and tops, flaxes, Chinese goat hair, hemp and jute sliver, orlon and nylon fleece and sliver, ramie, Samoyed, eight types of silks, wool tops in 13 colors, yak, goat, cashmere, alpaca and sisal slivers. Spinning equipment is available from Louet. Carding equipment is offered, as are looms and accessories from Louet, Beka, New Zealand, and other suppliers. A large selection of natural dyes and mordants, chemicals and synthetic dyes are offered, as are over 300 books. Yarns come in over 140 varieties, including wools and silks (1, 2, 3, and 4-ply), bouclés, cottons, linens, novelties, odds and ends, and rug yarns.

Many discounts are offered. See catalog for full details.

Send $1.00 for a very extensive catalog. You won't be sorry!

THE RUG HUT

#6 University Avenue
Los Gatos, CA 95030
(408) 354-9316

Mail Order, Retail Shop; V/MC;
Established in 1966

Karen Brayton-McFall, owner of THE RUG HUT, offers spinning wools, wool by the pound, Cushing dyes, supplies for rugmaking, braiding and hooking, and crochet and knitting yarns. Karen also gives lessons in rug braiding, hooking, and weaving.

Write for a current price list.

RUMPLESTILSKEINS

12018 Queens Place
Huntsville, AL 35803
(205) 883-9034

Mail Order, Retail hours by
appointment; Established in 1981

RUMPLESTILSKEINS offers wool yarns by Harrisville Designs, Tahki, Oregon Worsted, Borgs, Ironstone, Manos and others. Other yarns are available in cottons, cotolin, linens, alpacas, silks, and cashmere/wool blends. Hand-dyed and spun wool yarns by Ann McBeth are also offered. Looms are available from Louet, Glimakra, Rasmussen, Harrisville, Norwood, Schacht, Tools of the Trade, and Beka, as well as other supplies.

Quantity discounts are given; write for details.

Send for a free price list.

RUNTEE FIBER

620 Broad Street
Chambersburg, PA 17201
(717) 263-9722

Manufacturer; Mail Order, Retail
hours by appointment; V/MC;
Established in 1973

RUNTEE FIBER is a multi-faceted manufacturing and fiber supply business owned by Pam Bartl and William Batts. They present a custom-dyed line of 185 colors of 18 wools, mohairs and alpacas, which can be combined to create different color and design effects. Over 3,000 yarn/color combinations are possible with this system. Runtee's yarns are dyed for each client's specific needs. Yarns from other companies can be dyed at Runtee. Runtee feels that their strongest point is the unique nature of their custom work —they can design a yarn, design a color, and tell you how it can be used.

A minimum order is $15.00; no discounts are given.

Send for general information and prices of sample sets.

ST. PETER WOOLEN MILLS

101 W. Broadway
St. Peter, MN 56082
(507) 931-3734

Manufacturer; Mail Order;
Established in 1867

ST. PETER WOOLEN MILLS is owned and operated by Charles and Mary Lue Bricker and Family, also owners of Mary Lue's Yarn Shop. The mill offers custom carding/washing or recarding of wools and acrylics for spinning or quilt batting. Fibers offered include domestic spinning wools in white and natural colors, dyed wool tops, camel down, angora, mohair, llama, alpaca, and silks.

Send a SASE and 25¢ for a brochure.

SAMMEN SHEEP FARM

Rt. 1, Box 153
Henning, MN 56551
(218) 583-2419

Mail Order; Established in 1976

Ron and Teresa Parker, shepherds and owners of SAMMEN SHEEP FARM, offer heavily skirted, prime spinning wools from their sheep. Sammen Selection is a Lincoln/Finn wool, and is very bright, lustrous, and has a sensational wave. These wools come in white, silver, and black. Sammen Selection Fine is from the same breed, but has a finer, shorter staple. Lincoln wools are also available.

Send a SASE for a copy of Sammen's annual "Woolletter" and price list.

SASSAFRAS MEADOW FARM

P.O. Box 380
Simpsonville, KY 40067
(502) 722-5023

Mail Order; Established in 1981

SASSAFRAS MEADOW FARM's main business is providing Romney fleece for handspinning, guaranteed clean and healthy. Classes in spinning are given, and custom spinning is available. Farm visits are also welcome by appointment.

Send $1.00 for fleece samples and price list.

SCHACHT SPINDLE COMPANY, INC.

P.O. Box 2157
Boulder, CO 80306
(303) 442-3212

Manufacturer; Mail Order;
Established in 1969

SCHACHT SPINDLE COMPANY, INC. is oe of the most respected manufacturers of quality weaving equipment. Schacht builds Table Looms with 4 and 8 harnesses in 15, 20, and 25-inch weaving widths, rigid heddle looms, tapestry looms, backstrap looms, and inkle looms. Floor looms include counterbalance looms in 36 and 45-inch widths and 4 harnesses, jack-type floor looms with 4 and 8 harnesses and 36 or 45-inch widths, the Baby Wolf Loom, and more. Accessories include benches, bench bag kits, lamp holders, shuttles, etc. Tools include tapestry beaters, shed sticks, "The Incredible Rope machine," curved back carders, spindles, warping and winding tools, reeds, and heddles.

Educational discounts are given; write for details. Wholesale discounts are given to qualified retailers only.

A catalog and list of Schacht dealers is free. If Schacht is not represented in your area, you may order directly from the company at regular retail prices.

Jack floor loom (Low Castle). © Schacht Spindle Co.

SCHOOL PRODUCTS, INC.

1201 Broadway
New York, NY 10001
(212) 679-3516

Mail Order, Retail Shop; V/MC;
Established in 1949

SCHOOL PRODUCTS, INC. carries quite a large inventory of fiber supplies. They offer looms by Meco, Schacht, Fanny, Leclerc, etc., and several tapestry looms by various manufacturers. A large line of accessories is also available, including heddling hooks, spinning wheels, carders, spindles, ball and cone winders, a Fraser cloth cutting machine, warping mills and beams, and a large number of shuttles, reeds, and other accessories. Hand knitting and weaving yarns are also sold by School Products.

Send $2.00 for a current catalog.

SCHOOLHOUSE PRESS

6899 Cary Bluff
Pittsville, WI 54466
or
Box 157
Babcock, WI 54413

Mail Order; Established in 1957

SCHOOLHOUSE PRESS is owned by a delightful mother and daughter team — Elizabeth Zimmerman and Meg Swansen — who are "attempting to liberate handknitters from instructions; to help them think and design for themselves." Mrs. Zimmerman is not afraid to tell her secrets. She says that she started putting out newsletters in 1957 when she became disgusted at the way knitting magazines would "emasculate and louse up" her original designs. That newsletter has now developed into *Wool Gathering,* a semi-annual catalog of books, original knitting designs by both Elizabeth and Meg, and general information which goes out to all mail order customers. Elizabeth has also written three books: *Knitting without Tears* (Scribners), *Knitter's Almanac* (Dover) and *Knitting Workshop* (Schoolhouse), designed to accompany her latest video series of knitting classes! Meg brings her talents to the business by taking care of the newsletter, and has assembled a large range of knitting books (many imported) for sale. They also sell a number of wool yarns from Iceland, Scotland, Canada, and other suppliers.

Mrs. Zimmerman's books can be ordered wholesale with various discounts; write for more information.

Send $1.00 for a wool sample card and booklist. The newsletter, *Wool Gathering,* is available for $1.50 each (published in March and September), or is available by subscription at $7.50 for three years (six issues).

SHADY CREEK FARM

54494 Eleven Mile
New Hudson, MI 48165
(313) 437-1233

Mail Order; Established in 1982

Barbara Cash of SHADY CREEK FARM is a source for adult and kid mohair (75%) and wool (25%) blended rovings in several pretty colors and whites. Barbara also does custom handspinning for others.

Send a SASE for a current price list and samples.

E. F. SHAW COMPANY, INC.

P.O. Box 17
Norristown, PA 19404
(215) 272-2228

Mail Order; Established in 1982

E. F. SHAW carries polyester yarns in 8 oz. tubes (white only), 100% cotton warp yarns, 100% cotton roving in 21 colors, cotton cable cords, and natural and colored jutes. For rugmakers, Shaw offers cotton-knit, velour, and terry selvage materials in long lengths sold by the pound, and wool rug braid.

Various discounts are given; write for details.

Samples and a price list are available for $1.25.

SHUTTLE & EWE STUDIO

P.O. Box 133
Webster, NY 14580
(716) 671-3793

Mail Order; Established in 1983

Ann L. Kreckel's SHUTTLE & EWE STUDIO carries a wide variety of exotic spinning fibers, including alpaca, camel down, cashmere, cotton, flax, ramie, mohair, silk, silk/wool blends, rainbow wool batts, raw fleece, and combed and carded wool top and sliver. Louet products, along with accessories, dyes, and mordants can also be ordered from this company. Custom handspun yarns are also available.

Minimum amount on any order is $10.00.

Send for a free price list.

SIGHT/FEEL CARDS

P.O. Box 176
Comptche, CA 95427
(707) 937-4298

Manufacturer; Mail Order;
Established in 1983

According to the manufacturer, the SIGHT/FEEL Coded Weaving Cards are the first real advance in cardweaving in 4,000 years. By changing traditional cards from straight edges to distinctively contoured edges (each edge is a different shape), the process of cardweaving is made easier and faster.

A price list and sample is available; write for information.

SILK CITY FIBERS

155 Oxford Street
Paterson, NJ 07522
(201) 942-1100

Manufacturer; Mail Order;
Established in 1980

SILK CITY FIBERS carries a variety of yarns and fibers that can be used for weaving, crochet, hand and machine knitting. The Milan Collection of Italian yarns includes 2-ply 100% silks and silk boucles, silk ribbons, a silk/wool blend, and kid mohair. The Fantasy Collection includes novelty metallic yarns. The Silk Collection includes pure wild silk yarns and blends from France. Cotton, chenille, alpaca and mohair/wool blends, are also offered in several different varieties. Silk City can also provide a large line of Mokuba Knitting Tapes in linen blends, cottons, synthetics, and leathers.

Wholesale discounts are given to qualified retailers with a $250.00 minimum initial order; write for information.

A Silk City Fibers Yarn Binder is $30.00; a Mokuba Booklet of ribbons and tapes is $15.00.

THE SILK TREE

26727 Ferguson Avenue
Whonnock, B.C.
CANADA V0M 1S0
(604) 462-9707

Mail Order; V; Established in
1980

THE SILK TREE specializes in high quality silk yarns and fibers. They carry over 45 different types of silk fibers, yarns, and cords, including Tussah fibers, baby camel down/Tussah blends, 2-ply medium cord, Tussah singles, bourette singles, silk boucles, chenilles, heavy Tussah, noil fleck, silk/wool/angora blend, silk ribbons, and others. All yarns and fibers are natural colored, and range in price from $17.50 to $69.40 per pound.

Wholesale prices are given to shops and professionals with a resale tax number. Other discounts are given to individuals.

Send $3.00 for a sample sheet and current prices.

KATHLEEN B. SMITH

Handweaver & Wool Dyer
P.O. Box 48
West Chesterfield, MA 01084
(413) 296-4437

Manufacturer; Mail Order;
Established in 1982

KATHLEEN B. SMITH specializes in 18th Century needlework and reproduction textiles. She carries a line of supplies and tools which have all been selected on the basis of their similarity to 18th Century counterparts. These include yarns, threads, tapes and handwoven fabrics, all of which have been dyed using the vegetable dyes commonly available in the 18th Century. These include Au Ver a Soie 100% silk flosses, linens, worsted wools in 50 naturally dyed colors, and more. Ms. Smith offers custom weaving and dyeing, and gives weekend workshops on vegetable dyeing.

A 30% discount is given on naturally dyed yarns to teachers, fiber artists, and other professionals. A 20% discount is given on all other items. A wholesale price list is also available to those who purchase for resale.

Send $1.00 for a current catalog, which includes two or three updates per year. A sample card of 50 vegetable dyed yarn samples is available for $4.00.

SMITH'S PLACE

Rt. 1, Box 33
Eldridge, MO 65463
(417) 426-5275

Mail Order; Established in 1975

SMITH'S PLACE, owned by Dorothy Smith, supplies raw mohair fibers, both adult and kid, which is sold by the pound.

Send for current prices and samples.

LINDA SNOW FIBERS

3207 Doctors Lake Road
Orange Park, FL 32073
(904) 264-4235

Mail Order; Retail Shop;
Established in 1976

LINDA SNOW FIBERS is an all-around fiber supplier that offers materials for basketry, weaving, spinning, dyeing, etc. Further information is not available at this time.

Send 75¢ for a current catalog.

SPIN 'N WEAVE

2725 N. Campbell Avenue
Tucson, AZ 85719
(602) 323-9787

Mail Order, Retail Shop; V/MC;
Established in 1980

The owners of SPIN 'N WEAVE are spinners, and say that they will not sell anything that they would not be happy spinning for themselves. Wools available include New Zealand fleece, scoured and carded, dyed wools, Australian colored Merino cross fleece, etc. Exotic fibers include yak, mohair, llama, camel, goat, cashmere, cottons, flax, ramie, and silks. Spinning wheels from several suppliers are available: Pipy Traditional, Wendy, Ashford, Lendrum, and Louet. Other equipment, as well as a line of books, are also available. Supplies for dyeing include Kiton Wool Dyes, reactive dyes, Cushing dyes, natural dye extracts, mordants and chemicals. If you would like to try your hand at handmade basketry, you can also order supplies and books from here. Yarns are offered from Harrisville Designs, Tahki, E'Lite, Brown Sheep Company, and hand-dyed yarns by Jan L. Nordlund. Looms are available from Schacht, Harrisville, Norwood, Leclerc, and Beka.

Various discounts are given; write for details.

Send a SASE for a current catalog and price list.

SPINCRAFT

P.O. Box 332
Richardson, TX 75080
(214) 235-0864

Mail Order; Established in 1969

SPINCRAFT specializes in a Beginner's Spinning Kit, which includes a regular spindle with wool starter, instructions, a pair of #8 Carders, fleece, and a booklet which gives basic instructions for carding and spinning. The Kit is currently $22.00 ppd. They also carry a hand spindle, Turkish cross bar spindle, carders, Belgian flax, Ashford spinning wheel kits and accessories, and many books of interest to spinners.

Some discounts are given; write for information.

Send a SASE for a brochure and price list.

SPINDLE YARNS

R.D. #1, Box R331-T/F
Williamsburg, MA 01096
(413) 296-4025

Mail Order; V/MC; Established in 1982

SPINDLE YARNS specializes in 100% handspun alpaca yarns from Peru. The company claims that these yarns are the only handspun alpaca yarns available in the U.S. and Canada. The yarns are available in white, light and dark ginger, bark, medium red brown, light and medium grey, black, and tweeds. Spindle yarns also carries 100% wool Fisherman Yarns from New England flocks.

Discounts are given with a minimum order of four ounces of yarn.

Send $2.00 for a current price list and set of samples.

SPINDLETOP

6617 Snider Plaza, #110
Dallas, TX 75205
(214) 691-2489

Retail Shop; V/MC; Established in 1974

Dorothy Cole's SPINDLETOP carries a wide variety of weaving tools and equipment, including looms by Beka, Harrisville Design, Glimakra, Leclerc, Schacht, and Willow Tree. Spinning wheels are offered by Ashford, Leclerc, Louet, and Pipycraft. Yarns are from many major companies, including Andean, Berroco, Brown Sheep Company, Crystal Palace, Gemini, Harrisville, Henry's Attic, Ironstone Warehouse, Lily, Merino, Novitex, Reynolds, Tahki, and Scheepjeswol. Bond Knitting Frames and Superba Knitting machines are available from here, also, as are a large number of specialty items such as hooks, buttons, note cards, and lots of "sheep items."

A 15% discount is given to local weavers and guild members or with a minimum order of $100.00 or more (paid by cash or check).

Although Spindletop is not really a mail order business, Ms. Cole says that she will take special orders, and will ship to out-of-town customers.

SPINDRIFTER

Rt. 1, Box 530
Chireno, TX 75937
(409) 854-2571

Manufacturer; Mail Order, Retail Shop; Established in 1974

SPINDRIFTER, owned by Sandy Willard, is a good source for white cotton sliver, white, blended grey, and dark wools. They also carry a line of yarns in cotton/wool blends, and one 100% wool yarn. Harrisville Design looms as well as other spinning and weaving tools are offered. Several books on spinning are also available. Sandy also has a "Learn to Spin" kit for sale, and lambs. Handspinning workshops, and 4-H and FFA farm tours are given.

Discounts are given on fibers with a ten-pound minimum order.

Send a SASE for a price list and samples.

THE SPINNERS HILL SHOP

R.D. #1, Box 118-Brackett Lake
Road
Bainbridge, NY 13733
(607) 843-6267 or (607) 967-8325

Manufacturer; Mail Order, Retail
Shop; V/MC; Established in 1981

THE SPINNERS HILL SHOP, owned by Lisa Ann Merian, offers spinning fleece in the grease from Dorset, Tunis, Finn, Rambouillet, Corriedale, and crossbred sheep, and washed and carded wools. Other spinning fibers include cottons, silks, mohairs, angoras, and flax. Lisa also offers beautiful handspun and dyed wool yarns in solids, naturals and rainbow colors. Looms are available from Glimakra, Beka, and Louet. Createx Liquid Fiber Reactive dyes, dyeing assistants, felting and carding equipment, buttons and books are offered. Ms. Merian can custom card and scour your wools or mohair into batts or rovings on a cottage industry carding machine.

Quantity discounts are given; write for details.

Send $3.00 for a current catalog and samples of yarns and wools.

A ballwinder from the Spinners Hill Shop.

THE SPINNERY, INC.

R.D. #2, Box 156
Route 202 North
Neshanic Station, NJ 08853
(201) 534-2360

Mail Order, Retail Shop; V/MC;
Established in 1974

THE SPINNERY, INC. (formerly Oldebrooke Spinnery), carries a number of supplies for weaving, spinning, knitting, etc. Looms are available from Beka, Harrisville, Schacht and Glimakra. Spinning wheels include Camelot, Louet and Ashford. Other accessories available include drum and hand carders, the Patrick Green Wool Picker, skein and ballwinders, spindles, the McMorran Yarn Balance, warping reels, rag cutters, temples, tapestry beaters, bobbins, shuttles, etc. Spinning fibers include silk and wool tops, flax, cottons, and rainbow batts. The Spinnery also handles several yarn lines, including Borgs, Harrisville, Henry's Attic, Plymouth, Tahki, Vintage Yarns and others. Knitting patterns include those by Penny Straker and Nancy M. Brown. Dyes include natural indigo, madder, logwood dust, brazilwood, fustic, and cochineal, as well as an Indigo Dye Kit and mordant set. A number of classes are also offered.

Quantity discounts are given with a minimum order of $50.00.

Send $1.00 for a current catalog.

SPINNING WHEEL YARNS

P.O. Box 5076
Asheville, NC 28813
(704) 274-0584

Manufacturer; Mail Order, Retail
Shop; V/MC; Established in 1983

SPINNING WHEEL YARNS offers 100% wool yarns in 120 stock colors and over 100,000 pounds of mill-end yarns. Mill-ends are available in four standard weights; stock colors in two weights. To order mill-end yarns, the company has devised a Color Fan Deck (looks like paint chip cards) which contains 1,000 shades, tints, and colors. Spinning Wheel Yarns believes that this is an effective alternative to individual yarn samples.

Various quantity discounts are available. Other specials are offered.

Write for a free general price list. Stock color cards are $5.00; Color Fan Decks are $10.00 each (free if ordered with 125 pounds of yarn or more).

STANISLAUS IMPORTS

75 Arkansas Street
San Francisco, CA 94107
(415) 431-7122

Manufacturer; Mail Order;
Established in 1965

STANISLAUS IMPORTS is a manufacturer and importer of craft supplies that sells wholesale to retail outlets only. They carry a very large line of supplies for various fiber arts, including macrame.

Retail outlets can send $5.00 for a complete catalog.

STILL WATERS FARM

18728 S.E. Cheldelin Road
Portland, OR 97236
(503) 661-7560

Mail Order, Retail hours by
appointment; Established in 1977

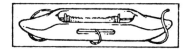

Lorraine Wells, owner and sole-operator of STILL WATERS FARM, raises Romney, Cotswold, "Salish" Karakul and Columbian sheep. She has been working for seven years towards a handspinners' fleece of extreme luster and silkiness in a range of colors. All wool tops and yarns are discounted. Yarns from Henry's Attic, Berroco, Nomis, Plymouth, Ironstone Warehouse, Shepherd's Icelandic Lava and others are priced at 25% below regular retail prices. Lorraine says that she tries to provide lower prices to those fiber artists who are trying to make a living selling their weavings, but also are not qualified to buy at wholesale prices. In addition to her wool tops, slivers and raw wools (both natural and dyed), other spinning fibers include silks (cocoons, Mawatas, factory waste, Bombyx mori, Tussahs), tow flax, line flax sliver, ramie sliver, pima cottons, alpaca, mohair, goat and yak hair top, camel hair and down, and cashmere. Ms. Wells also provides natural and synthetic dyes and mordants, J. A. Meck's Mini-Picker and wool comb, and spinning wheels from Ashford, Charkha, Clemes, Pipy, Restoration Arts, and others. Looms are also available from Louet. A large list of books, tools, and accessories are also offered. Classes on spinning, dyeing, weaving, and knitting are given, and a custom dyeing service is offered.

Send for a free price list.

STONEWOOD FARM & FIBRE SHOP

Rt. 1
Kewaskum, WI 53040
(414) 626-4650

Manufacturer; Mail Order, Retail
hours by appointment;
Established in 1974

STONEWOOD FARM & FIBRE SHOP, owned by Glenn, Sheila and Tammy Clement, specializes in mohair, angora and wool fibers and blends. Spinning fleece are available in raw, washed, carded or dyed forms by the pound or in batts. The rainbow dyed mohairs are indescribably beautiful in greens, blues, and lavender shades. Also available are raw, washed or carded mohairs and blends, angora rabbit wools, silks and cottons. Colored sheep, angora rabbit and angora goat breeding stock are also available. Sheila Clement states that her main purpose is to "produce quality breeding stock for sale and to provide quality fibers for handspinners." She also gives classes in felting, with an emphasis on using mohair and angora fibers in the felt.

Send $1.00 each for wool, mohair or angora samples — you won't be sorry!

STRAW INTO GOLD, INC.

3006 San Pablo Avenue
Berkeley, CA 94702
(415) 548-5241

Mail Order, Retail Shop; V/MC;
Established in 1971

STRAW INTO GOLD, INC. is another one of those popular, all-around fiber suppliers that provide materials for spinning, weaving, basketmaking, dyeing, knitting, etc. The large list of spinning fibers includes many silks (Tussah brick, Tussah carded sliver, bleached Tussah combed top, Tussah silk staple, combed Bombyx white silk top, combed Bombyx brick, Bombyx noils and batts, Bombyx cut silk staple, carded Bombyx silk sliver), wools (New Zealand Romney, Australian Merino, carded rainbow batts), and exotic tops from alpaca, Turkish mohair, pearl white mohair, camel hair, white goat hair, yak, and yak hair. Other fibers include cottons, flax, ramie, loose camel hairs, camel down, Chinese cashmere hair, white Persian, dark Iranian, and Chinese light grey cashmeres. Straw Into Gold also carries the entire line of Ashford products — wheels, accessories, and equipment. Two main lines of yarns are offered: Crystal Palace Yarns imported 100% silks from France and Italy, and Chanteleine Yarns from France in all wools and blends. Other yarns include coned silks, cottons and cotton blends, rayons, linens, wools, and other special import yarns.

Wholesale prices are available to qualified buyers only under "Textile Artist's Supply" label. Write for wholesale information.

Send a SASE for a current, complete catalog and yarn sample prices.

Ashford "Scholar" spinning wheel from Straw Into Gold

SUNRISE FARM

R.D. #1
East Freetown, NY 13055
(607) 863-3554

Mail Order; V/MC; Established
in 1977

Vince and Erica Rowe, owners of SUNRISE FARM, raise French and German angora rabbits, and specialize in the finest quality handspun angora yarns. These yarns are available in regular, fine, and weaver's singles sizes, and are offered in three natural colors: white, fawn, and grey. All yarns are spun to order, and most are shipped within one week of receipt of order. Erica also offers several kits to help you get started with angora. Also available is custom spinning of any fiber, custom dyeing, classes and seminars on angora spinning and rabbit raising. The Rowes also supply a line of custom-spun, millspun 100% wool yarns, available in natural cream, light and dark grey colors.

Quantity discounts are given with a minimum order of $100.00.

Send a SASE for a free brochure and information on angoras. Angora yarn samples are $5.00, and are all over one-yard long. Wool samples are $2.00.

THE SWEATER WORKSHOP

Box Five
Hingham, MA 02043
(617) 749-3649

Mail Order, Retail hours by appointment; V/MC; Established in 1979

THE SWEATER WORKSHOP, owned by Jacqueline Fee, offers Perlinox knitting needles imported from Germany, a needle gauge in millimeters, a Braidkin, gauge pages, a needlecase, a sheep tote, and selected Bartlett yarns. Janetta Dexter's Double Knitting Patterns are also offered. Ms. Fee has also come to the salvation of knitters with her comprehensive reference book for sweater knitting, "on your own," also titled *The Sweater Workshop,* published by Interweave Press.

Send for a free brochure.

TALON AMERICAN

High Ridge Park
Stamford, CT 06905
(203) 329-8111

Manufacturer; Mail Order;
Established in 1898

TALON is a large manufacturer of knitting, craft and rug yarns, crochet threads and embroidery flosses.

Retailers should write for wholesale prices. Educational/group discounts are given; write for more information.

JAN TARR WOOL IMPORTS

P.O. Box 164
Albion, CA 95410
(707) 937-0377

Mail Order; Established
in 1975

JAN TARR WOOL IMPORTS supplies high quality, raw greasy fleece from New Zealand. The wool is very clean and well-skirted, with a five to eight inch staple that permits spinning directly from the fleece. Currently available are wools from Romney, Romney Hogget, Border Leicester, Border X, Coopworth, Perendale, Corriedale, Merino, and colored sheep.

Various discounts are given with orders of 50 and 100 pounds of wool.

Send $1.00 for a price list and samples.

OBADIAH THARP COMPANY

8406 S.W. 58th Avenue
Portland, OR 97219
(503) 244-2594

Manufacturer; Mail Order;
Established in 1976

Lew Turner, along with his wife, Katy, are continuing the tradition set by Lew's great, great-grandparents, Obadiah and Sarah Tharp. The couple crossed the plains in 1858 to settle in Oregon, and took their spinning wheel with them. The current "Sarah" Great Wheel, updated, but inspired by the original, and the "Molly," are constructed of Eastern maple and hickory. The wheels feature life-time bronze bearings, and metal tension devices. There are no restricting orifices on the wheels, so wool, flax, silk or cotton can be spun in any desired diameter. The "Sarah" features an accelerating head which will enable an experienced spinner to produce up to 600 yards of fine yarn per hour. Both wheels can be assembled or disassembled in minutes. The wheels stand 63-inches high, 70-inches in length, and 16-inches wide. Also available are free-standing distaffs, large skeiners, spinning oil, belt dressing, and several books.

Due to high costs, wheels, skeiners and distaffs are sold by direct mail only. Other items are available to dealers for sale.

Send 25¢ for postage for a current brochure and price list.

THOUGHT PRODUCTS INTERNATIONAL

R.D. #2, Box 124A
Somerset, PA 15501
(814) 445-6039

Manufacturer; Mail Order;
Established in 1972

THOUGHT PRODUCTS INTERNATIONAL are manufacturers of the Cassandra I "Counter-Shed" (patented) looms made of cherrywood in 28 and 40-inch weaving widths. They also provide the Studio II "Fully-Adjustable" patented benches, and a full line of handweaving accessories such as shuttles, tapestry combs, raddles, lease sticks, etc.

Quantity discounts are given; write for details.

Send for a free brochure on all products.

TOOLS OF THE TRADE

R.F.D.
Fair Haven, VT 05743
(802) 537-3183

Manufacturer; Mail Order;
Established in 1970

TOOLS OF THE TRADE looms, handbuilt by Arthur Weitzenfeld, are available in a variety of models and sizes. Table looms are available with 4, 8, or 12-harnesses, and in 15, 25, or 32-inch weaving widths. Small floor looms are available in 25 and 32-inch widths, with 4 or 8 harnesses, 8-harness castle and 4 harnesses, or 4 additional harnesses. Large jack-type floor looms are built with 4, 8, or 12-harnesses in widths of 36, 45, 54, and 60-inches. Benches and a full line of accessories are also offered.

Wholesale discounts are given to qualified buyers; write for details.

Send for a free brochure and price list.

TRADITIONAL FIBER TOOLS

885 Glendower
Ashland, OR 97520

Manufacturer; Mail Order;
Established in 1983

TRADITIONAL FIBER TOOLS is a small woodworking shop in southern Oregon. They manufacture Squirrel Cage Swifts (floor model) and Yarn Blockers from Brazilian hardwoods called "goncalvo alves." The Yarn Blocker comes in two sizes (54 or 72-inch skeins) and it may also be ordered in kit form. The company also makes a drum carder needle which is used to remove batts from the carders. The Squirrel Cage Swifts are invaluable tools for holding skeins while making balls of yarn or winding shuttles.

Wholesale discounts are given to qualified retailers with a minimum purchase of two units; write for prices.

Send $1.00 for a colorful brochure and ordering information.

TRADITIONAL HANDCRAFTS, INC.

154 Mary Alexander Court
Northville, MI 48167
(313) 349-7509

Mail Order, Retail Shop; V/MC;
Established in 1973

John and Gloria Teeter, owners of TRADITIONAL HANDCRAFTS, INC. handle a full line of weaving, spinning, and fiber supplies. They carry over 20 different kinds of raw fibers for spinning, including alpaca, angora, camel, cashmere, cotton, flax, goat, mohair, ramie, raindeer, silk, sisal, and wools in many natural colors. Spinning wheels are available from various manufacturers, as well as spinning equipment. Over 38 types of natural dyestuffs are available, and include alkanet, bloodroot, butternut bark, cutch, elderberries, fustic, hemlock, indigo, lichens, madder, nutgalls, pine bark, and many more. Chemicals and mordants are also available. Weaving supplies include looms as well as a large number of accessories. They carry cottons, wools, linens, and rayons from Lily, CUM, Davidson's Old Mill, Fawcett, Folklorico, Harrisville, Henry's Attic, Plymouth, Tahki, Conshohocken, Ironstone Warehouse, and many others.

Quantity discounts are given; write for details.

Send for a free catalog and price list.

TREADLE I

18 Mildred Road
West Hartford, CT 06107
(203) 561-2299

Mail Order, Retail hours by
appointment; Established in 1977

TREADLE I carries the entire line of Schacht products, and Marks Linen, cotton and cottolin yarns. The company also offers a loom rental plan.

Discounts are given on yarns with a $200.00 minimum order.

Send for a current price list.

TUMBLEWEED WEAVING

2408 Carter
Cody, WY 82414
(307) 587-9568

Mail Order, Retail Shop;
Established in 1975

Vernice Myers, owner of TUMBLEWEED WEAVING, carries all Leclerc items, as well as a number of yarns and books. Classes, custom work and workshops are also offered.

Write or call for prices; a catalog is not available at this time.

TWIN BIRCH PRODUCTS

P.O. Box 50W
Winslow, ME 04902
(207) 873-0420

Manufacturers; Mail Order;
Established in 1981

L. Lincoln Brown, Jr., along with his brother Paul and sister Ann, of TWIN BIRCH PRODUCTS, are currently the only manufacturers of wooden knitting needles and crochet hooks. These handmade needles and hooks are especially good for people with arthritis, since the birch wood is never cold to the touch, unlike steel and aluminum needles. The wood also absorbs lanolin from wool yarn, and becomes smoother and silkier with use. The knitting needles come in various sizes and lengths, including an unusual 12-inch size. The company also makes double point needles. The wooden crochet hooks are available in four sizes, two lengths, and are also available with double ends. Other handmade items are also offered.

Discounts are given to schools and other groups; write for details.

Send $1.25 for a current catalog.

THE UNIQUE

21½ E. Bijou Street
Colorado Springs, CO 80903
(303) 473-9406

Mail Order, Retail Shop; V/MC;
Established in 1965

THE UNIQUE, owned by Eva Gerd Asher, carries a large inventory of yarns for weaving, knitting, crochet, stitchery, and other fiber arts, specializing in Scandinavian and European yarns. The Unique stocks the full line of Rauma and Roros Norwegian Spel-Sheep yarns, as well as other wools from Sweden, England, Scotland, and several domestic sources. Among these are Henry's Attic, Scott's, Harrisville, Eclectic, Ironstone, Plymouth, E'lite, and Lily. Imported linen yarns from Ireland are also offered, as are several Egyptian cottons and silks. The Unique also carries all products by Schacht, Leclerc, J-Made, Glimakra, Toika, Harrisville Designs, Clemes and Clemes, Ashford, and others.

The Unique gives many special offers, such as $25.00 worth of yarn free with purchase of any floor loom; $10.00 free with a 4-or-more harness table loom; 10% discount on all equipment purchased with loom; 10% discount on all yarns purchased within a year of loom order, etc. In addition to these, the company also gives a discount of up to 20% on quantity orders. Ms. Asher also offers classes and custom work, and promises continued expert help and advice for her customers.

Send $3.50 for a current catalog with some yarn samples. For $5.00, you will receive a Sample Kit including approximately 90-100 yarn samples, booklist, equipment catalogs, and price list.

VIKING FIBERS

Rt. 2, Box 2289
Benton City, WA 99320

Mail Order; Established in 1980

Julie Busch, owner of VIKING FIBERS, offers black wool fleece, mohair roving, washed kid mohair, adult mohair, and mohair/wool blend rovings. The easy-to-spin rovings consist of one-third yearling mohair and two-thirds lamb's wool, and come in black, grey and white.

Send a SASE for fiber samples and current prices.

THE WARPED WEAVER

P.O. Box 2520
Petaluma, CA 94953
(707) 763-YARN

Mail Order; V/MC; Established in 1981

Carol Larson, owner of THE WARPED WEAVER, says she started her business in order to provide high quality natural fiber yarns to weavers and knitters at below suggested retail prices. Since the business is mail-order only, you can save a considerable amount on your purchases. Yarns available are as follows: 100% Canadian wools from Condon in 30 colors, several 100% wool worsteds, 100% wool Berber yarns, 100% wools from Manos del Uruguay, wool bouclés, wool tweeds, white mohair/wool/nylon blends, linens, cottons, raw silks, and silk blends.

Since the Warped Weaver's prices are always 40-60% below suggested retail, they feel that this is a built-in discount.

Send $1.50 for a catalog and samples; this includes periodic updates as new yarns become available.

THE WEAVER'S LOFT

215 W. Center
Sandwich, IL 60548
(815) 786-2233

Mail Order, Retail Shop; V/MC; Established in 1981

THE WEAVER'S LOFT, owned by Shirley Seppla, carries a variety of weaving and spinning supplies, including yarns and threads from Unger, Pingouin, Berroco, Lily, School Products, Ironstone Warehouse, Henry's Attic, Harrisville Designs, Maysville, Fawcett, Conshohocken, Scheepjeswol, Heirloom, and others. Looms and accessories are available from Norwood, Schacht, Harrisville Designs, and Rick Reeves. Spinning wheels are from Country Craftsman, Ashford, and Clemes and Clemes. They also carry other supplies, books, and a large selection of knitting and crochet patterns. Various classes in weaving, spinning, knitting, and crocheting are offered.

Send for a current price list and class schedule.

THE WEAVER'S SHOP & YARN COMPANY

P.O. Box 457
Rockford, MI 49341
(616) 866-9529

Mail Order, Retail Shop; V/MC; Established in 1968

THE WEAVER'S SHOP carries looms by Leclerc, Schacht, Glimakra, and others. Also offered are many spinning fibers and yarns, Cushing dyes, books, spinning wheels, and accessories.

Discounts are given to those with a resale tax number and a $100.00 minimum order.

Send $2.50 for a current catalog (applied to first order).

THE WEAVER'S STORE

11 South 9th Street
Columbia, MO 65201
(314) 442-5413

Mail Order, Retail Shop; V/MC;
Established in 1977

THE WEAVER'S STORE is a full-line weaving and knitting supply source. They represent many major equipment manufacturers, including Harrisville Designs, Glimakra, Schacht, Leclerc, Beka, Ashford, Louet, Clemes and Clemes, and others. The store also has basketry supplies, whole skirted Corriedale fleece, carded wool rovings, rainbow batts, pima cotton, brown cotton, long line flax, ramie, mohair, alpaca, and silk. Natural dyes and mordants, as well as Cushing synthetic dyes, are offered. A huge variety of yarns are stocked from such companies as Oregon Worsted, Borgs, Novitex, Tahki, Simpkins, Perendale, Ironstone Warehouse, Berroco, Brown Sheep Company, Plymouth, Pingouin, Patons, Candide, Scheepjeswol, Henry's Attic, and more. The Weaver's Store also carries a *huge* book inventory. On-going classes and workshops are offered in weaving, spinning, basketry, knitting — many of them taught by nationally known experts.

Discounts are given with a minimum order of $200.00.

Send $2.00 for a current catalog. A packet with all loom and spinning equipment catalogs included is $5.00 (refunded with loom or wheel order). Fiber samples are $2.00. Write for information on specific yarn samples.

WEAVER'S WAY

P.O. Box 230
Crown Point, IN 46307
(219) 663-1406

Mail Order, Retail Shop; V/MC;
Established in 1975

WEAVER'S WAY supplies cotton and modacrylic yarns under their own label, in addition to yarns by others. They also sell the entire line of Leclerc looms and accessories, spinning wheels from Lendrum, wool carders from Clemes, and drum carders from Mark IV. A large list of books are also offered. Weaver's Way promises one day shipping on most orders.

Volume discounts are given; see catalog for details.

Send $1.00 for a current catalog. Yarn sample cards may be purchased individually (prices listed in catalog), or by the complete set for $20.00.

THE WEAVER'S WEB

12 Wall Street
Asheville, NC 28801
(704) 252-3221

Mail Order, Retail Shop; V/MC;
Established in 1980

THE WEAVER'S WEB carries wholesale yarns, mostly cottons. Classes and seminars are also offered.

Discounts are given on certain yarns, with a minimum order of $100.00.

Send for a free price list.

WEAVING LADY STUDIO

4001 Cresthill Road
Chester, VA 23831
(804) 748-9036

Manufacturer; Mail Order, Retail hours by appointment; V/MC;
Established in 1977

Although Gladys Strong of THE WEAVING LADY STUDIO says that mail orders are not her primary function, she does offer it as a service. The Studio carries Leclerc, Schacht, and Glimakra looms, Louet and Ashford spinning wheels, New Zealand and Australian wool fibers, yarns by Harrisville, Borgs, Kolmes, LeMeiux, Scott's, and others.

Write or call for specific prices.

WEAVING WORKS, INC.

5049 Brooklyn Avenue, N.E.
Seattle, WA 98105
(206) 524-1221

Mail Order, Retail Shop; V/MC;
Established in 1974

WEAVING WORKS, INC. carries a large number of fiber supplies, with over 37 types of yarns. Some of these are from Berga, Harrisville, Condon, CUM, Manos, Paternayan, Berroco, Tahki, El Molino, Lily, Tahki, Fawcett, etc. Spinning fibers include alpaca, angora, camel down and hair, cashmere, cottons, doghair, flax, goat hair, guanaco, jute, llama, mohair, ramie, silks, sisal, yak, and raw wools. A variety of weaving and spinning equipment is offered, including looms by Cranbrook, Herald, Leclerc, Rasmussen, Schacht, and others. Spinning supplies are offered by Ashford, Clemes, Kircher, Louet, Pipy, etc. Weaving Works also carries basketry supplies and books — over 150 of them, with more coming in. A full selection of classes are given, including such subjects as Weaving, Knitting, Machine Knitting, Spinning, Dyes of the Americas, Feltmaking, Papermaking, etc.

A 10% discount is given on orders of $150.00 or more.

Send 50¢ for a brochure and price list; also inquire about class schedules.

WEAVING WORKSHOP

817½ E. Johnson Street
Madison, WI 53703
(608) 255-1066

Mail Order, Retail Shop;
Established in 1971

WEAVING WORKSHOP carries yarns from several companies, including Henry's Attic, Berroco, Scott's, Tahki, LeMieux, Condon, Harrisville, Ironstone Warehouse, Brown Sheep Company, etc. Spinning fibers include raw wool and wool tops, ramie, flax roving, Mawata, Bombyx and Tussah silks, cotton sliver, mohair, cashmere, alpaca and angora rabbit. They are dealers for Leclerc, Herald, Norwood, Schacht, Harrisville Designs, and Kyra looms, as well as Ashford and Louet spinning wheels. A wide range of supplies for knitting and crochet are also offered.

A 5% discount is given to guild members, and a 15% discount is given on special orders over $125.00.

Send 50¢ for a current catalog.

WEBS

P.O. Box 349
Amherst, MA 01004
(413) 253-2580

Mail Order, Retail hours; V/MC;
Established in 1974

WEBS sells a full assortment of fiber supplies, and represents such manufacturers as Harrisville Designs, Tools of the Trade, Leclerc, Schacht, Glimakra, Willow Tree, Beka, Northfield, Ashford, Louet, Clemes, and Restoration Arts. They also stock a wide variety of yarns from Oregon Worsted, Borgs, Novitex, Harrisville Designs, Kolmes, Ironstone, Berroco, E'lite, Tahki, Charity Hill Farm, Anthea, Bernat, LaMieux, Silk City, and Reynolds. Webs' book inventory includes basic texts and monographs as well as new and/or lesser known publications. They also carry knitting patterns and books. A wide variety of classes are also offered.

Webs does not charge for shipping on looms, wheels and equipment orders over $50.00. They also offer a 20% discount on yarn purchases of $60.00 or more and a 25% discount on purchases of $120.00 or more.

Send for a free basic catalog. Catalogs on all looms are $3.50 (refunded with loom order).

YARNS/FIBERS/WEAVING/SPINNING/KNITTING/CROCHET/OTHER

A WESTSIDE WEAVER

P.O. Box 478, Planetarium Station
New York, NY 10024

Manufacturer; Mail Order;
Established in 1983

A WESTSIDE WEAVER offers tools for the weaver that are not commonly available. Among these are clear, acrylic warping paddles with the capacity for 32 warp ends, drawing-in hooks with one or two blades, the McMorran Yarn Balance used to calculate the length per weight (or yards per pound) in any given amount of yarn, and a spindle spinning kit. Two books are also available: *Warp with a Paddle and Beam Without Paper,* by Landis, and *Henry Moore's Sheep Sketchbook.*

Send for a free brochure.

THE WHITAKER REED COMPANY

P.O. Box 172
Worcester, MA 01602
(617) 752-8385

Manufacturer; Mail Order;
Established in 1869

THE WHITAKER REED COMPANY manufactures custom made loom reeds with either carbon or stainless steel dents. Metric dentages are also available.

Note: Whitaker does not carry basketry reed, in spite of the fact that they are listed in many basketry books.

Quantity discounts are given; check price list for details.

Send for a free price list.

WHITE LLAMA WEAVING SUPPLY

R.R. #1
Tallula, IL 62688
(217) 632-3732

Manufacturer; Mail Order, Retail hours by appointment;
Established in 1980

Lynn Barnett-Westfall started her WHITE LLAMA WEAVING SUPPLY business when she realized that people living in rural central Illinois had to travel a minimum of three hours to get to a weaving supply source. She now carries a wide variety of supplies such as looms by Norwood and Harrisville Designs, spinning wheels by Ashford, Louet, and Restoration Arts. Her inventory also includes a large number of weaving and spinning tools. Lynn specializes in unique handcrafted weaving and spinning tools. Spinning fibers include New Zealand Romney wools, wool rainbow batts, combed flax top, cottons, alpaca, mohair, yak, camel, silks, etc. Yarns are available by Harrisville, Crystal Palace, E'lite, Forté Fibers, Scott's, and others. An interesting assortment of natural dyes include cochineal, logwood powder, cutch and fustic extracts, quebracho extract, and others. Superba Knitting Machines can also be ordered from White Llama.

Some discounts are given; write for details.

Send $1.00 and a SASE for a catalog; spinning fiber samples are $3.00. Other sample prices are listed in catalog.

WILD WEFT YARNS

407 N. 5th Avenue
Ann Arbor, MI 48104
(313) 761-2466

Mail Order, Retail Shop; V/MC;
Established in 1972

WILD WEFT YARNS carries various types of weaving and spinning supplies, including looms by Schacht, Beka, Harrisville, Glimakra, and Norwood, and spinning wheels by Ashford and Louet. Other items include yarns on cones, mill-end yarns, books, basketry supplies, and fibers for spinning. They also offer classes in weaving, spinning, knitting, and basketry.

Discounts are given; write for details.

Send 50¢ for a price list and sample sheet.

WILDE YARNS

3705 Main Street
Philadelphia, PA 19127-2198
(215) 482-8800

Manufacturer; Mail Order, Retail
Shop; Established in 1880

John Wilde & Brother, Incorporated, owners of WILDE YARNS, currently offers eight different lines of yarn, plus unspun, washed and carded wools for handspinners, feltmakers, and weavers. The yarns include a sturdy 3-ply wool, available in 16 shades, all white wool yarns (scoured but not bleached), natural color wool yarns in three weights, Berber Yarns (characterized by flecks of color that appear irregularly against a background of a different shade) in five colors and two weights. One of Wilde's finest yarns is a blend of soft New Zealand wools, and is available in 28 colors. The heaviest of the yarns is a bulky 4-ply which is skein dyed in 9 bold colors; the softest is a wool that is designed for weaving and knitting clothing and blankets. This is available in 18 muted shades and eight undyed, natural shades. Wilde's unspun wools have been scoured, blended and carded in loose batting form, and come in five shades and nine dyed colors.

Wholesale discounts are given to qualified buyers only; write for details. Educational discounts are also available.

A brochure is free. Samples of all wools are $3.00.

WILLOW POND WOOLS

Rt. 1, Box 166F
Ware Shoals, SC 29692
(803) 861-2031

Mail Order, Retail hours by
appointment; Established in 1983

WILLOW POND WOOLS raises purebred Romney and Lincoln sheep, both white and colored. Their fleece are long, soft and lustrous, require little preparation and are ideal for spinning and dyeing. The company also raises angora goats for the mohair and angora rabbits for their fine, fluffy fur. All of these fibers are sold in the raw forms, and all (except angora) are available in washed, picked and carded forms. Also available are naturally dyed wools and a wool/mohair blend. A custom carding service is available for your own fleece. Willow Pond Wools Handspun Yarns are produced entirely on the farm, and are offered in white, natural, and natural dyed colors. Other items include spinning wheels by Louet, Ashford, and Lendrum, and looms from Harrisville, Herald, Tools of the Trade, and Louet. Yarns are available from Harrisville, Brown Sheep Company, Condon, Plymouth, Tahki, Berroco, Henry's Attic, Lily, and a variety of mill-ends. A large number of natural dyes and mordants are also offered.

A general price list is free. Fleece samples are $1.00, dyed fleece samples are $1.50, and handspun yarn samples are $2.00.

WINDHOVER WOOLS

R. D. #1
Fort Plain, NY 13339
(315) 823-1077

Mail Order, Retail Shop; V/MC;
Established in 1983

WINDHOVER WOOLS is a complete weaving and spinning supply shop that also offers a beautiful "flock of sheep to see." Some of the shop's supplies include Schacht and Kyra looms, Louet, Camelot and Peacock spinning wheels. Raw, washed, and carded fleece is available, as are silk bricks, noils and roving, flax roving, ramie, cotton, camel down, and handspun wools. Yarns are available from several companies. Patterns by Paula Straker and Maine Maid are also offered.

Send for a free brochure and ordering information.

WINDSOR FARMS

Rt. 1, Box 76
Amesville, OH 45711
(614) 448-2771

Mail Order, Retail hours by
appointment; Established in 1976

WINDSOR FARMS, managed by Ron Chacey, offers Lincoln and Lincoln crossbred fleece, skirted, washed and picked or washed and carded, natural grey mulespun yarns, longwooled sheepskins, and prize winning breeding stock (specializing in black sheep).

Quantity discounts are given with a minimum order of $125.00.

Send a $1.00 for an information sheet and samples; or send $2.00 for a set of four-yard samples of each of the yarns that are currently available.

WINDSPUN FIBERS

P.O. Box 1461
Valdez, AK 99686
(907) 835-2278

Mail Order, Retail Shop;
Established in 1982

WINDSPUN FIBERS is an importer in the only free trade zone in Alaska. They carry the full line of supplies from Ashford, Louet, Rasmussen, Beka, and Textile Artists' Supply. Yarns are available from Marks, Berga, Tahki, Wilde, etc. Spinning fibers include raw wools, silks, camel, musk ox, yak, dog, alpaca, llama, Icelandic wools, etc. Classes in weaving, spinning, dyeing, felting, basketry, beading, knitting, and crocheting are offered.

Discounts are given with a minimum order of $250.00.

Send for a free brochure and price list.

Angora goat.

WONDER CRAFT

1 Constitution Street
Bristol, RI 02809
(401) 253-2030

Manufacturer; Mail Order, Retail
Shop

WONDER CRAFT, a division of Robin Rug, Inc., carries a large assortment of odd lot yarns, most of which are wools, wool blends, cottons and synthetics.

Quantity discounts are given with a minimum order of $25.00. Further discounts are given with larger orders.

Send $1.00 for a current price list with samples; periodic mailings are sent out.

WOOL AND FEATHERS

Box 1123
Stowe, VT 05672
(802) 253-9653

Manufacturer; Mail Order, Retail
Shop; V/MC; Established in 1980

WOOL AND FEATHERS is owned by Gisela Gminder. She carries a line of 100% wool yarns in 18 heathery, beautiful colors. Other supplies are available from Tools of the Trade, Leclerc, Louet, Northfield, and Ashford. Raw wools and tops are available, as are dyes and other fiber supplies.

Discounts are given with a minimum order of $250.00.

Send a SASE for yarn samples and a current price list.

WOOL BASKET

R. D. #1, Box 207
Canonsburg, PA 15317
(412) 745-0397

Mail Order, Retail Shop;
Established in 1981

Sally Young, owner of the WOOL BASKET, carries spinning wheels by Ashford, Louet, Peacock, Nagy and Camelot. Spinning fibers include Romney and Dorset wools, cashmere, camel down, angora, silks, and mohair. Other accessories and supplies are available, such as spindles, carders, shuttles, etc.

Send a SASE for price list and fiber samples.

THE WOOL GALLERY

459 High, S.E.
Salem, OR 97301
(503) 363-9665

Mail Order; Retail Shop; Established in 1979

Caryl Gertenrich, owner of THE WOOL GALLERY, distributes a full range of Berga yarns imported from Sweden, in wool, alpaca, cotton, and linen blends.

Discounts are given with a minimum order of $1,000.00.

Send $10.00 for a complete set of ten sample cards (each containing from 22 to 130 colors per card).

WOOLEN HARVEST

365 Dairy Road
Auburn, CA 95603
(916) 823-5545

Mail Order

Dorothy Zelle of WOOLEN HARVEST sells New Zealand wools in batt or roving form, in dyed colors and white. She also offers a washing, teasing, and carding service, and can make 72-inch batts or continuous roving from your wool.

Send a SASE for a price list.

THE WOOLERY

R. D. #1
Genoa, NY 13071
(315) 497-1542

Mail Order, Retail hours by appointment; Established in 1981

THE WOOLERY, managed by Tim and Marianne Horchler, tries to support U.S. sheep producers by only selling domestic wools. In turn, they also have a flock of 75 sheep of their own, including Registered Finns (white and colored), Registered Black Border Leicesters and Finn/Dorsets. Wools from these are offered for spinning, in addition to carded cottons, Tussah silk sliver, ramie, mohair, and alpaca top. The Woolery was also one of the first shops to carry knitting machines, and now stock a large number of Studio Knitting Machines. Also available are spinning wheels from Ashford, Louet, Country Craftsman, and Charkha. Spindles, carders, accessories and books are also offered.

Send a SASE for samples of fleece or yarns and a price list; specify desired breed or color.

THE WOOLMARK

322 Fifth Street
Eureka, CA 95501
(707) 442-9272

Mail Order, Retail Shop;
Established in 1975

THE WOOLMARK offers an extensive list of fiber supplies. Spinning fibers include wools (domestic, New Zealand Perendale, Farol and Dark Merino fleece, rovings and tops), alpaca, mohair, camel hair, ramie, jute sliver, rayon and linen roving, uplands sliver cotton, silks, and six types of cashmere and angora rabbit fur. Yarns include natural fibers only from Berroco, Brown Sheep Company, Christopher Sheep Heathers, Condon, Dorothee Bis, E'lite, Forté Fibers, Harrisville, Indiecita Alpaca, Lane Borgosesia, Lily, Maypole, Reynolds, Tahki, Unger, Wilde, Berga, Swedish wools, Irish singles, Scottish Shetland wools, and many more. Looms are available from Schacht, Leclerc, Harrisville, and wheels from Ashford, Clemes, Louet and Nagy. Many other supplies and tools are offered, including an extensive list of natural dyes, mordants and assistants.

Some quantity discounts are given; write for details.

Send for a free catalog and workshop schedule.

WOOLS & WEAVES

5731 Cowell Road
Brighton, MI 48116
(313) 231-2455

Manufacturer; Mail Order, Retail
Shop; Established in 1980

Charlotte Morgan, owner of WOOLS & WEAVES, carries a large assortment of spinning and weaving equipment, including Louet spinning wheels, looms and accessories, Mark IV carding machines, Studio and KnitKing Knitting Machines, and yarns from Scott's and Plymouth. Spinning fibers include wools, silk, and natural sharla. As far as she knows, Ms. Morgan is the only source of natural sharla in the U.S., and perhaps in North America.

A 10% discount is given on all Louet products. Educational discounts are also given; write for details.

Send 50¢ for a current catalog.

WOOLWORKS

3254 E. Kelly Road
Bellingham, WA 98226
(206) 592-5818

Mail Order, Retail hours by
appointment; Established in 1978

Jan Witcraft, of WOOLWORKS, can provide colored fleece, Glimakra looms, Borgs yarns, and custom woven items. Jan also teaches tapestry and "Weaving as a Business" workshops.

Wholesale discounts are given to qualified buyers; write for details. A 10% discount is given to schools/groups, etc.

Send for prices and a brochure on various workshops.

WOOLY ACRE FARM

R. #2, Box 39
Royal Center, IN 46978
(219) 889-2662

Mail Order; Established in 1942

WOOLY ACRE FARM is owned and operated by L. E. Zimmer and Family. They can supply white spinning fleece from Corriedale sheep. They also have Corriedale sheep for sale, in addition to sheep supplies.

Quantity discounts are given; write for prices.

Send a SASE for wool samples and current prices.

THE WOOLY WEST

208 South 13th East
Salt Lake City, UT 84102
(801) 583-9373

Mail Order, Retail Shop; V/MC;
Established in 1980

THE WOOLY WEST carries a large line of yarns from such companies as Tahki, Candide, Crystal Palace, Scheepjeswol, Andean, Pingouin, Berger du Nord, Brown Sheep Company, and others. Workshops are also offered throughout the year.

A 10% discount is given on purchases of two or more bags of yarn.

Send $2.00 for current price list and newsletter.

V & E WRENSCH RANCH

Rt. 1, Box 75
Johnson Creek, WI 53038
(414) 699-2996

Mail Order; Established in 1961

The V & E WRENSCH RANCH sells raw wool in black, brown, silver, white and tan, and carded wool batts. They also offer tanned hides, both shorn and unshorn. You can even buy your own sheep from this source —rams, ewes, or lambs!

Quantity discounts are given; write for details.

Write for a current price list.

YARN & WEAVERS THINGS

2558B Cottage Way
Sacramento, CA 95825
(916) 485-7648

Mail Order, Retail Shop; V/MC;
Established in 1973

YARN & WEAVERS THINGS stocks yarns by Berroco, Plymouth, Tahki, Harrisville Designs, Lily, Robinson-Anton, Nevada, Phildar, Novitex, and others. They are also dealers for Leclerc looms and accessories. Also offered is an assortment of basketry supplies and books.

Quantity discounts are given to those with a resale tax number.

Call or write for specific information and prices; a catalog is not available at this time.

YARN BARN

Box 334
Lawrence, KS 66044
(913) 842-4333

Mail Order, Retail Shop; V/MC;
Established in 1971

The YARN BARN is another of those in-depth fiber suppliers that seem to have just about everything. Looms are available from J-Made, Norwood, Loomcraft, Beka, Leclerc, Schacht and Harrisville Designs. Spinning wheels and accessories are available from Ashford, Louet, and Lendrum. Spinning fibers include raw wools, rovings and tops, cotton, ramie, flax, silks, camel, alpaca, cashmere, mohair, and acrylic roving. A large selection (over 45) of natural dyestuffs are available, along with the required mordants. A full line of supplies for printing on or dyeing fabrics are also offered, including dyes, silkscreen and batik supplies, fabrics, stenciling supplies, and much more. They also carry supplies for rugmaking, knitting, crochet, tatting, and bobbin lace. Over 400 books on all aspects of the fiber arts are included in Yarn Barn's extensive catalog.

Quantity discounts are given; write for details.

Send $1.00 for a complete catalog (refunded with order). A basic yarn sample card is $2.00.

YARN BARN OF SAN ANTONIO

4803 Broadway
San Antonio, TX 78209
(512) 826-3679

Mail Order, Retail Shop;
Established in 1971

THE YARN BARN OF SAN ANTONIO is a multi-service fiber shop, carrying supplies for weaving, all types of needlework, knitting, etc. They offer Leclerc looms and accessories, the full line of DMC products, Paternayan Persian yarns, knitting machines, all major brands of knitting yarns, foreign and domestic books and patterns, and much more.

Discounts are given to designers and teachers with a $150.00 minimum order.

Write or call for specific information or prices; a catalog is not available at this time.

YARNS + MORE

2249 S. Brentwood Blvd.
St. Louis, MO 63144
(314) 961-4377

Mail Order; V/MC; Established in 1983

YARNS + MORE carries the full line of Chat Botté yarns and patterns imported from France, along with Marjorie Ivey Pattern Kits. Marjorie Ivey is a nationally known knitting designer whose garments have appeared most recently in *Vogue Knitting, McCall's Needlework and Crafts* and *Family Circle Annual*. The kits also include knitting needles, crochet hooks and other accessories. Finishing services are also available for those garments ordered from this company.

Send $1.00 for an illustrated brochure.

YARNWORKS

1938 N. First Street
Grand Junction, CO 81501
(303) 243-5365

Mail Order, Retail Shop; V/MC;
Established in 1984 (continuation of a ten-year business under another name)

YARNWORKS is the only store in Colorado designated as an "authorized" Glimakra Weaving School. The store, recently opened by Constance La Lena, an internationally known textile artist and writer, is called a "one-stop service center for all the textile arts." Many different yarns are offered for knitting, weaving, machine knitting, crochet, etc., and accessories are available, too. Looms are available from Glimakra, Schacht, Beka, and Northfield. Spinning fibers, dyes, books, and exclusive knitting patterns will all be available from Yarnworks. A full load of classes and workshops will be held at the store, and Connie will also travel to give workshops at your location.

Quantity discounts are given with a minimum order of $150.00.

A new catalog is in progress; write for current price.

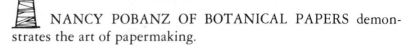 NANCY POBANZ OF BOTANICAL PAPERS demonstrates the art of papermaking.

1. Plant material (in this case, cedar bark) is boiled in water with caustic soda to remove the fleshy parts of the plants and isolate cellulose, which becomes the substance of the paper. The fibers are then rinsed thoroughly.

2. Pulp is made by beating the fiber.

3 & 4. The pulp is mixed with water in a vat. A mold and deckle (the frames with screen shown) are lowered into the vat and with a quick scooping motion, lifted and rocked back and forth to catch the pulp and intertwine the fibers on the screen of the mold.

5. A piece of cotton is laid onto the wet, matted fibers, pressed with a sponge and lifted off the screen, pulling the fibers with it.

6. It is then laid on a board, brushed on and left to air dry.

(The photographer is Scott Woodcock).

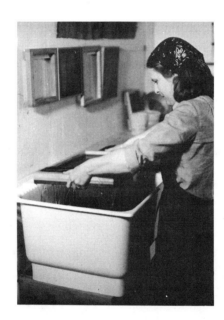

CHAPTER
6

Papermaking Supplies and Equipment

For those fiber artists who work in the area of handmade paper, this chapter contains supplies such as raw fibers (cotton linters, abaca, kozo, Belgian line flax, Indian hemp, khus-khus, and other exotic fibers), basic tools and equipment, instruction books, Hollander-style paper beaters, moulds and deckles, etc. A full line of supplies for Japanese style papermaking are also listed.

BASIC CRAFTS CO.

1201 Broadway
New York, NY 10001
(212) 679-3516

Mail Order; MC/V

BASIC CRAFTS CO. supplies cotton linters and softwood pulps for hand papermaking. They also offer a large number of basic supplies for bookbinding, including several how-to books.

Send for a current "Bookbinding" catalog and price list.

BOTANICAL PAPERS

P.O. Box 31032
Seattle, WA 98103-1032
(206) 789-3379 or (206) 784-0155

Manufacturer, Mail Order;
Established in 1981

BOTANICAL PAPERS is the handmade papermaking studio of Nancy Pobanz. She makes papers that are not available for sale anywhere else in the country. These are made from willow, yucca, straw, pampas grass, fig, cedar, and cattail. All papers are acid free; special sizes and shapes of paper are made on request. Nancy teaches classes and workshops, and gives lectures and demonstrations.

Quantity discounts are negotiable; write for information.

A price list, general information, and samples of all papers is $3.00.

CARRIAGE HOUSE HANDMADE PAPER WORKS

8 Evans Road
Brookline, MA 02146
(617) 232-1636

Manufacturer, Mail Order;
Established in 1975

CARRIAGE HOUSE is owned and operated by Elaine and Donna Koretsky, a well-known mother and daughter team of handmade paper artists. Primarily, the studio was established to research and experiment with handmade paper as an art form. Carriage House provides information and technical assistance in the field of papermaking, as well as a full line of supplies. Papermaking kits and prepared pulps such as manila hemp (abaca), cotton linters, sisal/Indian hemp are available. Bark fibers widely used in Asian papermaking include kozo, mitsumata and daphne. Other supplies available include Tororo-Aoi seeds, Chiri-Tori tweezers, papermaking additives such as retention agents, formation aids, soda ash, calcium carbonate, and colorants (Aardvark Colors). Elaine Koretsky has written an extremely useful book, *Color for the Hand Papermaker,* which is also available from this source. Workshops and other studio programs are offered, and handmade papers are available.

A catalog and price list is 50¢.

*A type of beater used to break down
materials into fibers (cut-away side view)*

CHENEY PULP & PAPER COMPANY

Box 215
Franklin, OH 45005
(513) 746-9991

Manufacturer, Mail Order;
Established in 1924

CHENEY PULP & PAPER COMPANY manufactures several grades of rag pulp. All pulp is half-stock, which means that further refining is necessary before it can be made into paper.

A free price list is available. Don't plan to order from Cheney unless you need a LOT of paper, since their minimum order is two bales of one grade of pulp — with each bale weighing approximately 500 pounds, and costing from $125.00 to $195.00 per bale, depending on grade.

DIEU DONNÉ PRESS & PAPER, INC.

3 Crosby Street
New York, NY 10013
(212) 226-0573

Manufacturer, Mail Order;
Established in 1977

DIEU DONNÉ PRESS & PAPER provides wholesale papermaking supplies to retailers. Along with ready-made 100% rag papers, they carry supplies for handmade papermaking such as pulps in 100% cottons and 100% linens, unbeaten raw materials such as sheet linters, dry abaca half-stock, and custom pulps. Dieu Donné also provides a studio rental service which can include consultation services, use of all papermaking equipment and mill, and preparation of raw materials. The company also teaches a workshop on handmade paper through the New School in New York City.

Wholesale discounts are given to qualified retailers; write for information.

A price list is free.

 WHAT ARE "COTTON LINTERS"...

After cotton is harvested, the long fibers are removed for use in textiles. The shorter, coarser fibers that remain attached to the cotton seed are known as "cotton linters". These are then cut from the seed, cooked, and used in making papers. The linters produce a low-shrinkage pulp that is good for paper casting. The fibers are too short, however, for making durable book papers.

FIBER DIRECTIONS/ COLOR CONNECTIONS, LTD.

P.O. Box 2143
Corrales, NM 87048
(505) 898-7345

Manufacturer, Mail Order, Retail Shop; V/MC; Established in 1983

FIBER DIRECTIONS/COLOR CONNECTIONS, LTD. is an all-around supplier for the fiber arts. In addition to dyes, yarns, fibers, and books, Coralie Jones and Trudy Maxwell of FD/CC has available supplies for hand papermaking. A simple student mould and deckle is available, as are abaca, sisal, flax, Indian hemp, cotton rag, and cotton linter pulps in dry sheet form. Sizings, felts, and special order pulps (linen, Belgian line flax, Kozo, Mitsumata) are also offered. Both Coralie and Trudy give classes and demonstrations in their retail location.

Send $2.00 for a catalog (applicable to first order); paper pulp samples are $2.00, and dye samples are $2.00.

GOLDS' ARTWORKS, INC.

2918 N. Elm Street
Lumberton, NC 28358
(919) 739-9605

Wholesale Distributor; V/MC;
Established in 1980

GOLDS' distributes linter pulp in various grades, dry pigments by Perma Color, methyl cellulose, calcium carbonate, a paper press and a vacuum table. The company also offers workshops at their art studio at Topsail Island, NC, as well as studio rental for private use. Golds' claims to have "met the needs of the papermaker when getting his materials was almost impossible."

Wholesale or quantity discounts are given to individuals; write for details.

A free brochure and price list is available.

ICOSA STUDIO AND PAPERMILL

Rt. 4, Box 279
Ellensburg, WA 98926
(509) 964-2341

Private Studio; Established in 1975

ICOSA is the papermaking studio of Margaret Ahrens Sahlstrand. The studio can be rented, which includes access to a Hollander beater, hydro-pulper, vacuum table and standing press. The fee also includes three Hollander loads of pulp beaten in advance and ready for use. In-studio workshops are also available for beginners, such as Introduction to Fibers for Sheet Forming and Casting, Use of the Hollander Beater and Hydro-pulper, and Relief and Flat Forms Constructed on the Vacuum Table.

Margaret will also travel to present workshops in papermaking and to lecture on Japanese and Korean papermaking techniques.

Linen, cotton, and Oriental paper fibers are also available.

Send for a free brochure on workshops and studio rental information.

LEE SCOTT MC DONALD FINE HAND PAPERMAKING EQUIPMENT

523 Medford Street
P.O. Box 264
Charlestown, MA 02129
(617) 242-2505

Manufacturer, Mail Order; V/MC; Established in 1979

LEE SCOTT MC DONALD has one of the most extensive lines of paper-making supplies around. Basic equipment consists of papermaking kits, "package deals" for schools and simple moulds. A complete selection of books on papermaking is offered, and includes works by such authors as Heller, Hunter, Barrett, Koretsky, etc. Fibers and pulps include kozo, gampi, mitsumata, line flax, cotton, unbleached abaca, sisal, and others. A new line of Barbados fibers are available, and include banana, breadfruit, sugar cane, coconut, papyrus, and Khus-khus. McDonald also offers a wide selection of coloring agents, sizings, buffers and other hard-to-find chemicals used in papermaking. As a special service, custom moulds and deckles are available, as are two types of watermarking: bentwire and photographic. For those who wish to make their own moulds and deckles, LSM offers all supplies needed, including brass hardware and wood finishes. A wide variety of felts are offered, as are vats, mixers, stampers, the David Reina Hollander Beater, the Charles Hilger Vacuum Table, and various presses. Equipment for Nagashizuki (Oriental) papermaking is also available.

Many items in the McDonald catalog are available wholesale. Send inquiries on your letterhead.

Send for a current catalog.

The Lee Scott McDonald basic papermaking kit includes mould and deckle, felts, abaca pulp, and instruction book. © Lee Scott McDonald

DAVID REINA DESIGNS, INC.

44 Mechanic Street
Millburn, NJ 07041
(201) 376-1725

DAVID REINA DESIGNS, INC. is a source for high quality, traditional Hollander-style paper beaters. This company also offers replacement parts for older beaters and new machines.

Quantity discounts are given with a minimum order of two beaters.

Send for a free brochure.

H. M. SPENCER, INC.

78 North Canal Street
P.O. Box 965
Holyoke, MA 01041
(413) 532-1525

Manufacturer; Established in 1896

H. M. SPENCER, INC. provides laid-wire covers for handmade paper moulds, a watermarking service, and all types of wire cloth.

Retailers can write for more information.

STRAW INTO GOLD, INC.

3006 San Pablo Avenue
Berkeley, CA 94702
(415) 548-5241

Mail Order, Retail Shop; M/V;
Established in 1971

STRAW INTO GOLD, INC. supplies cotton linters for handmade papermaking. The linters are sold in large sheets by weight only. Sheets are available in five, ten, and 20 pound sizes.

Send a SASE for more information and current prices on papermaking supplies.

TWINROCKER HANDMADE PAPER

RFD 2
Brookston, IN 47923
(317) 563-3210

Manufacturer, Mail Order, Retail Shop; V/MC; Established in 1971

Kathryn and Howard Clark formed TWINROCKER HANDMADE PAPER COMPANY in 1971. They feel that (and many agree) their business has played a major role in the revival of hand papermaking in the United States, and has aided the development of many artistic techniques. In addition to specializing in custom handmade paper to order, Twinrocker offers a wide range of supplies for papermaking. The owners feel that after thirteen years of experience as professional papermakers they are qualified to give their customers good advice on using the supplies they sell. Twinrocker has also been at the same location for twelve years, and the Clarks intend to be there "for many years to come."

The company offers a wide variety of fibers and ready-to-use pulps from those fibers. These include cotton linters, cotton rag, raw flax, linen rag, abaca (two types), ramie, kapok, sisal cuttings and pulps, Russian hemp, kozo (Oriental mulberry bark), mitsumata and gampi. Also available are lightfast, waterbased pigments for coloring papers, books about papermaking, sizings, kits and moulds.

Quantity discounts are given to individuals, schools and other groups. Write for information.

A general catalog is free; samples are $3.00.

MICHAEL JOHN
VERLANGIERI

790 Santa Barbara Drive
Claremont, CA 91711
(714) 624-6987

Manufacturer, Mail Order;
Established in 1976

As well as being a professional artist and lecturer, Mr. Verlangieri owns and operates a small custom handmade paper mill. In addition to offering custom handmade papers, Michael also sells sheets of cotton linter pulp from Alpha Cellulose in bleached white and unbleached tan colors.

Orders over 400 sheets are discounted.

Write for more information and current prices.

 WHAT IS "ABACA"?

Abaca is a fiber obtained from the leafstalk of a banana plant native to the Philippines; also called "Manila hemp".

WEI T'O ASSOCIATES, INC.

21750 Main Street, #27
P.O. Drawer 40
Matteson, IL 60443
(312) 747-6660

Manufacturer, Mail Order;
Established in 1972

WEI T'O is said to be an ancient Chinese god who protects books against destruction from fire, worms, insects, and robbers, big or small. The company, WEI T'O ASSOCIATES, INC., offers nonaqueous preservation equipment for books, prints, and works of art on paper. Artists who work in handmade paper or printmaking will be interested in the process which the company uses to deacidify papers.

A free brochure and price list is available.

ZELBUR PORCELITE
CER-ART PRODUCTS

Box 964
Plainfield, NJ 07061
(201) 755-1828

Manufacturer, Mail Order;
Established in 1950

ZELBUR distributes a heavy-duty fifteen gallon fiberglass pulp mixer for making ready-to-use paper pulp. Along with the mixer, they supply half-stock rag fiber and prepared wet pulp. For making cast paper, Zelbur carries latex rubber and rubber filler for moulds. They also offer various seminars.

Quantity discounts are offered with a five pound minimum order.

Send for a free information sheet and price list.

CHAPTER 7   Basketry Supplies

This chapter contains basic supplies for handmade baskets: canes, cords, seagrass, bamboos, reeds, hoops, bases, splints, tools, and kits.

THE BACK DOOR - COUNTRY BASKETS

10 Batchellor Drive
North Brookfield, MA 01535
(617) 867-3079

Mail Order; V/MC; Established in 1983

THE BACK DOOR - COUNTRY BASKETS carries a full line of basket-making kits, instructions, and some supplies. These include reeds in various sizes, handles and eight-inch round hoops.

Basketweaving classes are also offered.

A 10% discount is given with a minimum order of $100.00.

Send 50¢ for a current brochure and price sheet.

BAMBOO & RATTAN WORKS, INC.

470 Oberlin Avenue, South
Lakewood, NJ 08701
(201) 370-0220

Mail Order, Manufacturer; Established in 1880

BAMBOO & RATTAN WORKS, INC. is a family-owned business that provides a large line of materials for basketmaking, including flat oval reed, flat reed, chair cane, binding cane, seagrass cord, round reeds, raffia, decorative bamboo and rattan, spline reed, twisted seagrass and bamboo poles. They also carry wallcovering and matting. Custom work is available.

Quantity discounts are given to individuals.

Send for a free brochure; samples are also available.

BASKET BEGINNINGS

P.O. Box 24815
San Jose, CA 95154-4815
(408) 269-4513

Mail Order, Retail Shop; V/MC; Established in 1983

BASKET BEGINNINGS is owned and operated by Maxine Kirmeyer, a basketmaker since 1975 and the director of the Kirmeyer School of Fiber Studies. She and her friend Shirley Fite try to provide interesting fibers for basketmaking, and do carry hand-gathered fibers from California that very few other places have. Included in their catalog is hand-dyed raffia and sisal, braided bamboo, coir rope, Danish seat cord, grass twine, hemp, mali mali, paper-rush, rattan, reed, seagrass, and shura nawa. Hand-gathered fibers include banana bark, date fruit stalks, dracaena palm fronds, pink palm leaves, and Ponderosa pineneedles. Hand-dyed reeds (flat and round) are also available, as are several books on basketry.

School or group discounts are given (if requested on letterhead) with a minimum order of $50.00.

A catalog is $2.00, and includes samples of all fibers.

THE BASKET WORKS

4900 Wetheredsville Road
Baltimore, MD 21207
(301) 448-0800

Mail Order, Retail Shop; V/MC; Established in 1977

Along with over 20 different books on basketmaking, THE BASKET WORKS carries a large list of supplies for the craft. Included in their brochure are such materials as round and flat reed, half-round reed, ash splints, seagrass, flat paper fiber, strand cane, wheat, binding cane, handles, "D" rings, raffia, and wooden hoops and frames. They also offer three different basket kits.

Discounts of 10% are given with orders over $75.00; 15% on orders over $150.00.

A brochure is free; orders usually take from two to three weeks for delivery.

BASKETRY STUDIO A

P.O. Box 300
West Barnstable, MA 02668
(800) 334-3317, Extension 25
(Toll-free for orders only)

Manufacturer, Mail Order; V/MC;
Established in 1979

Along with many basketmaking kits for beginners, BASKETRY STUDIO A carries basketry supplies for sale. Included in their catalog are round and flat reeds, Hong Kong grass, medium cane, wide binding cane, wooden hoops, raffia, and hickory handle stock from Kentucky.

A 10% discount is given on retail orders over $100.00. Wholesale minimum is 50 kits. Write for more information.

An illustrated catalog is $1.00.

BECK'S WARP 'N WEAVE & NEEDLECRAFTS

2815 34th Street
Lubbock, TX 79410
(806) 799-0151

Mail Order, Retail Shop; V/MC;
Established in 1976

BECK'S carries a fair number of supplies for basketry in addition to their full line of weaving and spinning supplies. These include raffia, round and flat reed in various sizes, Fiber Flex, imitation fiber rush, seagrass, and wooden bases. Several books on basketmaking are also offered.

Some quantity discounts are given; check catalog for prices.

Send $1.00 for a complete catalog.

DICK BLICK CO.

Box 1267
Galesburg, IL 61401
(309) 343-6181

Manufacturer, Mail Order, Retail Shop; V/MC; Established in 1911

DICK BLICK CO. is famous for the large number of craft supplies that they offer. Basketry supplies include reed spline, natural stand cane, binding cane, reed and cane cutters, fiber rush, natural reed in bulk, raffia, drilled plywood bases, kits, and books.

Send for a current catalog.

THE CANING SHOP

926 Gilman Street
Berkeley, CA 94710
(415) 527-5010

Mail Order, Retail Shop; V/MC;
Established in 1969

THE CANING SHOP is owned and operated by Jim Widess, co-author of *The Caner's Handbook,* published in 1983 by Van Nostrand Reinhold. In addition to tools and supplies for chair caning, the shop also carries many materials suitable for basketry. Included are reed splines, cane webbing, hand caning supplies, binder cane, Danish seat cord, rawhide, rubber webbing, reed splint, fiber rush, Hong Kong grass, ash splint, Shaker tapes, round reeds (whole and split), wicker braid, handles, rattan poles, Kooboo rattan and whole rattan. A large selection of books are offered, both on caning and basketmaking. Bonsai tools, very useful for gathering your own fibers, are sold, too.

Basketry classes are offered; write for schedule.

Some quantity discounts are given; write for information.

The CANING SHOP catalog is $1.00, and is applicable to the first order.

CONNECTICUT CANE & REED COMPANY

P.O. Box 1276
Manchester, CT 06040
(203) 646-6586

Mail Order, Retail Shop;
V/MC/AMEX; Established in
1980

CONNECTICUT CANE & REED COMPANY is owned by artists who recognize "the need for quality service and communication" in the field. The company carries a large line of supplies for basketmaking: chair cane in seven sizes, ash splint, reed splint in ten sizes, binding cane, fiber rush, flat and flat oval reed, round reed, seagrass, raffia, hoops, bases, books and accessories.

Quantity discounts are given to individuals and schools/groups, etc. Write for more information.

Send 50¢ for a current catalog and price list.

Basketmaking tools from Connecticut Cane & Reed Company.

CREATE-A-CRAFT

2961 E. Highland
Highland, MI 48031
(313) 887-5445

Mail Order, Retail Shop; V/MC;
Established in 1976

CREATE-A-CRAFT carries a large supply of basketry materials, such as cane, pressed cane, webbing, spline, ¼ inch slab rattan, seagrass, sweetgrass, rush, raffia, broom corn, round reed in 13 sizes, split and smoked reeds, flat reed splints, flat oval splints, oak and ash splints, and handles in white oak and black ash. Over 25 books on basketmaking are also available.

Send for a free catalog.

DAY BASKET COMPANY

Ross A. Gibson, President
110 West High Street
North East, MD 21901
(301) 287-6100

Manufacturer, Mail Order, Retail
Shop; V/MC; Established in
1876

DAY BASKET COMPANY claims to be the only oak basket manufacturer in the United States. Besides offering a large number of handmade baskets, they also carry top grade hand-drawn white oak splints, hoops and handles for those who want to make their own baskets. Tours of the company are given on weekends.

Quantity discounts are available to anyone with a minimum order of $100.00.

Send for a free brochure and price list.

FIBER DIRECTIONS/COLOR CONNECTIONS, LTD.

P.O. Box 2143
Corrales, NM 87048
(505) 898-7345

Manufacturer, Mail Order, Retail
Shop; V/MC; Established in
1983

In addition to a full line of other fiber supplies, FIBER DIRECTIONS/ COLOR CONNECTIONS carries a number of supplies for basketry, including reed, buri, lauhala, raffia, jute, cane, etc.

Send $2.00 for a complete catalog (applicable to first order).

FLORIDA FIBER CO-OP

630 May Street
Jacksonville, FL 32204
(904) 354-6661

Mail Order, Retail Shop; V/MC;
Established in 1981

In addition to a large inventory of supplies for other fiber arts, FLORIDA FIBER CO-OP stocks materials for basketmaking. They carry reed from Hong Kong and Taiwan in sizes #0 to #7, 3/16 inch and 1/4 inch flat oval reed, smoked reed, ash splints, flat paper fiber, braided buri, seagrass, raffia in natural and brown colors, Belgian flax, Canton rope, wire grass, handspun Spanish moss, wild grasses, etc. They also offer a miscellaneous assortment of wooden beads, leather strips, and other embellishments.

Bulk prices are available by ordering more than ten of any one item. Other discounts may apply.

Send for a price list of basketry supplies, or send $2.00 for a complete fiber catalog (includes yarn samples, loom and spinning wheel brochures, etc.).

FRANK'S CANE & RUSH SUPPLY

7252 Heil Avenue
Huntington Beach, CA 92647

Mail Order; V/MC; Established in 1975

FRANK'S CANE & RUSH SUPPLY promises fast service on their high quality supplies for natural basketry. They offer reeds, fiber rush, caning supplies, round reed, raffia, tools, implements, and books.

Quantity discounts are given; write for information.

Send for a free price list.

SHEREEN LAPLANTZ

899 Bayside Cutoff
Bayside, CA 95524
(707) 822-6009

Manufacturer, Mail Order;
Established in 1970

SHEREEN LAPLANTZ is an active lecturer, workshop leader, author, and exhibitor in the area of handmade baskets. From time to time she has exotic basketry fibers for sale by mail order. She has also published her own book titled *Plaited Basketry — The Woven Form,* and publishes a newsletter called *The News Basket.* Shereen is available for workshops, too.

Write for information on publications and available fibers; quantity discounts are given to individuals.

LEMCO

P.O. Box 40545
San Francisco, CA 94140

Mail Order; Established in 1974

LEMCO carries a wide selection of basketry supplies, including wheat stock braid, agas straw, bamboo braid, smoked braided buri, bleached abaca, Madagascar raffia (fireproof), round rattan core, rattan peel, flat rattan core, seagrass twine, lauhala strips, rope Canton, and rattan webbing.

A 10% discount is given with a minimum order of $50.00 or more.

Send $3.00 for fibers catalog, including basketry supplies.

ROSS-HILL HANDCRAFTS

29 Seventh Avenue, NE
Hickory, NC 28601
(704) 328-3645

Manufacturer, Mail Order, Retail Shop; Established in 1975

ROSS-HILL HANDCRAFTS, owned by Linda Burnside, carries a complete line of basketry supplies — reed, hoops, books, kits, etc. Classes, tours, seminars, and custom work are offered, also.

Quantity discounts are available to individuals with a minimum order of $50.00.

Send for a free brochure and price list.

STRAW INTO GOLD

3006 San Pablo Avenue
Berkeley, CA 94702
(415)548-5241

Mail Order, Retail Shop; V/MC;
Established in 1971

STRAW INTO GOLD carries many materials for basketmaking: fiber rush, Fiber Flex, reed, raffia, untreated pigtail raffia, and seagrass in various sizes.

Send a SASE for a current catalog and price list.

THE WEAVER'S STORE

11 South 9th Street
Columbia, MO 65201
(314) 442-5413

Mail Order; Retail Shop; V/MC

In addition to its full line of weaving supplies, THE WEAVER'S STORE carries some supplies for basketry. These include round reed in eleven sizes, flat basket reed in seven sizes, round wooden hoops in eleven sizes, oval hoops, hand-split market basket handles, fiber rush, seagrass, and natural raffia.

Send for current prices.

WEAVING WORKSHOP

817½ East Johnson Street
Madison, WI 53703
(608) 255-1066

Mail Order, Retail Shop;
Established in 1971

WEAVING WORKSHOP offers basketry supplies along with their regular line of spinning and weaving materials. Some of these include round, fat and half-round reeds, natural jute, raffia, fiber rush and splint, Hong Kong grass, and Fiber Flex.

Send 50¢ for a sample card of basketry fibers, and a current price list.

WOVENWARE

3465 Edgewater Drive
Orlando, FL 32804
(305) 425-7001

Mail Order, Retail Shop

WOVENWARE supplies a number of materials for making baskets, including round reed in eight sizes, oval, flat and half-round reed, round or flat paper rush, chair cane, seagrass, philodendron sheaths, longleaf pine needles, and colored reed.

Send for a current price list and ordering information.

YARN BARN

P.O. Box 334
Lawrence, KS 66044
(913) 842-4333

Mail Order, Retail Shop; V/MC;
Established in 1971

In addition to their large selection of weaving and spinning supplies, THE YARN BARN carries basketry supplies. These include pine needles, raffia (natural and dyed), round and flat reed, flat paper rope, fiber rush, grass rope, seagrass, palm rope, wheat, wooden and metal hoops, horsehair, oak splint handles, Hong Kong cane, Scandia-Braided Straw, and three basic dyes for reeds. Approximately 25 different books on basketmaking are available, including such authors as Hart, LaPlantz, Meilach, and Rossbach.

Some quantity discounts are given; write for details.

Send $1.00 for a complete catalog (applicable to first order).

CHAPTER
8

Publications
Books
Magazines

Whether you need a basic book on fiber technique or a technical treatise of the most complicated kind, you will find a source for it in this chapter.

AMERICAN CRAFT

401 Park Avenue South
New York, NY 10016
(212) 696-0710

American Craft (formerly *Craft Horizons*) is a high-quality, full color magazine published bimonthly by the American Crafts Council.

The magazine primarily serves as a showcase for contemporary, professional crafts (including fibers), historical movements, important exhibitions, new books, and more. The magazine also includes regular columns such as "Where to Show," "Calendar," "Gallery," and "Craft Marketplace."

The magazine is included in the membership dues for the American Craft Council (currently $35.00 for one year). Write for more information.

AYOTTES' DESIGNERY

P.O. Box 287
Center Sandwich, NH 03227
(603) 284-6915

Manufacturer, Mail Order, Retail Shop; Established in 1958

Robert and Roberta Ayotte, of AYOTTE'S DESIGNERY, publish a home study program titled *Handweaving with Robert and Roberta*. The program, now in its sixth year of publication, has become the leading step-by-step home study handweaving course available. The four-volume program is designed to build your fundamental weaving knowledge and skills.

Subscribers to the home study program also receive special discounts on yarns and equipment.

Send for free information on the course.

B. R. ARTCRAFT, CO.

6701 Cherry Hill Road
Baldwin, MD 21013
(301) 592-2847

Mail Order; Established in 1935

B. R. ARTCRAFT, CO. handles out-of-print, new, and imported books on the arts and crafts. Their catalog includes sections on needlework and weaving. A book-search service is also available.

Send $2.00 for a current catalog.

THE BASKETMAKER QUARTERLY
MKS Publications, Inc.

P.O. Box 005
Belleville, MI 48111-005
(313) 753-4920

Publisher; Established in 1984

Karen Mida, Sue Kurginski and Lori Summers publish *THE BASKETMAKER QUARTERLY* magazine for weavers, designers and collectors of baskets. Features include various patterns, interviews, book reviews, etc. —all related to basketry. Karen, Sue and Lori say that their magazine is special because it promotes networking between basketweavers from all over the United States, Canada and Australia.

Send for a free brochure on the magazine. Quarterly subscriptions are currently $8.95 per year.

BLACK SHEEP NEWSLETTER

28068 Ham Road
Eugene, OR 97405
(503) 344-964

Publisher; Established in 1974

The *BLACK SHEEP NEWSLETTER* is a delightful, useful little publication edited by Sachiye Jones. The newsletter is written for black sheep breeders, handspinners, and any craftspeople who work with wools. Recent issues included articles on purebred and crossbred sheep, shows, fairs, an annual directory of breeders and suppliers, veterinarian's corner, The Spinner's Page, classified ads, book reviews, etc.

The newsletter is published five times a year; the current subscription price is $8.00. Write for more information.

 PENELOPE B. DROOKER, AUTHOR OF *Embroidering with the Loom,* earned degrees in both geology and hydrology. She then worked as a scientist, engineer, and technical manager. However, because of a growing interest in embroidery, weaving, and other fiber arts, she gave up her career as a scientist in order to develop her proficiency as a handweaver. She was one of the first recipients of the Handweavers Guild of America Certificate of Excellence in Handweaving, and now lectures and teaches courses in fiber techniques. Ms. Drooker also does commissioned fiber work and is a freelance writer.

BOOKS FOR EMBROIDERY

96 Roundwood Road
Newton, MA 02164
(617) 969-0942

Mail Order, Retail Shop;
Established in 1979

Bette S. Feinstein's BOOKS FOR EMBROIDERY catalog contains new, rare, out-of-print, and one-of-a-kind books and magazines on needlework.

Bette's inventory of over 10,000 books includes such subjects as antiques, blackwork, canvaswork/needlepoint, counted thread work, cut work, lacemaking, quilting, smocking, textiles/fabrics, weaving/dyeing, basketry, and many others.

A free search service for out-of-print books is also offered.

Send $1.00 for a complete catalog.

MARGARET BOYD

P.O. Box 6232
Augusta, GA 30906

Publisher

MARGARET BOYD, author of *Catalog Sources for Creative People,* also publishes a *News and Updates* newsletter as a sequel to her book. Both the book and the newsletter are useful for tracking down all-purpose craft supplies and equipment.

Ms. Boyd has also written a new book, *The Sew and Save Source Book,* published by Betterway Publications. The book is packed with mail order sources for creative and general sewing supplies. Fiber artists who work in appliqué, quilting, dollmaking, soft sculpture, or any of the needle arts will find this to be a very useful resource book.

Write to the author at the address above for more information.

BARBARA BRABEC PUBLICATIONS

P.O. Box 2137
Naperville, IL 60566

Publisher, Mail Order;
Established in 1981

BARBARA BRABEC loaned herself $1,000 four years ago to start her present business. In a very short time, she has established herself as one of the country's leading authorities on homebased businesses.

Barbara's monthly newsletter, *NATIONAL HOME BUSINESS REPORT* (formerly *SHARING BARBARA'S MAIL*), is a valuable tool featuring timely business and marketing information and resources. The newsletter is special because of the amount of unselfish networking and sharing that goes on between the readers.

Barbara has also written two books which should be of interest to anyone who is trying to effectively market their work. The two books, *CREATIVE CASH* and *HOMEMADE MONEY*, both offer detailed information on getting started in your own business, pricing for profit, planning for success, tips on mail order, etc. *HOMEMADE MONEY,* published by Betterway Publications, includes an A-to-Z Business Encyclopedia and a 500-address Resource Directory.

Barbara is also available for crafts marketing and home business workshops and consultation.

Send for a free brochure on all publications.

BROOKLYN BOTANIC GARDEN

1000 Washington Avenue
Brooklyn, NY 11225

The BROOKLYN BOTANIC GARDEN carries several low-cost handbooks of interest to fiber artists: *Dye Plants and Dyeing* and *Natural Plant Dyeing*. They also offer a film titled "Nature's Colors — The Craft of Dyeing with Plants," for sale or rental.

Send for copies of the Plants and Gardens Handbooks and Films for Sale or Rent brochures.

JO BRYANT BOOKS

Selected Needle Art Publications
630 Graceland, S.E.
Albuquerque, NM 87108
(505) 268-7775

Mail Order, Retail hours by
appointment; Established in 1983

JO BRYANT carries a selection of new, used, and out-of-print books on the needle arts. She also offers a book search service.

A 20% discount is given to libraries.

Send $1.00 for a current catalog.

CHEAP THREADS: ROSS BOOK SERVICE

Box 12093, Seminary Post Office
Alexandria, VA 22304-0993
(703) 823-1919

Mail Order; Established in 1981

Miriam Ross, owner of CHEAP THREADS, stocks and sells bargain books, remainders, and other books that she considers to be good buys. Subjects covered include fibers, spinning, weaving, dyeing, lace, collecting, textile history, sewing, rugs, stitchery, design, etc. Prices are very low, but most books are in limited supply.

An additional 10% discount is given to schools/shops/groups, etc. with a minimum order of $100.00.

Send $1.50 for a current book catalog.

COATS & CLARK, INC.

P.O. Box 1966
Stamford, CT 06904
(203) 327-3005

COATS & CLARKS, INC. publishes a large number of low-cost educational publications leaflets and craft and needlework books. Leaflets include such titles as "ABC of Crochet," "Patchwork," "Machine Embroidery," and more. Craft and needlework books include pattern and project books, as well as basic instructional books on knitting, crochet, embroidery, etc.

Send for a free list of available publications.

COVE COTTAGE CRAFTS

P.O. Box 220
Sanbornville, NH 03872
(603) 522-3144

Publisher, Mail Order; Established in 1979

Penelope B. Drooker, owner of COVE COTTAGE CRAFTS, has written and self-published a book titled *Hammock Making Techniques.* The book includes all necessary information, from materials and equipment to shapes, dimensions and finishing touches, for a wide variety of hammock types. Ms. Drooker is also the author of *Embroidering with the Loom: Creative Combinations of Weaving and Stitchery,* published by Van Nostrand Reinhold (1979).

Quantity discounts are available on books; write for more information.

Send for a free brochure on books and lecture topics.

CRAFT INTERNATIONAL

247 Centre Street
New York, NY 10013
(212) 925-7320

Publisher; Established in 1980

CRAFT INTERNATIONAL, the official publication of the World Crafts Council, states that their purpose is to provide the best coverage of the contemporary international arts and crafts movement.

Edited by Rose Slivka, the periodical includes articles about international craftspeople in all areas: fibers, pottery, metals, etc. It also includes news and reports on the World Crafts Council and lists show deadlines, jobs, commissions and fellowships.

A yearly subscription is currently $14.00; send for more information.

THE CRAFTS REPORT

3632 Ashworth North
Seattle, WA 98103
(206) 632-7222

Publisher; V/MC/AMEX;
Established in 1975

THE CRAFTS REPORT - A Newsmonthly of Marketing, Management and Money for Crafts Professionals — that just about says it all. This is a professional publication for craftspeople who are serious about selling their work. Regular features include: Protecting your Health, Craft Photography, Wholesale Show Dates, New Products, Crafts Available (listings from craftspeople), Book Reviews, Exhibitions/Competitions, Workshops/ Seminars and Crafts Wanted (listings by shop owners looking for specific crafts).

On top of all this, Michael Scott, the editor of Crafts Report, still finds room to include articles on such topics as trade shows, IRS audits, individual craftspeople, computers in design, consignment controversies, pricing, and much more.

The Crafts Report Book Service also has two books available: *The Crafts Business Encyclopedia,* written by Michael Scott, and *The Law (In Plain English) for Craftspeople,* by Leonard D. DuBoff. *The Crafts Business Encyclopedia* covers the basics of Management, Insurance, Labor and Employees, Finances, Accounting, Credit, Taxes, Selling and Marketing, Promotion and Publicity, Production, Shipping, etc. for craftspeople.

Dr. DuBoff, a professor of law, practicing attorney, and recognized expert on law and the arts, has written a much-needed book. The book gives detailed information on different forms of business organization, trademarks, contracts, consignment, working at home legally, keeping taxes low, copyright, insurance, product liability, getting paid for your work, and how to find a lawyer — much valuable advice!

The Crafts Report is currently $16.75 per year (11 issues). Send for more information and book prices.

CRAFTSWOMAN MAGAZINE

Daedalus Publications, Inc.
1153 Oxford Road
Deerfield, IL 60015
(312) 945-1769

Publisher, Mail Order;
Established in 1981

CRAFTSWOMAN MAGAZINE, edited and published by Anne Patterson Dee, serves as a bi-monthly business and marketing publication for the home-based craftswoman, needleworker, and designer. Past issues have included articles on selling your patterns to magazines, pricing, an advertising co-op, low-budget promotions, developing a wholesale product, designing an effective catalog on a small budget, teaching, designing and marketing crafts kits, obtaining publicity and much more.

The magazine provides information that is not included in other periodicals — you owe it to yourself to give it a try!

Write or call for current subscription prices, or send $3.00 for a sample copy.

CRAZY QUILT STITCHES

34706 Row River Road
Cottage Grove, OR 97424

Publisher; Established in 1978

Dorothy Bond has written and published a delightful little book called *CRAZY QUILT STITCHES,* in which she has illustrated over 1,000 decorative embroidery stitch variations from old crazy quilts.

Dorothy, a quilt designer, became fascinated with the many variations of basic stitches such as the herringbone, satin, chain and stem stitch while studying crazy quilts for the past ten years. Her book is a result of that research. The 112-page book is completely handwritten and illustrated with 22 chapters of stitches and combinations ranging from the very basic to the very decorative — no quilter should be without this one.

A 35% discount is given on orders of six or more copies.

The book is currently $10.00, plus $1.50 postage.

DAEDALUS PUBLICATIONS, INC.

1153 Oxford Road
Deerfield, IL 60015
(312) 945-1769

Publisher; Mail Order;
Established in 1981

In addition to publishing *Crafts Woman Magazine,* Anne Patterson Dee, owner of DAEDALUS PUBLICATIONS, INC. also has written and published a very helpful booklet called *How to Have a Successful Craft Show in Your Home - A Guide to Planning and Publicizing Your Own Holiday Boutique.* The booklet will be of use to any craftsperson who wants an effective alternative to galleries and retail shops for selling their work.

Daedalus Publications, Inc. has also published *101 Art Fairs - The Best in the Midwest* and *Handmade Dolls and Related Delights - A Marketing and Resource Guide.*

Write for more information and current prices.

DAVIS PUBLICATIONS, INC.

50 Portland Street
Worcester, MA 01608
(617) 754-7201

Publisher, Mail Order; V/MC;
Established in 1901

DAVIS PUBLICATIONS, INC. publishes books in the fields of art, art education, crafts, and technical education. Some of the titles offered by Davis include *The Art of Papermaking* by Toale, *Photo Art Processes* by Howell-Koehler, *Soft Sculpture* by Vosburg Hall, *Designing in Batik and Tie-Dye* by Belfer, *Contemporary Quilting and Contemporary Basketry* by Robinson, and many others.

Quantity discounts are given to schools and retail establishments; write for more information.

Send for a free Art and Craft Books catalog.

MARGUERITE P. DAVISON, PUBLISHER

Box 263
Swarthmore, PA 19081
(215) 729-6254

Publisher, Mail Order;
Established in 1944

MARGUERITE P. DAVISON has published three very helpful books of interest to weavers: *Weaving Lessons for Hand Looms* by Edith Huntington Snow and Laura L. Peasley, *A Handweaver's Source Book* and *A Handweaver's Pattern Book,* both of which were also written by Ms. Davison.

School/group discounts are given; write for more information.

Send for a free descriptive brochure on all three books.

DESIGNER'S CHOICE

P.O. Box 687
Manchester, NH 03105
(603) 622-6134

Mail Order; V/MC; Established in 1983

DESIGNER'S CHOICE specializes in fabric and fiber related craft and art books. They feel that they have compiled the most extensive catalog of books (over 1,000) on the subject available today. New publications, as well as an extensive selection of hard-to-find books are offered.

The catalog covers such subjects as art and art education, basketry, business, design sources, dyeing, ethnic and folk art, interior design, papermaking, felting, knitting and crochet, needlework, quilting, sewing, silkscreen, stenciling, weaving and spinning, and many more.

A 20% discount is given to individuals and schools with a minimum order of five copies of one title.

An extensive catalog is available for $1.00. With your first purchase, you will receive a coupon good for 10% off the price of any single book included in your next order.

DOS TEJEDORAS FIBER ARTS PUBLICATIONS

3036 North Snelling
St. Paul, MN 55113
(612) 636-0205

Publisher, Mail Order;
Established in 1976

DOS TEJEDORAS FIBER ARTS PUBLICATIONS handle several books on ethnic textile techniques with the emphasis on how these art forms fit into the culture. Books for weavers include *Finishes in the Ethnic Tradition* and *Latin American Brocades* by Baizerman and Searle, and *Textures and Patterns for the Rigid Heddle Loom* by Davenport. Books for knitters include *Latvian Mittens* by Upitis, and *Cornish Gurnseys and Knitted Frocks* by Wright.

Send for a free brochure on all publications.

DOVER PUBLICATIONS, INC.

31 East 2nd Street
Mineola, NY 11501
(516) 549-1815

Manufacturer, Mail Order;
Established in 1940

If you haven't seen the book catalogs from DOVER, you are missing a real treat. They now carry over 2,800 high-quality paperback books, including an extensive selection of arts and crafts books. Dover also publishes over 250 books in their Pictorial Archive Collection. This collection contains thousands of motifs, emblems, patterns, drawings, symbols, etc., "from ancient Egypt to Op Art," all of which can be used without permission.

All books are unconditionally guaranteed, and only cost from $2.00 to $5.00 each. I have many of these books — I recommend them highly!

All Dover catalogs are free. Write for a complete list of books in all fields, or the craft and needlecraft catalogs.

ERIC'S PRESS

Box 1680
Tahoe City, CA 95730
(916) 583-1445

Publisher, Mail Order;
Established in 1980

ERIC'S PRESS is owned by Lois Ericson, designer and widely-exhibited fiber artist. Along with her daughter, Diane Ericson Frode, Lois has written and published three very useful books: *Print It Yourself, Design and Sew It Yourself,* and *Belts . . . Waisted Sculpture.*

Print It Yourself describes several fabric printing and decorating techniques. *Design and Sew It Yourself* is advertised as a workbook for creative clothing. The book features specific design exercises using ideas for innovative closures, sewing techniques, surface decoration, structural effects, and much more. *Belts . . . Waisted Sculpture* includes techniques that can be used to embellish belts: quilting, smocking, weaving, piping, etc. and includes a section on fundamentals of belt construction. All three of these books will be extremely helpful to those who work with wearable art.

Lois is also available for design workshops/seminars.

Discounts are given with a minimum order of 12 books.

Send for a free brochure on books and workshops.

ETHNIC ACCESSORIES

Box 250
Forestville, CA 95436
(707) 887-2909

Mail Order; Established in 1978

ETHNIC ACCESSORIES offers several books of interest to the fiber artist: *Japanese Costume and Textile Arts* by Noma, *Cut My Cote* by Brunham, *Bolivian Indian Textiles* by Wasserman & Hill, *Molas* by Auld, *Patterns for Guernseys, Jerseys & Arans* by Thompson, and many more. In addition to these, Ethnic Accessories also carries the entire line of Folkwear patterns and clothing embellishments.

Send $1.50 for a current catalog and price list.

FIBERARTS MAGAZINE

50 College Street
Asheville, NC 28801
(704) 253-0467

Publisher, Mail Order

FIBERARTS should be one of the first magazines on your list of fiber-related publications. The magazine is informative, inspirational, and provides an overview of all fiber arts. Special issues have focused on tapestry, soft sculpture, papermaking, surface design, wearables, rugs, and much more.

The magazine covers such subjects as historical design, technique, and individual artists, as well as news in international fibers. Exhibit and book reviews are included, as is information on competitions, shows and educational opportunities.

Send for current subscription prices.

FIBERWORKS QUARTERLY

P.O. Box 49770-FW
Austin, TX 78765

Publisher; Established in 1984

FIBERWORKS QUARTERLY, published by Bobbi A. McRae, serves as a constant source of up-to-date information on new supplies, services, publications, markets, etc. for those working/writing/designing in all areas of the fiber arts: weaving, spinning, quilting, knitting, crochet, soft-sculpture, stitchery, basketry, surface design, felting, handmade paper, rugmaking, etc. The quarterly newsletter also serves as an update to this book, *The Fiberworks Source Book,* listing address changes, new product information, catalog price changes, etc.

Send $3.00 for a sample issue and further information.

FIBRE FORUM

R. L. Shep
Box C-20
Lopez Island, WA 98261

Publication, Mail Order

FIBRE FORUM is the tri-annual (April, August, and November) magazine of the textile arts in Australia. R. L. Shep, former publisher of The Textile Booklist, is the subscription agent for the magazine.

Write for more information and current subscription prices.

FOX HOLLOW FIBRES

Rt. 1, Box 161A
Glasgow, VA 24555
(703) 463-2878

Publisher, Mail Order;
Established in 1980

FOX HOLLOW FIBRES publishes the book, *Australian Locker Hooking: A New Approach to a Traditional Craft,* by Joan Z. Rough. The book offers step-by-step instruction in the art of Australian locker hooking, showing you how loops of unspun wool are held in place on rug canvas by a hidden "locking" yarn. The 60-page book includes several projects, illustrations, a source directory, and a locker hook.

Quantity prices are given with an order of ten or more books and hooks.

Send a SASE for a descriptive brochure. The book is currently $6.95 plus $1.35 for postage and handling.

GLP INTERNATIONAL

560 Sylvan Avenue
Englewood Cliffs, NJ 07632
(212) 736-7455

Publisher; Established in 1964

GLP INTERNATIONAL imports several high quality European magazines for knitters, crocheters, needleworkers, and other fiber artists. *ANNA-Knitting and Needlecrafts Magazine* contains many knitting, crochet, sewing, fashion and other practical projects and patterns. Many issues include re-usable iron-on transfers and pattern sheets.

Another magazine available through GLP is *CARINA BURDA,* which contains more than 25 patterns and projects for teens and young women in each issue.

GLP also has other magazines and books available on embroidery, lacework, crafts, knitting, crochet, and sewing.

Discounts are given to retailers; write for more information.

Others should send for a complete publications list and current prices.

HANDMADE

Lark Communications
50 College Street
Asheville, NC 28801
(704) 253-0467

Publisher, Mail Order

HANDMADE Magazine is published by the same wonderful people at Lark Communications who bring you *Fiberarts* Magazine. *Handmade* focuses more on practical how-to projects in all crafts. Each issue contains a full-size pullout designer pattern, articles on knitting, crochet, sewing and quiltmaking, as well as woodworking, stained glass, jewelry, etc.

Retailers interested in handling *Handmade* should contact the publisher.

Send for more information and current subscription rates.

HANDWOVEN MAGAZINE

Interweave Press, Inc.
306 N. Washington Avenue
Loveland, CO 80537
(303) 669-7672

Publisher, Mail Order

HANDWOVEN MAGAZINE, edited and published by Linda Ligon of Interweave Press, is a truly inspirational magazine for weavers, spinners, and other interested fiber artists. *Handwoven* contains many well-designed weaving projects with instructions, as well as articles on dyeing, spinning, tricks of the trade, book reviews, other weavers, and more. If you are a weaver — beginning or advanced — you will love this magazine.

Send for current subscription information.

THE HEDDLE

A Canadian Publication for
Spinners and Weavers
Box 220
Goderich, Ontario
CANADA N7A 4B6
(519) 524-8331

Publisher, Established in 1983

THE HEDDLE, edited by Shirley J. Keller, is a relatively new publication for Canadian spinners and weavers, although there is much here to interest those in the United States as well. The delightful newspaper contains news on Canadian guilds, fiber artists, helpful hints for weavers and spinners, book reviews, projects with instructions, classified ads, and ads for other mail order sources (U.S. and Canadian).

The Heddle will only be continued if enough interest is shown, so PLEASE support this paper. The cost is very low (only $5.00 for four issues), and is worth every penny!

Write for more information.

BARBARA HUMES

Box 29TF
Orcas, WA 98280
(206) 376-4370

Publisher, Mail Order;
Established in 1983

BARBARA HUMES has written and published a 112-page book called *Easy Knit Family Patterns for Your Homespuns* (currently $11.50 + $1.50 postage and handling). After spinning and knitting for eighteen years, Barbara got tired of trying to adjust commercial patterns to handspun yarns. This book has taken the guesswork out of knitting with handspun and describes how to make the process as easy as possible. So far, this is the only book published for homespun yarns that also includes patterns, given in charts for sizes 1-48.

Quantity discounts are given to schools/groups, etc.

Send for more information.

INDIGO PRESS

5950 Fern Flat Road
Aptos, CA 95003
(408) 688-8543

Publisher, mail Order;
Established in 1978

INDIGO PRESS publishes the book *Indigo from Seed to Dye* by Dorothy Miller. Included in each book is an order form for free indigo seeds. Dorothy also gives workshops and lectures on indigo dyeing, fibers of Far East Textiles, Shifu, Japanese paper weaving, and others.

A 20% discount is given on orders of three or more books; 40% on 10 or more.

Write for more information.

INTERWEAVE PRESS, INC.

306 N. Washington Avenue
Loveland, CO 80537
(303) 669-7672

Publisher, Mail Order; V/MC;
Established in 1975

INTERWEAVE PRESS, INC. started out in 1975 as a small magazine called "interweave: mountain/plain fiber crafts." Since then, Linda Ligon, editor and founder of the company, has watched her first project grow into a corporation that now publishes *Handwoven* magazine, *Spin-Off,* and an interesting array of books on weaving and spinning. The magazines exist as a showcase for fine functional weaving, teaching, and inspiration for weavers of all skill levels. If you do any weaving at all, take a look at the publications by Interweave Press.

Discounts are given to schools, libraries, guilds, and retail establishments.

Send for a free book catalog and descriptive brochure on the magazines.

J. ARVIDSON PRESS

P.O. Box 4022
Helena, MT 59601
(406) 442-0354

Publisher, Mail Order;
Established in 1976

Joanne Hall, owner of J. ARVIDSON PRESS, has written and published a book titled *Mexican Tapestry Weaving.* She also owns and operates Elkhorn Mountain Weaving School.

Send for more information and current price of Joanne's book and a free weaving school class schedule.

JOSEPH'S COAT

26 Main Street
Peterborough, NH 03458
(603) 827-3205

Mail Order; Retail Shop; AMEX;
Established in 1980

JOSEPH'S COAT carries over 100 books on quilting and clothing design. Some of the featured authors are Puckett, Gutcheon, Martin, Birren, James, Chase, Laury, Avery, Bishop, Porcella, Gostelow, Leman and many others.

Send for a free catalog which also includes other quilting supplies

DORAMAY KEASBEY

5031 Alta Vista Road
Bethesda, MD 20814
(301) 530-5031

Publisher, Manufacturer, Mail Order; Studio Hours by appointment; Established in 1978

DORAMAY KEASBEY wrote and published the book *Pattern Devices for Handweavers.* Ms. Keasbey regularly shows her work at the Torpedo Factory Art Center in Alexandria, VA, holds a Master Weaver rating from her local guild, and a Certificate of Excellence in Handweaving from the Handweavers Guild of America. Her experiments and research into unusual techniques are shared readily with other weavers through lectures, workshops, and her published works. She is also the author of numerous technical articles appearing in major periodicals.

Quantity discounts are given on orders of five or more books.

Send for an order form and a list of workshop topics.

KNITKING MAGAZINE

1128 Crenshaw Blvd.
Los Angeles, CA 90019
(213) 938-2077

Publisher, Mail Order; V/MC;
Established in 1934

KNITKING MAGAZINE has been internationally acknowledged as the finest English language machine knitting magazine in the world. The quarterly magazine includes top quality patterns (approximately 25 per issue) for clothing, gifts, and household items, practical knitting hints, and more. *Knitking* subscribers are also eligible for discounts on machines, yarns, books and accessories.

The current subscription price for one year is $18.00; write for additional information.

THE KNITTING MACHINE STUDIO BOOKSHELF

P.O. Box 746
Englewood, NJ 07631
(201) 568-3369

Mail Order; Established in 1980

THE KNITTING MACHINE STUDIO BOOKSHELF, owned by Marlene Cuniberti, offers a large number of professional books for the serious knitter, many of which are imported titles. Pattern books and a large number of magazines especially for machine knitters are available. Learn-at-Home Cassette Tapes for several different knitting machines are also offered.

The Studio also offers an annual week-long course, given in two locations each year, on various aspects of machine knitting.

Quantity discounts are given to retailers, write for more information.

Send for a free Bookshelf Catalog and a brochure on the next annual machine knitting course.

KROLL PUBLICATIONS

P.O. Box 264
Jefferson, WI 53549
(414) 593-2338

Publisher, Mail Order;
Established in 1976

KROLL PUBLICATIONS publishes the book *Putting on the Dog,* which covers the subject of making yarns from pet fur — dog, cat, rabbit, etc. The book contains many photos and drawings to help the novice spinner. A sample page of dog and cat fur yarns is included with each book.

Quantity discounts are given to guilds/schools, etc. with a minimum order of 10 copies.

Send $3.00 + 50¢ postage for the book, or write for more information.

LA PLATA PRESS

P.O. Box 820
Evans, CO 80620
(303) 353-9164

Jean Dubois, owner of LA PLATA PRESS, publishes *The LaPlata Review,* a quarterly newsletter which reviews quilt books, events and products, and runs features on quilting — a pattern centerfold, a collector's corner, Jean's Notebook, and Kathy's Sketchbook. They also sell other books on quilting, pamphlets and patterns published by them.

Jean also writes articles on quilting, lectures at national and regional meetings, and gives quilt workshops.

Various discounts are given; write for details.

Send for a free price list.

LARK COMMUNICATIONS

50 College Street
Asheville, NC 28801
(704) 253-0468

Publisher, Mail Order

LARK COMMUNICATIONS, publishers of *Fiberarts, Handmade,* and *Yarn Market News,* also publish a large line of books that will be of interest to the fiber artist. These books can be obtained from Lark, as well as many others: *The Fiberarts Design Book, Fiberarts Design Book II, A Machine Knitter's Guide to Creative Fabrics* by Lewis and Weissman, *Color-and-Weave Design* by Sutton, and *The Craft of the Weaver* by Collingwood, Sutton and Hubbard.

Discounts are given to retailers; write for more information.

Send for a current list of publications.

R. LUBOW PUBLISHING

The Art Marketing Letter
3608 Douglas Avenue, Suite 404
Racine, WI 53402
(414) 681-3195

Publisher, Seminar Leader,
Consultant; Established in 1980

The Art Marketing Letter, offered by R. LUBOW PUBLISHING, was started to "teach artists how to be better business people." Seminars on How to Market Your Art are available, as is a cassette tape library on the Business of Art.

Quantity discounts are given to schools/guilds, etc.; write for more information.

Send for a free brochure on the publication and other services offered.

MACHINE KNITTERS NEWSLETTER

130 West 29th Street
New York, NY 10001
(212) 564-8103

Publisher, Mail Order;
Established in 1982

THE MACHINE KNITTERS NEWSLETTER is published once every two months, and offers "a lot of information for a reasonable cost." Each issue includes news on events, seminars and workshops, Reader's Forum, projects, yarn information, book reviews, trade show and conference information, helpful tips, and more. The publisher also offers patterns designed by C. Dadisman, Gene Bailey, and others for sale.

Discounts are given with a minimum order of ten copies.

The current subscription price for one year is $12.00; write for more information on the newsletter and a list of patterns for sale.

MADRONA PUBLISHERS, INC.

P.O. Box 22667
Seattle, WA 98122

Publisher, Mail Order; V/MC;
Established in 1974

MADRONA PUBLISHERS, INC. has published several books of interest to fiber artists: *The Law (in Plain English) for Craftspeople* by DuBoff, *Complete Book of Seminole Patchwork* by Rush and Wittman, *Spinning for Softness and Speed* by Simmons, *Synthetic Dyes for Natural Fibers* by Knutson, *Color and Design in Macrame* by Harvey, and others.

Discounts are given to guilds (40%), schools and libraries (20%); write for specific information and minimum order requirements.

Send for a free list of publications.

MIDMARCH ASSOCIATES

Box 3304 Grand Central Station
New York, NY 10163
(212) 666-6990

MIDMARCH ASSOCIATES is a New York state not-for-profit corporation, which publishes various books on the arts and *Women Artists News* magazine. The publisher states that *Women Artists News* is "the only independent periodical serving the community of women in the visual arts." Each issue reviews exhibits, books, film, theatre, music, and dance events, and includes the nation's most comprehensive listing of women's exhibitions and arts activities. The magazine also includes call-for-slides, job opportunities, exhibitions, panels and conferences.

Midmarch also offers several books: *Women Artists of the World, Guide to Women's Art Organizations,* and *Directory for the Arts.*

The corporation organizes and coordinates conferences, seminars and exhibits, and covers "all aspects of the arts and crafts made by women."

Send for a free brochure on all publications.

MIND YOUR OWN BUSINESS AT HOME NEWSLETTER

P.O. Box 14850
Chicago, IL 60614
(312) 472-8116

The MIND YOUR OWN BUSINESS AT HOME NEWSLETTER, published by Coralee Smith Kern, offers helpful information to the home-based business or craftsperson. The newsletter covers such subjects as business organizational methods, marketing and promotion, successful home businesses, and includes business sources, book reviews, questions and answers, legal information, and more.

A sample copy of the newsletter is $5.00. Subscription price is currently $24.00 per year (bi-monthly issues).

Write for more information.

MUSEUM BOOKS, INC.

6 West 37th Street
New York, NY 10018
(212) 563-2770

Mail Order, Retail Shop; V/MC;
Established in 1948

MUSEUM BOOKS, INC. specializes in the Applied and Decorative Arts and Crafts, and offers many books on these subjects.

Send 50¢ for a current ctalog of fiber-related books.

NATIONAL STAMPAGRAPHIC

1952 Everett St.
North Valley Stream, NY 11580
(516) 285-5587

Publisher; Established in 1982

NATIONAL STAMPAGRAPHIC, edited by Melody Hope Stein, is published to "inspire and inform rubber stampers." The magazine contains articles, ads, sources, etc. for those who have fallen in love with the art of rubber stamping. In the past, the magazine has included several articles on rubber stamping on fabric, and the July 1984 issue focused on Wearable Stampart. If you use rubber stamps in your work, it may be to your advantage to check out this magazine.

Write for more information, or send $3.50 for a sample issue.

NATURAL FIBER BASKETRY

3544 Hilltop Road
Fort Worth, TX 76109
(817) 924-1134

Manufacturer, Mail Order;
Established in 1980

Sue M. Smith, a contemporary basketmaker, writer, lecturer and workshop leader, has written a book titled *NATURAL FIBER BASKETRY.*

The book can be ordered from Sue at the address above. In addition, she is available for workshops and seminars.

Quantity discounts are given with a minimum order of ten books.

Send for more information on book or available seminar topics.

THE NEWS BASKET

LaPlantz Studios
899 Bayside Cutoff
Bayside, CA 95524

Publisher, Mail Order

THE NEWS BASKET is a new newsletter/newspaper published by Shereen LaPlantz, the well-known basketmaker, author, lecturer and teacher.

The News Basket takes a personal, informal approach, and contains information on all types of basketry, basket artists, projects, classes and workshops, book reviews, guild news, mail bag and Swap Meet — ads for basketry artists who want to exchange or sell supplies.

Write to Shereen at the address above for current subscription price.

OLIVER PRESS

917 Lakeview
St. Paul, MN 55117
(612) 488-0974

Publisher; V/MC; Established in 1983

OLIVER PRESS, owned by Jeannie M. Spears, publishes *The Professional Quilter,* a bimonthly business, marketing and educational publication for the home-based businesswoman/quilter. The magazine features articles on organizing your business, improving your teaching skills, learning new techniques, increasing your profits, etc.

Ms. Spears has also written *Mastering the Basics of Quiltmaking — How to Evaluate your Workmanship and Improve Your Skills.* This 40-page booklet describes what judges look for in quilts, and includes illustrated tips and techniques to get that professional look.

The Confidence Quilting Home Study Course is also offered by Oliver Press, and consists of ten lessons which teach you to quilt at home, working at your own pace and skill level.

Ms. Spears also sponsors a national seminar for professional quilters in April of each year; write for information.

Send a SASE for complete information on all publications, or send $3.00 for a sample copy of *The Professional Quilter.*

PACIFIC SEARCH PRESS

222 Dexter Avenue North
Seattle, WA 98109

PACIFIC SEARCH PRESS publishes several books on the fiber arts. Among these are two books by Nancy Harvey — *Patterns for Tapestry Weaving: Projects and Techniques,* and *The Guide to Successful Tapestry Weaving.*

The Handspinner's Guide to Selling, and *Spinning and Weaving with Wool,* both by Paula Simmons, are also published by Pacific Search Press, as is Cheryl Samuel's book, *The Chilkat Dancing Blanket.*

Quantity discounts are given to retailers; write for more information.

Send for a current book catalog.

THE QUALITY CRAFTS MARKET

15 West 44th Street
New York, NY 10036
(212) 575-0140

Publisher, Mail Order; V/MC

THE QUALITY CRAFTS MARKET is a service publication of the National Information Center for Crafts Management and Marketing. The magazine, geared toward professional craftspeople, gives step-by-step information on how to price your products, how to use consignment, marketing tips from other craftspeople, and more. Each issue lists shop and gallery owners and department store buyers who are looking for specific crafts.

Send for more information, current subscription price, and a list of back issues still available.

QUILTING BOOKS UNLIMITED

156 S. Gladstone
Aurora, IL 60506
(312) 896-7331

Mail Order, Retail Hours by Appointment; V/MC; Established in 1980

QUILTING BOOKS UNLIMITED carries over 500 books on quilting and related topics (exhibit catalogs, stenciling, etc.). Also offered are fabrics for quilting.

A 10% discount is given to individuals and schools with a minimum order of $100.00; all book orders are postage paid.

Send for a free catalog.

RAINBOW DESIGNS

P.O. Box 151108
San Diego, CA 92115
(619) 583-8009

RAINBOW DESIGNS, owned by Susi Torre-Bueno, publishes *The Index of Needlwork,* the annual trade directory for the needlework industry. The 600-plus page publication has completely cross-indexed information on hundreds of suppliers, valuable trade information, and a cross-indexed directory of needlework publications.

Although the Index is not available to the retail consumer, it is sent to needlework/stitchery/fiber store owners and others in the trade.

Rainbow Designs also rents mailing lists of needlework and craft stores and manufacturers.

Suppliers of needlework/fiber materials should write for advertising rates in *The Index of Needlework,* which also includes yarns, knitting patterns, fiber supplies, etc. Qualified persons should write to Susi at the address above to find out about receiving a copy of the Index.

KATHERINE RAMUS BOOKS

2100 East Eastman Avenue
Englewood, CO 80110
(303) 789-3115

Mail Order, Retail Hours by Appointment; Established in 1938

KATHERINE RAMUS carries books on all crafts, particularly weaving, spinning, dyeing, embroidery, and quilting. She also acts as a "Book Service" to many weavers, guilds, and quilters.

Katherine always gives a 10% discount on books to individuals (occasionally more) and 20% off to libraries and shops.

Send for a list of available books.

THE RICHLAND WOOL MONGER

1922 Mahan
Richland, WA 99352
(509) 946-4409

Mail Order, Retail Hours by
Appointment; Established in 1974

Betty L. Davenport, owner of THE RICHLAND WOOL MONGER, has written a book titled *Textures and Patterns for the Rigid Heddle Loom,* a basic reference manual for frame loom weavers.

Betty also offers classes and workshops on rigid heddle weaving.

Send for more information on the book.

MAGGIE RIGHETTI DESIGNS

P.O. Box 49707
Atlanta, GA 30359
(404) 325-5122

Manufacturer, Mail Order; V/MC;
Established in 1981

MAGGIE RIGHETTI has written a time-saving book for knitters titled *The Universal Yarn Finder.* The *Yarn Finder* categorizes yarns into four weights: fingering, sport, heavy or bulky, and specialty. In each of the categories, Ms. Righetti has listed yarn manufacturers, suggested needle sizes, suggested gauge/tension, approximate yardage or meters, and approximate number of skeins necessary to make a simple sweater. The *Yarn Finder* enables you to tell how much length there is in a ball of yarn that weighs a certain number of ounces or grams. With this, you can compare lengths of yarns in two different skeins of yarn.

Ms. Righetti also has video cassettes available on Basic Knitting, Finishing, Intermediate Knitting, and Pattern Stitches.

Wholesale discounts are given to retailers; write for more information.

Send for more information and current prices.

RUBBERSTAMPMADNESS

P.O. Box 168
Newfield, NY 14867
(607) 564-7673

Publisher; Established in 1979

RUBBERSTAMPMADNESS is a bimonthly publication for rubber stampers and stamp lovers. Begun by Lowry Thompson, co-author of *The Rubber Stamp Album,* the magazine is now published by Roberta Sperling.

Each issue includes information on stamping techniques, rubber stamp artists, mail art exhibits, and rubber stamp suppliers. *Rubberstampmadness* also includes periodical articles on stamping on fabric.

Send for a free brochure listing back issues and subscription prices.

THE RUG HOOKER: NEWS AND VIEWS

Kennebunkport, ME 04046

Publication

THE RUG HOOKER: NEWS AND VIEWS is edited by Joan Moshimer. Joan is a believer in the philosophy that rug hooking is "an art form and you should use it to express yourself freely." The magazine takes the attitude that rug makers should experiment, be flexible and adventurous, and enjoy themselves. A recent issue of *The Rug Hooker* included a column answering reader's questions on dyeing, exhibit and club news, projects, classified ads, book reviews, etc.

The magazine staff also offers to send you a "Teacher List" of people in your area that offer instruction in rug hooking. Other books on rugs and hooking are available from this address also.

Send $1.00 for a sample copy of the magazine or write for current subscription prices.

THE RUGGING ROOM

10 Sawmill Drive
Westford, MA 01886
(617) 692-8600

Manufacturer, Mail Order;
Established in 1970

Jeanne H. Fallier, owner of THE RUGGING ROOM, has written and published three books for rug hookers. Jeanne's *Traditional Rug Hooking Manual* gives an introduction to rug hooking, and includes sections on Planning Your Materials, Preparation of Wools, Hooking Your Design, Backgrounds and Finishing, Tricks and Trade Secrets, etc. She also lists several suppliers and recommended books.

Her other two books, *Designs for Rug Hooking* and *Little Critters,* are both pattern books.

Ms. Fallier also offers several special services, such as rug hooking classes, hooked rug repairs, custom rugs on commission, slide-lecture on traditional rug hooking history, and a slide talk on a museum rug reproduction project.

A 30% discount is given to teachers/schools/groups, etc. with a minimum order of five books.

Send $1.50 for a current catalog and brochure of publications.

SELECT BOOKS

Rt. 1, Box 129C
Mountain View, MO 65548
(417) 934-6775

Mail Order; Established in 1963

SELECT BOOKS says that they are special because they keep valuable books in print that would otherwise become unavailable. Books currently offered are by such authors as Elsie G. Davenport, Katy Turner, Eliza Leadbeater, K. Grasett, Mary Kirby, and Betty E. M. Jacobs.

Send for a current list of available books.

SHADES OF WOOL

Rt. 4, Box 263-B
Yakima, WA 98908
(509) 966-8402

Mail Order; Established in 1981

Linda Knutson, owner of SHADES OF WOOL, is the author of the very helpful book, *Synthetic Dyes for Natural Fibers,* published by Madrona Publishers. The book is 160-pages of comprehensive information on working with chemical dyes on natural fibers, written specifically for the fiber artist and dyer. She is also the author of a dye sample notebook appropriately titled *Shades of Wool.* Although the notebook is only 25-pages long, it contains 373 dye samples in both pale and medium values with formulas for each one (based on Ciba-Kiton Acid type dyes), and is representative of all areas of the red-yellow-blue and magenta-yellow-turquoise color wheels. If you work with dyes or wools at all, this book will save you hours of time.

Linda also gives Synthetic Dye Workshops called "Dyeing for Color."

Send a SASE for brochure describing both books and workshops.

SHEEP TALES

Box 146
Hadley, MI 48440
(313) 664-7387

Mail Order; Established in 1982

SHEEP TALES is a bimonthly publication dedicated to the needs of the small shepherd and the fiber artist who works with wool. The magazine covers such subjects as lambing, sheep health, raising good wool, handspinning, etc. The magazine strives to "reach both the small shepherd and the home crafter with timely articles and interesting features."

Subscription discounts are given to 4-H and FFA members.

Send $1.00 for a sample copy, or write for current subscription price.

SHUTTLE, SPINDLE & DYEPOT

65 La Salle Road
West Hartford, CT 06107
(203) 233-5124

Publisher, Mail Order

SHUTTLE, SPINDLE & DYEPOT is the official publication of The Handweaver's Guild of America. The magazine, edited by Jane Bradley Sitko, contains technical and inspirational features for weavers, spinners, and dyers of all levels.

Other information includes guild news, exhibit calendars, Where to Show, Test and Report on new equipment and yarns, and more.

The magazine is included in the HGA membership fee; write for more information.

PAULA SIMMONS

48793 Chilliwack Lake Road
Sardis, B.C.
CANADA V2R 2P1
(604) 858-6020

Mail Order; Established in 1945

Anyone who is interested in weaving and spinning should have all of PAULA SIMMONS' books in their library. Paula has been spinning and weaving professionally for 30 years, so she knows what she's talking about! Her books are all available from her, and include: *Spinning and Weaving with Wool, Handspinner's Guide to Selling, Spinning for Softness and Speed, Raising Sheep the Modern Way,* and *Patterns for Handspun.*

Wholesale prices are given to qualified retailers; write for more information.

Send for a free price list.

SPIN-OFF

Interweave Press, Inc.
306 N. Washington Avenue
Loveland, CO 80537
(303) 669-7672

Publisher

SPIN-OFF, edited by Lee Raven, also comes from Interweave Press, home of *Handwoven* Magazine. A recent issue of the quarterly magazine aimed at spinners featured articles on raising silkworms, textile traditions of Yugoslavia, the spinning jenny, Peruvian spinners, dealing with dog hair, projects from handspun yarns, etc. Regular departments cover book reviews, spinning guild news, events calendar, product news, and classified ads.

The current subscription price for one year is $10.00. Write for additional information.

STERLING PUBLISHING COMPANY

Two Park Avenue
New York, NY 10016
(212) 532-7160

Publisher, Mail Order;
Established in 1949

STERLING PUBLISHING COMPANY handles several books of interest to fiber artists: *Antique Needlework* by Synge, *Bobbin Lacemaking for Beginners* by Dawson, *Create Your Own Natural Dyes* by Schultz, and others.

School discounts are given; write for information.

Send for a free book catalog.

STRAW INTO GOLD

3006 San Pablo Avenue
Berkeley, CA 94702
(415) 548-5241

Mail Order, Retail Shop; MC/V;
Established in 1971

STRAW INTO GOLD, INC. publishes The Textile Artist's Newsletter, a publication which emphasizes technical articles, history, in-depth information on techniques, book reviews and news items aimed at the serious textile artist and interested layman.

Over 500 books are also available from the company, and feature such subjects as weaving, knitting, needlework, crochet, spinning, dyeing, color, printing, basketry, papermaking, felting, lace, costume design, history, ethnic design, etc.

Send $1.00 and a SASE for a current Book Catalog and more information on The Textile Artist's Newsletter.

CAROL STRICKLER

1690-F Wilson Ct.
Boulder, CO 80302
(303) 444-0610

Mail Order; Established in 1978

CAROL STRICKLER has compiled three volumes in her *Portfolio of American Coverlets*. Each volume contains 25 looseleaf information sheets on 19th Century American woven bed coverlets. The information sheets include weaving drafts, pattern references, annotated bibliography, photo, computer drawdowns, technical notes, and historical information.

Discounts are given with orders of eight or more Portfolios.

Send a long SASE for complete information on all books.

SURFACE DESIGN JOURNAL

311 E. Washington Street
Fayetteville, TN 37334
(615) 433-6804

The SURFACE DESIGN JOURNAL, edited by Stephen Blumrich, is the official publication of the Surface Design Association. Published four times a year, the Journal includes technical, historical and inspirational articles, all on the subject of surface design on fabrics. Past issues have included articles on Shigeko Spear, Indigo Recipes, Copyright, Cyanotype, Wearable Art, etc. Each issue also contains news of regional Association activities, the yearly Surface Design Conference, questions and answers on dyeing, book reviews, deadlines for shows, and much more.

If you work in the area of fabric design, whether it be batik, silkscreen, hand painting, or dyeing — you should be reading this magazine.

A subscription to the Journal is included in membership dues for the Surface Design Association. Write for current price and more information.

THE TEXTILE MUSEUM

2320 "S" Street, NW
Washington, DC 20008
(202) 667-0441

Publisher, Retail Shop, Museum;
V/MC/AMEX

If you haven't become acquainted with THE TEXTILE MUSEUM in Washington, DC, it's about time you did. In addition to their educational activities and exhibits, they also publish a shop catalog, which includes a list of their publications. These include books on costume and fashion history, textiles, textile history, wearable art, techniques, international textiles, and many more. The Museum also offers t-shirts, publications for children, notecards, etc. for sale through the catalog. Memberships are also available.

Discounts are given to Museum members and retailers; write for more information.

Send $1.00 for a current, detailed catalog.

THE UNICORN

Books for Craftsmen, Inc.
Box 645
Rockville, MD 20851
(301) 933-5497

Mail Order, Retail Shop; V/MC;
Established in 1969

THE UNICORN carries a large number of books on spinning, dyeing, weaving, and many forms of needlework. Basic books, as well as more technical volumes, are available.

Discounts are given with a minimum order of $50.00.

Send for a current free catalog.

UNIVERSITY OF
WASHINGTON PRESS

Seattle, WA 98105
(206) 543-4050

Publisher, Mail Order

The UNIVERSITY OF WASHINGTON PRESS publishes several books of interest to fiber artists. One of the recent books is *Surface Design for Fabric,* by Richard M. Proctor and Jennifer F. Lew.

Fundamentals of surface design are covered with explanations of repeat patterns, an introduction to color and color effects, an overview of natural and manmade fibers and fabrics, and textile structure. The "Dyes and Colorants" chapter finally unravels the mystery of the different types of dyes, listing them one-by-one and explaining in detail how to use them. The categories of dyes included are acid dyes, Fezan Batik dyes, Inko dyes, Ciba Kiton series dyes, Indigo, Fiber Reactive dyes (Procion M and H Series), Disperse dyes, Naphthol or Azoic dyes, and household dyes. Other areas covered are discharge substances, pigments, and blue-brown-printing on fabric.

Part Two of the book covers Techniques and Examples of Surface Design. This section includes chapters on Direct Dyeing, Liquid Resists, Bound Resists, Direct Printing, Stencil Printing, and Needlework. Each of the chapters gives how-to directions in easy to follow steps. They are also illustrated with many photographs and examples of finished work to ignite your imagination. Some less familiar techniques are also discussed, such as the Japanese paste resist methods, sgraffito on fabric, "canning," and color application on leather. There is also good information on preparing a printing table, registration, and fabric finishing methods.

The 192-page book currently sells for $24.95 (cloth) and $14.95 (paper). Four color plates are included.

Write to the address above for more information on this and other publications.

VAN NOSTRAND REINHOLD

Mail Order Service
7625 Empire Drive
Florence, KY 41042

Publisher, Mail Order;
V/MC/AMEX

VAN NOSTRAND REINHOLD publishes a large number of books on weaving, spinning and other fiber arts. Several of these include *Yarns for Textile Crafts* by Lorant, *Overshot Weaving* by Saltzman, *Woven Fashions* by Bateson, and many more.

Retailers should inquire about shop discounts.

Send for a current book catalog.

VISIBILITY ENTERPRISES

450 West End Avenue
New York, NY 10024
(212) 787-9239

Mail Order; V/MC; Established in
1979

Kate Kelly, a public relations instructor at The New School in New York and business consultant, has written a very useful book titled *The Publicity Manual.* Based on her experiences with business owners, the book gives details on getting media exposure with a minimum of time and money spent. The book provides a wealth of information on the tools, techniques, and ideas that will enable the entrepreneur, home-based businessperson or craftsperson to get publicity in newspapers, magazines, newsletters, and trade publications, as well as on radio or television. Some of the subjects covered in *The Publicity Manual* include: what publicity can do for you, your publicity budget, how to write an effective press release, how to announce news of a new product or service, other types of press materials, the importance of photographs, contacting and working with the press, your image as a business, how to handle an interview, and much more. The book also contains sample press releases, a worksheet and chart for publicity planning, a resource directory of media outlets and other publicity aids.

The 184-page manual is currently priced at $29.95 and can be ordered from the address above. Ms. Kelly has also written a guidebook titled *How to Write Press Releases that Work,* which sells for $7.00. Both of these books are recommended to those who want to take the success of their home-based business into their own hands!

A 20% discount is given on orders of five to nine books; 40% on orders of ten or more.

Write for more information.

**WATSON-GUPTILL
PUBLICATIONS**

1515 Broadway
New York, NY 10036

Publisher, Mail Order

WATSON-GUPTILL PUBLICATIONS offers many books on the fiber arts and related subjects. Two of these include *Ikat* by Van Gelder and *Feltmaking* by Gordon.

Write for a current book catalog.

THE WEAVER'S JOURNAL

P.O. Box 14-238
St. Paul, MN 55114

Publisher, Mail Order;
Established in 1976

THE WEAVER'S JOURNAL, a quarterly magazine, offers "education and inspiration" for handweavers and spinners. Previous issues have included articles on tanning rabbit furs, fashion trends, design by computer, spinning cotton, basketry, and many projects. The Journal also handles books by Clotilde Barrett: *Boundweave, Shadow Weave, Double Two-Tie Unit Weaves, Summer and Winter and Beyond,* etc. *Sling Braiding of the Andes* by Adele Cahlander is also available.

Discounts are given on books only with a minimum order of ten.

Send for a free brochure on all publications.

WOODEN PORCH BOOKS

Rt. 1, Box 262
Middlebourne, WV 26149
(304) 386-4434

Mail Order; V/MC; Established in
1975

Lois J. Mueller, owner of WOODEN PORCH BOOKS, sells out-of-print
and rare books and magazines on the Fine, Applied and Textile Arts. Some
of the subjects currently covered include basketry, knitting, batik, quilting,
etc. Lois also has back issues of Fiberarts and the Ciba Review.

A book search service is also available.

Send $1.00 for a current catalog.

WWH PRESS

P.O. Box 237
Norwood, NJ 07648
(914) 725-3632

Publisher, Mail Order

WWH Press publishes *Women Working Home: The Homebased Business
Guide and Directory*. The directory contains much useful information on
computer systems for home business use, advertising, marketing and promotion, simplified record keeping, setting fair prices, homebased work and
the disabled, rural homebased industry, coping with kids at home, successful networking, and A-Z Suggestions for Businesses.

The book, written and compiled by Marion Behr and Wendy Lazar, also
contains a directory of women in diverse occupations — a nationwide
network at your fingertips!

The book is currently $12.95 + $1.25 postage and handling. Write for more
information.

YARN MARKET NEWS

50 College Street
Asheville, NC 28801
(704) 253-0468

YARN MARKET NEWS also comes from Lark Communications, publishers of *Fiberarts* and *Handmade*. The magazine is currently the only trade
publication for yarn retailers, and contains regional market reports as well
as business-oriented articles on advertising, management, direct mail,
supplier profiles, etc.

The magazine also includes New Products and News and Notes columns.

Retailers, qualified wholesalers and manufacturers of yarn products should
write for more information. Current subscription prices for others are
$24.00 per year (U.S.A.), $26.00 (Canada), and $30.00 (Foreign).

CHAPTER 9

Schools
Colleges
Workshops

This chapter lists a multitude of educational opportunities in the fiber arts. From colleges and schools who offer advanced degrees, to individual weaving studios that give basic workshops — they are all listed here.

"The lyf so short, the craft so long to learn . . ."
Chaucer

ADIRONDACK LAKES CENTER FOR THE ARTS

Blue Mountain Lake, NY 12812
(518) 352-7715

ADIRONDACK LAKES CENTER FOR THE ARTS offers various workshops in batik, quilting, natural dyeing, and other fiber arts.

AEOLIAN OF MARTHA'S VINEYARD

Box 1867
Vineyard Haven, MA 02568
(617) 693-4675

AEOLIAN OF MARTHA'S VINEYARD is directed by Sally Coker. Various workshops in the fiber arts are offered by guest lecturers, as is individual instruction in spinning and weaving.

ALBANY STATE COLLEGE

Art Department
Albany, GA 31705

ALBANY offers a B.A. in Art, and gives several classes in textile design.

ANTIOCH COLLEGE

The Visual Art Center
6100 Foreland Garth
Columbia, MD 21045

ANTIOCH COLLEGE offers both a B.F.A. and an M.F.A. in Fibers.

APPALACHIAN CENTER FOR CRAFTS

Rt. 3, Box 347A-1
Smithville, TN 37166
(615) 597-6801

THE APPALACHIAN CENTER FOR CRAFTS provides the opportunity for students to explore contemporary art as well as traditional crafts in five basic media: clay, fibers, glass, metals and wood. Currently a B.F.A. degree is offered in conjunction with Tennessee Technological University in Cookeville, which operates the Center. A unique B.S. degree in Crafts Marketing has also been established. Short workshops and classes are also offered on a year-round basis.

ARIZONA STATE UNIVERSITY

School of Art
Tempe, AZ 85281

ARIZONA STATE offers a B.F.A. in Crafts with a concentration in Fibers, and an M.F.A. in Fiber Arts.

ARROWMONT SCHOOL OF ARTS AND CRAFTS

P.O. Box 567
Gatlinburg, TN 37738
(615) 436-5860

ARROWMONT offers a summer craft program, which includes courses in Fibers and Fabric Design. Credit is available through the University of Tennessee.

ART INSTITUTE OF CHICAGO

Fiber/Fabric Department
280 South Columbus Drive
Chicago, IL 60603

The ART INSTITUTE OF CHICAGO offers both a B.F.A. and an M.F.A. in Textile Design.

ARTS AND CRAFTS CENTER OF PITTSBURGH

1047 Shady Avenue
Pittsburgh, PA 15232

The ARTS AND CRAFTS CENTER OF PITTSBURGH offers various classes in fabric design techniques.

AUBURN UNIVERSITY

School of Home Economics
Auburn, AL 36830

AUBURN offers both undergraduate and graduate degrees in Textile Design.

AUGUSTA COLLEGE

Rock Island, IL 61201

AUGUSTA COLLEGE offers a general B.A. degree in Art, and individual courses in Surface Design during the summer.

AUGUSTA HERITAGE ARTS WORKSHOPS

Davis and Elkins College
Elkins, WV 26241
(304) 636-1903

The AUGUSTA HERITAGE ARTS WORKSHOP was started by local people who were concerned that the folk arts were in danger of disappearing. The workshop has now grown into a year-round organization for the promotion and preservation of the traditional arts. Fiber arts workshops include basketry, bobbin lacemaking, crewel embroidery, natural dyeing, lace net weaving, loom-shaped weaving, papermaking, quilting, rug hooking, spinning, tatting, and many others.

AUSTIN PEAY STATE UNIVERSITY

Department of Art
Clarksville, TN 37040

AUSTIN PEAY STATE UNIVERSITY offers a B.A., B.S., and a B.F.A. in Textile Design.

THE BANFF CENTER

Box 1985
Banff, Alberta CANADA
T0L 0C0
(403) 762-6100

THE BANFF center offers courses in Textile Arts in both the summer and the winter; no degrees are given.

THE BATIK ART PLACE

530 A Miller Avenue
Mill Valley, CA 94941

THE BATIK ART PLACE offers credit through other schools and colleges on their batik and fabric printing courses.

BERNICE P. BISHOP
MUSEUM

Box 6037
Honolulu, HI 96813
(808) 847-5311

The BERNICE P. BISHOP MUSEUM offers workshops in batik, quilting, soft sculpture, and other fiber arts.

BOSTON UNIVERSITY

Program in Artisanry
620 Commonwealth Avenue
Boston, MA 02215
(617) 353-2022

BOSTON UNIVERSITY offers an Associate of Fine Arts (two year) degree, a B.F.A., and an M.F.A. degree in Weaving and Surface Design.

BOSTON YWCA

Workshops in Creative Arts
140 Clarendon Street
Boston, MA 02116

The BOSTON YWCA offers various classes in batik, printing, and fabric dyeing.

BOWLING GREEN STATE
UNIVERSITY

Art Department
Bowling Green, OH 43403

BOWLING GREEN STATE UNIVERSITY offers a degree program in Textile Design.

BRENAN COLLEGE

Art Department
Gainesville, GA 30801

BRENAN COLLEGE offers a B.A. in Crafts, and various courses in textile design.

BROOKFIELD CRAFT CENTER

P.O. Box 122
Brookfield, CT 06804
(203) 775-4526

BROOKFIELD CRAFT CENTER is primarily a craft school, with unique classes taught by the "best craftspeople in the country." Workshops include: weaving, quilting, basketry, papermaking, computers for craftsmen, painting on silk, shibori, cardweaving, etc. The Brookfield faculty includes such persons as Michael James, Virginia Jacobs, Patricia Malarcher, and others. The school also supports a retail shop that sells handmade crafts by its members.

CALIFORNIA COLLEGE OF ARTS AND CRAFTS

Textile Arts Department
5212 Broadway
Oakland, CA 94618
(415) 653-8118

The B.F.A. and M.F.A. Textile Arts Programs at CALIFORNIA COLLEGE OF ARTS AND CRAFTS offer a wide range of beginning to advanced courses in five major areas: weaving, printing, hand construction, costume and history. Noted instructors include Lia Cook and Nance O'Banion. Special summer classes are also offered.

CALIFORNIA INSTITUTE OF THE ARTS

24700 McBean Parkway
Valencia, CA 91355

CALIFORNIA INSTITUTE OF THE ARTS offers a degree in Textiles.

CALIFORNIA STATE UNIVERSITY, FULLERTON

Art Department
800 North State College Blvd.
Fullerton, CA 92631

CALIFORNIA STATE UNIVERSITY at FULLERTON offers a B.A. and an M.A. in Crafts with a concentration in Fibers.

CALIFORNIA STATE UNIVERSITY, LONG BEACH

Art Department
6101 East 7th Street
Long Beach, CA 90804

CALIFORNIA STATE UNIVERSITY at LONG BEACH offers both a B.F.A. and an M.F.A. in Textile Designs.

CALIFORNIA STATE UNIVERSITY, LOS ANGELES

5151 State University Drive
Los Angeles, CA 90032

CALIFORNIA STATE UNIVERSITY at LOS ANGELES offers a B.A. in Textiles with a concentration in fabric printing.

CALIFORNIA STATE UNIVERSITY, NORTHRIDGE

Art 3-D Media Department
Northridge, CA 91330
(818) 885-2784

The most complete studio facilities in the western U.S. are housed in the Art and Design Center of CALIFORNIA STATE UNIVERSITY at NORTHRIDGE. The school offers a B.A. in Design on Fabric/Fiber Art which covers such subjects as weaving, non-loom, printing, dyeing, silk-screen, Fabric as Art, Design for the Textile Industry, etc.

CAMBRIDGE CENTER FOR ADULT EDUCATION

42 Brattle Street
Cambridge, MA 02138

The CAMBRIDGE CENTER FOR ADULT EDUCATION offers many classes in batik, printing and dyeing, quilting, stitchery, textiles, textile design, etc.

CARNEGIE-MELON UNIVERSITY

Art Department
Schenley Park
Pittsburgh, PA 15213

CARNEGIE-MELON UNIVERSITY offers several classes in the fiber arts.

CATHOLIC UNIVERSITY OF AMERICA

Art Department
620 Michigan Avenue, N.E.
Washington, DC

The CATHOLIC UNIVERSITY OF AMERICA offers various courses in textiles.

CEDAR ART CENTER

171 Cedar Street
Corning, NY 14830
(607) 936-4448

The CEDAR ART CENTER offers a variety of fiber workshops in batik, quilting, soft sculpture, dyeing, etc.

CEDAR LAKES CRAFTS CENTER

Ripley, WV 25271
(304) 372-6263

CEDAR LAKES CRAFTS CENTER offers workshops in weaving, quilting, stitchery, soft sculpture, spinning, fabric and surface design.

THE CENTER FOR TEXTILE ARTS

326 Fifth Street
Eureka, CA 95501
(707) 443-0602

The CENTER FOR TEXTILE ARTS, a non-profit institution, offers a variety of classes in the fiber arts, including weaving, silk painting, coiled basketry, color theory for quilters, wool dyeing, machine knitting, beginning knitting, spinning, and more. Other services include individual instruction, a certificate program, textile studio and loom rental with very reasonable rates.

CENTRAL MICHIGAN UNIVERSITY

Department of Industrial
   Education and Technology
204 Wightman Wall
Mt. Pleasant, MI 48859
(517) 774-3033

CENTRAL MICHIGAN UNIVERSITY offers a degree in Textiles.

CHADRON STATE COLLEGE

Fine Arts Department
Chadron, NE 69337
(308) 432-4451

CHADRON STATE COLLEGE offers a Crafts degree, as well as courses in batik and other fiber arts.

CLEVELAND INSTITUTE OF ART

11141 East Boulevard
Cleveland, OH 44106

CLEVELAND INSTITUTE offers a B.F.A. in Textile Printing and courses in various fiber arts.

CLEVELAND STATE UNIVERSITY

1983 E. 24th Street
Clevelnd, OH 44115

CLEVELAND STATE UNIVERSITY offers a B.A. in Fibers and various related courses.

COLLEGE OF ART AND DESIGN

245 E. Kirby
Detroit, MI 48202

The COLLEGE OF ART AND DESIGN offers both B.F.A. and M.F.A. degrees, including a summer program which features fiber courses.

COLORADO STATE UNIVERSITY

Department of Art
Fort Collins, CO 80523
(303) 491-6774

COLORADO STATE UNIVERSITY offers a B.A. and B.F.A. in Fibers, and an M.F.A. in other subjects.

COLUMBUS COLLEGE

Art Department
Columbus, GA 31907
(404) 568-2047

COLUMBUS COLLEGE offers both a B.S. and a B.A. in Art, with courses in Textile Design.

CORNELL UNIVERSITY

Design and Environmental
   Analysis Department
Martha Van Resselaer hall
Ithaca, NY 14850

CORNELL UNIVERSITY offers a B.F.A. and an M.F.A. in Textile Design.

CRANBROOK ACADEMY OF ART

Fiber Department
500 Lone Pine Road
Bloomfield Hills, MI 48103

CRANBROOK offers a B.F.A. and an M.F.A. in Surface Design and Weaving.

DuCRET SCHOOL OF THE ARTS

559 Route #22
North Plainfield, NJ 07060

DuCRET offers various classes in textile design.

EAST CAROLINA UNIVERSITY

School of Art, Department of
   Design
Greenville, NC 27834
(919) 758-6563

EAST CAROLINA UNIVERSITY offers both a B.F.A. and an M.F.A. in Textile Design.

EASTERN CONNECTICUT
STATE COLLEGE

Extension Division
Winham Street
Willimantic, CT 06226

Through their Extension Department, EASTERN CONNECTICUT STATE COLLEGE offers various fiber courses in printing and dyeing.

EASTERN ILLINOIS
UNIVERSITY

Art Department
Charleston, IL 61920
(217) 581-3410

EASTERN ILLINOIS UNIVERSITY offers both a B.A. and an M.A. in Art, along with various courses in Textiles.

EASTERN MICHIGAN
UNIVERSITY

Art Department
Ypsilanti, MI 48197
(313) 487-1268

EASTERN MICHIGAN UNIVERSITY offers courses in Textile Design.

EDINBORO STATE COLLEGE

Art Department
Edinboro, PA 16412

EDINBORO STATE COLLEGE offers B.A., B.F.A., M.F.A., and M.Ed. degrees in Textile Design.

EK TRADET-EK GARDEN

9533 Highway 57
Baileys Harbor, MI 54202
(414) 839-2154

Normajean Johnson Ek, owner of EK TRADET (means "The Oak Tree" in Swedish) offers various workshops and college credit courses in such subjects as spinning, papermaking, Beginning and Intermediate Weaving, Knitting Loom Seminar, Felting, etc.

ELKHORNS MOUNTAIN
WEAVING SCHOOL

SR Box 165
Clancy, MT 59634
(406) 442-0354

Joanne Hall, author of *Mexican Tapestry Weaving* owns the ELKHORNS MOUNTAIN WEAVING SCHOOL. Small Beginning, Intermediate and Advanced classes are held each summer in tapestry, traditional and pictorial 4-harness weaving, Scandinavian weaves, fabric and rug weaves, color, design, spinning, dyeing, etc.

FASHION INSTITUTE OF
DESIGN AND
MERCHANDISING

The FASHION INSTITUTE OF DESIGN AND MERCHANDISING offers Certification Programs and summer studies in various design areas.

818 W. 7th Street
Los Angeles, CA 90017

FASHION INSTITUTE OF
TECHNOLOGY

The FASHION INSTITUTE OF TECHNOLOGY offers an A.A.S., B.S., and B.F.A. in Textile Design.

227 West 27th Street
New York, NY 10001

THE FIBER AND PRINT
WORKS SCHOOL

The FIBER AND PRINT WORKS SCHOOL offers courses and seminars in various textile techniques.

1030 Mission Street
South Pasadena, CA 91030

FIBERWORKS
CENTER FOR THE TEXTILE
ARTS

The FIBERWORKS CENTER FOR THE TEXTILE ARTS offers a Certification Program along with classes in all areas of the textile arts.

1940 Bonita Avenue
Berkeley, CA 94704
(415) 548-6030

FLORIDA STATE
UNIVERSITY

FLORIDA STATE UNIVERSITY offers an M.A. in Textiles, along with related classes.

Fine Arts Building
Tallahassee, FL 32306
(904) 644-5474

FRANCONIA COLLEGE

FRANCONIA COLLEGE offers a variety of courses and instruction in Textile Design.

Art Department
Franconia, NH 03580

GEORGIA COLLEGE

Art Department
Willedgeville, GA 31061

GEORGIA COLLEGE offers a B.A. in Art, with related courses in textile design.

GEORGIA INSTITUTE OF TECHNOLOGY

Textile Department
Atlanta, GA 30332

GEORGIA INSTITUTE OF TECHNOLOGY offers a degree in Textiles, along with courses in fibers.

GEORGIA SOUTHERN COLLEGE

Art Department
Statesboro, GA 30458

GEORGIA SOUTHERN COLLEGE offers a B.A. in Art with courses in Textile Design.

GEORGIA STATE UNIVERSITY

Art Department
University Plaza
Atlanta, GA 30303

GEORGIA STATE UNIVERSITY offers a B.V.A. and an M.V.A. in Textile Design.

GLASSBORO STATE COLLEGE

Art Department
Glassboro, NJ 08028

GLASSBORO STATE COLLEGE offers a B.A. in Fibers and Fabrics.

GLENDALE COMMUNITY COLLEGE

6000 West Olive
Glendale, AZ 85301

GLENDALE COMMUNITY COLLEGE offers various classes in fabric design.

GLENVILLE STATE COLLEGE

Department of Art
Glenville, WV 26351
(304) 462-7186

GLENVILLE STATE COLLEGE offers classes in textile design.

GODDARD COLLEGE

Fine Arts Department
Plainfield, VT 05669

GODDARD COLLEGE offers an off-campus study program in textiles with degree plans designed by students. A summer program is also offered.

GUILFORD HANDCRAFTS CENTER

Rt. #77, Box 221
Guilford, CT 06437
(203) 243-4393

GUILFORD HANDCRAFTS CENTER offers many classes in all areas of crafts, including fibers and textiles

HALIBURTON SCHOOL OF FINE ARTS

Sir Sanford Fleming College
Box 339
Haliburton, Ontario
Canada, K0M 1S0

HALIBURTON offers a variety of fiber courses during the summer. These include courses in rugmaking, silk painting, hand embroidery, Introduction to Weaving, Knitting, Innovative Quilting, Silkscreen, Basic Photography, Basketry, Spinning and Dyeing, Navajo Weaving, 3-D Textile Construction, and Ikat Weaving. The instructors include such fiber artists as Clotilde Barrett, Ankaret Dean, and others.

NANCY HARVEY TAPESTRIES

5834 Riddio Street
Citrus Heights, CA 95610
(916) 967-9359

Nancy Harvey, author of both *The Guide to Successful Tapestry Weaving,* and *Patterns for Tapestry Weaving, Projects and Techniques,* is available for seminars, lectures, and classes on Tapestry Theory, Tapestry: Past and Present, Getting the Business (the Commission Process), and Tapestries for Interiors (A Personal View).

HAYSTACK MOUNTAIN SCHOOL OF CRAFTS

Deer Isle, ME 04627
(207) 348-6946

HAYSTACK MOUNTAIN SCHOOL OF CRAFTS offers two-to-three week sessions in clothing design, quilts, weaving, basketry, papermaking, fibers, fabric, etc. Some past instructors have been Susan Lyman, Jack Lenor Larsen, Bernie Toale, Sheila Hicks, and others.

HAYWOOD TECHNICAL COLLEGE

Production Crafts Department
Freelander Drive
Clyde, NC 27101
(704) 627-2821

HAYWOOD TECHNICAL COLLEGE offers a Production Crafts-Fiber Program which includes courses in weaving, clothing and costume, production weaving, fiber studio, textile industry, portfolio development, color and dyeing, machine knitting, etc.

HILL COUNTRY WEAVERS

918 West 12th Street
Austin, TX
(512) 474-6773

HILL COUNTRY WEAVERS, owned by Suzanne Middlebrooks and Marta Shannon, offers a variety of workshops throughout the year on such subjects as Rigid Heddle Loom Weaving, Beginning Floor Loom Weaving, Basic Knitting and Beyond, Feltmaking, Tapestry, Natural Fiber Basketry, and others. The store also stocks a large supply of yarns, looms, fibers, etc.

HINCKLEY SCHOOL OF CRAFTS

Box 66
Hinckley, ME 04944
(207) 453-9991

The HINCKLEY SCHOOL OF CRAFTS offers a summer crafts program which includes several courses in Fabric Design.

HOFSTRA UNIVERSITY

Long Island Craftsmen's Guild
Hempstead, NY 11550
(516) 560-3313

HOFSTRA UNIVERSITY offers various fiber courses, including some in batik, quilting, soft sculpture, etc.

HUNTER COLLEGE

Fine Arts Department
695 Park Avenue
New York, NY 10021

HUNTER COLLEGE offers various courses in Textiles and Design.

ILLINOIS STATE UNIVERSITY

Art Department, Center for the
   Visual Arts
Normal, IL 61761
(309) 438-5621

ILLINOIS STATE UNIVERSITY offers B.A., B.S., B.F.A., M.A., M.S., M.F.A., and Ed.D. and Doctorate degrees in Weaving and Textiles.

INDIANA UNIVERSITY

Fine Arts Department
Bloomington, IN 47405

INDIANA UNIVERSITY offers a B.A., B.F.A., and an M.F.A. in Textile Design.

IOWA STATE UNIVERSITY

Department of Art and Design
Ames, IA 50011

IOWA STATE UNIVERSITY offers a B.A., B.F.A., and an M.A. with an emphasis in Fibers. They also offer various courses in printing and dyeing fabrics.

KANSAS CITY ART
INSTITUTE

4415 Warwick
Kansas City, MO 64111

The KANSAS CITY ART INSTITUTE offers a B.F.A. degree with courses in fabric printing and other fiber arts.

KEAN COLLEGE OF NEW
JERSEY

Fine Arts Department
Morris Avenue
Union, NJ 07083

KEAN COLLEGE offers a degree program and various courses in Textiles.

KENT STATE UNIVERSITY

School of Art
Kent, OH 44242
(216) 672-2192

KENT STATE UNIVERSITY offers B.A., B.F.A., M.A. and M.F.A. degrees in Fiber Arts.

KIRMEYER SCHOOL OF FIBER
STUDIES

P.O. Box 24815
San Jose, CA 95154-4815
(408) 269-4513

Maxine Kirmeyer offers classes in all aspects of fiber, but specializes in basketmaking classes. These include such subjects as Plaiting, Coiling and Knotting, Twining, Pineneedle Baskets, and others. She offers a special environment, an extensive collection of crafts to study and quality teachers.

LAWRENCE ART CENTER

9th and Vermont
Lawrence, KS 66044
(913) 843-9444

LAWRENCE ART CENTER offers workshops in batik, quilting, needle-crafts, and other fiber arts.

LOUISIANA STATE
UNIVERSITY

Department of Fine Arts
Baton Rouge, LA 70803

LOUISIANA STATE UNIVERSITY offers a B.F.A. and an M.F.A. in Textiles.

LOUISIANA TECHNICAL
UNIVERSITY

Box 6277, Tech Station
Ruston, LA 71270

LOUISIANA TECH in Ruston offers a B.F.A. and an M.F.A. in Textile
Design

LOUISVILLE SCHOOL OF ART

100 Park Road
Anchorage, KY 40223
(502) 245-8836

LOUISVILLE SCHOOL OF ART offers a B.F.A. in Surface Design or Fiber
Construction.

JAMES MADISON
UNIVERSITY

Art Department
Harrisonburg, VA 22807
(703) 568-6216

JAMES MADISON UNIVERSITY offers a B.F.A. in Crafts with a concentration in Textiles.

MANHATTANVILLE COLLEGE

Art Department
Purchase Street
Purchase, NY 10577

MANHATTANVILLE COLLEGE offers a B.A. and a B.F.A. in Textile
Design.

MARLBORO COLLEGE

Office of Admissions
Marlboro, VT 05344

MARLBORO COLLEGE offers off-campus study programs in textiles
designed by students.

MARYLAND INSTITUTE
COLLEGE OF ART

Craft Department
1300 Mount Royal Avenue
Baltimore, MD 21217

MARYLAND INSTITUTE COLLEGE OF ART offers a B.F.A. and an
M.F.A. in Crafts, along with a number of courses in Weaving, Surface
Design, Quilting, Soft Sculpture, etc.

MARYWOOD COLLEGE

Adams Avenue
Scranton, PA 18509

MARYWOOD COLLEGE offers a B.F.A. and an M.F.A. in Textiles.

MASSACHUSETTS COLLEGE
OF ART

Craft Department
364 Brookline Avenue
Boston, MA 02215

MASSACHUSETTS COLLEGE OF ART offers a B.F.A. in Textile Design.

MEMPHIS STATE
UNIVERSITY

Art Department
Memphis, TN 38152

MEMPHIS STATE UNIVERSITY offers a B.A. in Art with a minor in Textiles.

MENDOCINO ART CENTER

Textile Apprenticeship Program
Box 765
Mendocino, CA 95460
(707) 937-0228

The MENDOCINO ART CENTER Textile Apprenticeship Program offers a three year certificate program in weaving and surface design. Some of the classes and workshops include Plaited Basketry (Shereen LaPlantz), Introduction to Weaving (Lolli Jacobsen), Paper/Fiber Mixed Media (Coleen Barry-Wilson), Shibori (Barbara Goldberg), Tapestry and Pictorial Weaving (Joanne Hall), Dyeing with Mushrooms (Miriam Rice), and many others. The Art Center also supports a gallery which carries high quality fine arts and crafts made by its members. They also do mail orders and wholesale, especially through Mendo Products, their Christmas mail order catalog.

For $3.00, the Art Center will add you to their mailing list for three years.

MIAMI UNIVERSITY

Department of Art
Hiestand Hall
Oxford, OH 45156
(513) 529-6010

MIAMI UNIVERSITY offers both a B.F.A. and an M.F.A. in Textile Design. They also sponsor a "Craftsummer" Program.

MICHIGAN STATE
UNIVERSITY

Department of Human
   Environment and Design
College of Human Ecology
East Lansing, MI 48824
(514) 355-7715

MICHIGAN STATE UNIVERSITY offers a B.F.A. and an M.F.A. in Weaving and Textile Design.

MIDDLE TENNESSEE
STATE UNIVERSITY

Art Department
Murfreesboro, TN 37172
(615) 898-2781

MIDDLE TENNESSEE STATE offers a B.S. and a B.F.A. degree with a minor in Fiber Arts.

MONTCLAIR STATE
COLLEGE

Fine Arts Department
Upper Montclair, NJ 07043
(201) 893-4307

MONTCLAIR STATE COLLEGE offers B.A., B.F.A., M.A. degrees and a graduate assistantship leading to an M.A. in Fine Arts or Art Education with a major concentration in fibers and fabrics. In addition, they also maintain apprenticeships in the textile industry in Manhattan, independent internships, and textile conservation and museum practice.

MOORE COLLEGE OF ART

20 and Race Street
Philadelphia, PA

MOORE COLLEGE OF ART offers a B.F.A. in Textile Design.

MORRIS BROWN COLLEGE

Art Department
Atlanta, GA

MORRIS BROWN COLLEGE offers a B.A. in Crafts, with various courses in Textiles.

MOUNT ALOYSIUS JUNIOR
COLLEGE

Art Department
Route #221
Cresson, NY 16630

MT. ALOYSIUS JUNIOR COLLEGE offers various courses in batik, tie-dye, textiles, etc.

MOUNT MARY COLLEGE

Milwaukee, WI 53222

MOUNT MARY COLLEGE offers a B.A. degree with various courses in fibers.

MURRAY STATE UNIVERSITY

Art Department
Murray, KY 42071
(502) 762-3784

MURRAY STATE UNIVERSITY offers B.S., B.A., B.F.A., M.A., M.Ed., and M.A.C.T. degrees in Fibers and Fabrics.

THE NEW SCHOOL

Crafts Department
66 West 12th Street
New York, NY 10011
(212) 741-5614

THE NEW SCHOOL offers courses in batik, printing, dyeing, quilting, stitchery, tie-dye, etc.

NEW YORK UNIVERSITY

Art Education Department
80 Washington Square
New York, NY 10003

NEW YORK UNIVERSITY offers various courses in textile design.

NORTH GEORGIA COLLEGE

Art Department
Route 4
Dahlonega, GA 30533

NORTH GEORGIA COLLEGE offers a B.A. in Crafts and Design, with various courses in fabric design.

NORTH TEXAS STATE
UNIVERSITY

Department of Art
Box 5098, N.T. Station
Denton, TX 76203
(817) 788-2398

NORTH TEXAS STATE UNIVERSITY offers a B.A. and B.F.A. in Weaving, Interior Design and Fashion Design, an M.A. and M.F.A. with a concentration in Weaving and Fabric Design, and a variety of courses in Surface Design.

NORTHERN ARIZONA
UNIVERSITY

P.O. Box 6020
Flagstaff, AZ 86011

NORTHERN ARIZONA UNIVERSITY offers both a B.F.A. and an M.A. degree in Textile Design.

NORTHERN ILLINOIS
UNIVERSITY

Department of Art
DeKalb, IL 60115
(815) 753-1473

NORTHERN ILLINOIS UNIVERSITY offers degrees of B.A., B.F.A., M.A., and M.F.A. in Fibers/Fabrics.

NOTRE DAME COLLEGE

Art Department
2321 Elm Street
Manchester, NH 03104

NOTRE DAME offers a B.A. in Textiles.

OHIO STATE UNIVERSITY

Division of Art
146 Hopkins Hall
128 North Oval Mall
Columbus, OH 43210

OHIO STATE UNIVERSITY offers a B.F.A. and an M.F.A. in Textiles.

OHIO UNIVERSITY

School of Art
Siegfried Hall
Athens, OH 45701
(614) 594-5667

OHIO UNIVERSITY offers a B.F.A. in Studio Art with a concentration in Fibers.

OKLAHOMA BAPTIST
UNIVERSITY

500 W. University
Shawnee, OK 74801

OKLAHOMA BAPTIST UNIVERSITY offers a B.A. degree with a concentration in Fabric Printing.

OKLAHOMA STATE
UNIVERSITY

104 Industrial Building
Stillwater, OK 74074
(405) 624-7414

OKLAHOMA STATE UNIVERSITY offers several courses in Textile Design.

OREGON SCHOOL OF ARTS
AND CRAFTS

8245 S.W. Barnes Road
Portland, OR 97225
(503) 297-5544

OREGON SCHOOL OF ARTS AND CRAFTS offers a B.A. in Crafts.

OREGON STATE
UNIVERSITY

Department of Art
Corvallis, OR 97331
(503) 754-4745

OREGON STATE UNIVERSITY offers a B.A., B.S. and a B.F.A. in Arts and Crafts, with instruction in batik.

PACIFIC BASIN SCHOOL OF
TEXTILE ARTS

1659 San Pablo Avenue
Berkeley, CA 94702
(415) 526-9836

PACIFIC BASIN is the only independent year-round school exclusively devoted to textiles. The school offers classes, lectures and workshops in such subjects as Professional Weaving Studio Skills, Computer Pattern Drafting, Textile Production, Marketing and Sales for Surface Design, The Knitting Machine, Textile Conservation, Marbling, Exploration in Painted Warp, Spinning, Basketry, and others. The school also has a unique marketing/business program for artists and craftspersons. The program, developed with a grant from the H.E.W. Fund for Postsecondary Education, covers such topics as Market Research, Business Records, Taxes and Legal Aspects, Portfolio Graphics, etc.

PARSONS SCHOOL OF DESIGN

Fine Arts Department
66 Fifth Avenue
New York, NY 10011

PARSONS offers various courses in Textile Design and Fibers.

PASADENA CITY COLLEGE

Art Department
1570 East Colorado Blvd.
Pasadena, CA 91106
(213) 578-7238

PASADENA CITY COLLEGE offers a degree in Crafts.

PENDLETON FABRIC CRAFT
SCHOOL

P.O. Box 233 (465 Jordan Road)
Sedona, AZ 86336
(602) 282-3671

Mary Pendleton, owner of the PENDLETON FABRIC CRAFT SCHOOL, offers a number of fiber classes, including Tapestry, Navajo and Hopi Weaving Techniques, Weaving with Rags, Designing with Soumak and a Swedish In-lay Technique, Beginning Spinning, Beginning Weaving on Floor Looms, and more. Individual and small group instruction is also offered.

PENLAND SCHOOL OF
CRAFTS

Penland, NC 28765
(704) 688-3386

PENLAND offers summer, fall and spring programs in fibers which include courses in papermaking, tapestry, beginning to advanced weaving, basketry, surface design, knitting, and more.

PENNSYLVANIA STATE
UNIVERSITY

102 Visual Arts
University Park, PA 16802
(814) 865-6570

PENNSYLVANIA STATE UNIVERSITY offers degrees of B.A., B.F.A., M.S., M.Ed., Ph.D, and D.Ed. in Fine Arts with a concentration in Fiber Arts.

PHILADELPHIA COLLEGE
OF ART

Broad and Spruce Streets
Philadelphia, PA 19102
(215) 546-0545

PHILADELPHIA COLLEGE OF ART offers a B.F.A. in Fibers and Fabrics.

PHILADELPHIA COLLEGE OF
TEXTILES AND SCIENCE

School House Lane and Henry
Avenue
Philadelphia, PA 19144
(215) 951-2700

PHILADELPHIA COLLEGE OF TEXTILES AND SCIENCE offers a B.S. degree in Apparel Management, Color Science, Fashion Merchandising, Textile Chemistry, Textile Design, Textile Engineering, Textile Management and Marketing, and Textile Technology. Individual courses include Weaving, Batik, Tapestry, Screen Printing, etc.

PHOENIX COLLEGE

Art Department
1202 West Thomas Road
Phoenix, AZ 85013

PHOENIX COLLEGE offers various courses in Textile Design.

PRATT INSTITUTE

215 Ryerson Street
Brooklyn, NY 11217
(212) 636-3600

PRATT INSTITUTE offers a degree in Textile Design.

PURDUE UNIVERSITY

Department of Creative Arts
West Lafayette, IN 47906

PURDUE offers a B.A. and an M.A. in Studio Art, with courses in Surface Design.

RHODE ISLAND SCHOOL OF DESIGN

Fine Arts Department
Two College Street
Providence, RI 02903

RHODE ISLAND SCHOOL OF DESIGN offers a B.F.A. in Textile Design.

RIVIER COLLEGE

429 S. Main Street
Nashua, NH 03060

RIVIER COLLEGE offers a B.A., B.F.A. and a B.S. degree, with various courses in fibers.

ROCHESTER INSTITUTE OF TECHNOLOGY

School for American Craftsmen
One Lomb Memorial Drive
Rochester, NY 14623

ROCHESTER INSTITUTE OF TECHNOLOGY offers degrees of A.A.S., B.F.A. and M.F.A. in Textile Design and Weaving.

SAM HOUSTON STATE UNIVERSITY

Art Department
Huntsville, TX 77340
(713) 295-9406

SAM HOUSTON STATE UNIVERSITY offers degrees of B.F.A. and M.F.A. in Fabric Design.

SAN FRANCISCO FIBER

3435 Army Street, #222
San Francisco, CA 94110
(415) 821-2568

SAN FRANCISCO FIBER offers a variety of fiber classes throughout the year. Some of these include Basketry, Cardweaving, Crochet, Feltmaking, Knitting, Spinning, Tapestry, Weaving, and many more. Weaving supplies are also available for sale at the shop.

SANTA FE WEAVER'S SCHOOL

Box 9001
Santa Fe, NM 87504
(505) 983-8058

SANTA FE WEAVER'S SCHOOL offers such courses as Basic Weaving, Intermediate/Advanced Weaving, Computer Designing, Woven Color, Twill Tricks, Shaft Switching, etc.

SCHOOL OF THE BOSTON MUSEUM OF FINE ARTS

230-C The Fenway
Boston, MA 02115
(617) 267-9300

The SCHOOL OF THE BOSTON MUSEUM OF FINE ARTS offers a B.F.A. and an M.F.A. degree, along with courses in Surface Design.

SCHOOL OF VISUAL ARTS

Fine Art Department
209 East 23rd Street
New York, NY 10010

The SCHOOL OF VISUAL ARTS offers various courses in Textile Design.

SCRIPPS COLLEGE

9th and Columbia
Claremont, CA 91711

SCRIPPS COLLEGE offers a B.A. degree with a major in Textile Printing.

SEADAD STUDIOS, INC.

130 W. 29th Street
New York, NY 10001
(212) 564-8103

SEADAD STUDIOS (also publishers of Machine Knitters Newsletter), gives lessons and seminars on all types of knitting machines. Monthly classes include such subjects as Beginning Machine Knitting, Designing Punch Cards, Deco for the Passap, Intarsia for Single Beds, Intermediate Machine Knitting, Finishing Workshop, Patternmaking, Buying a Knitting Machine, etc.

SHORTER COLLEGE

Art Department
Rome, GA 30161

SHORTER COLLEGE offers a B.A. in Art, with various courses in Surface Design and Basic and Advanced Crafts.

SKIDMORE COLLEGE

Art Department
Saratoga Spring, NY 12866
(518) 584-5000

SKIDMORE COLLEGE offers a B.S. and a B.A. in Studio Art, with various textile courses.

SOUTH GEORGIA COLLEGE

Art Department
Douglas, GA 31533

SOUTH GEORGIA COLLEGE offers various courses in fabric design and printing.

SOUTHEASTERN
MASSACHUSETTS
UNIVERSITY

North Dartmouth, MA 02747

SOUTHEASTERN MASSACHUSETTS UNIVERSITY offers a B.F.A. in Design, Textile Design, and Fine Arts. An M.F.A. degree is offered in Visual Design and an M.A.E. with a concentration in Textile Design.

SOUTHERN ILLINOIS
UNIVERSITY

School of Art
Carbondale, IL 62901

SOUTHERN ILLINOIS UNIVERSITY offers a B.F.A. and an M.F.A. in Textiles

---

SOUTHERN MASSACHUSETTS
UNIVERSITY

Design Department
North Dartmouth, MA 02738

SOUTHERN MASSACHUSETTS UNIVERSITY offers a B.F.A. and an M.F.A. in Textile Design.

SOUTHWEST CRAFT CENTER

300 Augusta Street
San Antonio, TX 78205-1296
(512) 224-1848

The SOUTHWEST CRAFT CENTER offers several classes and workshops in fibers. Recent ones included Natural Dyeing, Spinning, Contemporary Quilting, On-Loom Weaving, Weaving Theory, Designing with a Computer, and others. Instructors have included Luisa Gelenter of "La Lana Wools," Rachel Brown, and Pamela Studstill, among others.

SOUTHWEST MISSOURI
STATE UNIVERSITY

Department of Art
Springfield, MO 65806

SOUTHWEST MISSOURI STATE UNIVERSITY offers a B.A., B.S. and a B.F.A. in Fibers with a concentration on Surface Design and/or Weaving.

SOUTHWEST TEXAS STATE
UNIVERSITY

Department of Fine Art
San Marcos, TX 78666

SOUTHWEST TEXAS STATE UNIVERSITY offers a B.F.A. in Studio Art with a concentration in Textiles.

STANFORD UNIVERSITY

Department of Art
Stanford, CA 95050

STANFORD UNIVERSITY offers a B.F.A. and an M.F.A. in Textile Design.

STATE UNIVERSITY
COLLEGE AT BUFFALO

Design Department
1300 Elmwood Avenue
Buffalo, NY 14222

STATE UNIVERSITY COLLEGE offers a B.F.A. and an M.F.A. in Textile Design.

STEPHEN F. AUSTIN
STATE UNIVERSITY

Department of Art
Box 3001
Nacogdoches, TX 75962
(713) 569-4810

STEPHEN F. AUSTIN STATE UNIVERSITY offers a B.F.A. and an M.F.A. in Fiber Design.

SYRACUSE UNIVERSITY

Department of Textile Arts
College of Visual and Performing
   Arts
Syracuse, NY 13210

SYRACUSE UNIVERSITY offers a B.F.A. and an M.F.A. in Surface Design and Fibers.

TEACHERS COLLEGE,
COLUMBIA UNIVERSITY

Art and Education Department
525 West 120th Street
New York, NY 10027

TEACHERS COLLEGE OF COLUMBIA UNIVERSITY offers various courses in Textile Design.

TENNESSEE STATE
UNIVERSITY

Home Economics Department
Nashville, TN 37203

TENNESSEE STATE offers a B.S. in Home Economics with a minor in Textile Design.

TENNESSEE TECHNOLOGICAL
UNIVERSITY

School of Home Economics
Box 5035
Cookeville, TN 38501

TENNESSEE TECHNOLOGICAL UNIVERSITY offers a B.A. in Home Economics with an emphasis on Textiles.

TEXAS CHRISTIAN
UNIVERSITY

Art Department
University Drive
Fort Worth, TX 76129

TEXAS CHRISTIAN UNIVERSITY offers both a B.F.A. and an M.F.A. in Textile Design.

TEXAS TECH UNIVERSITY

Box 4720
Lubbock, TX 79401

TEXAS TECH offers a B.F.A. and an M.F.A. in Textile Design.

TEXAS WOMEN'S
UNIVERSITY

Department of Art
TWU Station, Box 22995
Denton, TX 76201
(817) 382-8923

TEXAS WOMEN'S UNIVERSITY offers various courses in printed and dyed textiles.

TOWSON STATE UNIVERSITY

Art Department
Osler Drive
Towson, MD 21204
(301) 321-2808

TOWSON STATE UNIVERSITY offers a B.S. and a B.A. in Studio Art with a concentration in Fabric Design and Weaving. An M.F.A. in Studio Art is also offered.

TYLER SCHOOL OF ART
OF TEMPLE UNIVERSITY

Beech and Penrose Avenues
Elkins Park
Philadelphia, PA 19126
(215) 224-7575

TYLER SCHOOL OF ART offers a degree program in Textiles.

UNIVERSITY OF ALABAMA

Department of Art
Box F University
Tuscaloosa, AL 35486

The UNIVERSITY OF ALABAMA offers an M.F.A. in Textiles degree.

UNIVERSITY OF ARIZONA

Art Department
Tucson, AZ 85721
(612) 626-4966

THE UNIVERSITY OF ARIZONA offers degrees of B.F.A., M.F.A. and M.A.E. with majors in Fibers.

UNIVERSITY OF CALIFORNIA
AT DAVIS

Department of Applied
    Behavioral Science
Davis, CA 95616

The UNIVERSITY OF CALIFORNIA AT DAVIS offers a B.S. in Design with an emphasis in Textile Design, Costume Design, Environmental or Graphic Design.

UNIVERSITY OF CALIFORNIA
AT LOS ANGELES

Art Department
405 Hilgurd Avenue
Los Angeles, CA 90024

The UNIVERSITY OF CALIFORNIA AT LOS ANGELES offers both a B.F.A. and an M.F.A. in Textile Design.

UNIVERSITY OF DELAWARE

Department of Art
Newark, DE 19711
(302) 738-2244

The UNIVERSITY OF DELAWARE offers a B.A. in Textile Design.

UNIVERSITY OF GEORGIA

Department of Art
Athens, GA 30602

The UNIVERSITY OF GEORGIA offers a B.F.A. and an M.F.A. in Textile Design.

UNIVERSITY OF HAWAII
AT MANOA

2535 The Mall
Honolulu, HI 96822

The UNIVERSITY OF HAWAII AT MANOA offers a B.F.A. and an M.F.A. in Textile Design.

UNIVERSITY OF KANSAS

Department of Design
Visual Arts Building
Lawrence, KS 66045

The UNIVERSITY OF KANSAS offers both a B.F.A. and an M.F.A. in Textile Design.

UNIVERSITY OF KENTUCKY

Department of Art
Lexington, KY 40506

The UNIVERSITY OF KENTUCKY offers a B.A. and an M.F.A. in Textiles.

UNIVERSITY OF LOUISVILLE

A. R. Hite Art Institute
Louisville, KY 40292

The UNIVERSITY OF LOUISVILLE offers a B.A. and a B.F.A. degree, with some fiber courses.

UNIVERSITY OF MICHIGAN

School of Art
2000 Bonisteel Blvd.
Ann Arbor, MI 48109

The UNIVERSITY OF MICHIGAN offers a B.F.A. and an M.F.A. degree, with various textile courses.

UNIVERSITY OF MINNESOTA

208 Studio Arts Building
Minneapolis, MN 55455

The UNIVERSITY OF MINNESOTA offers a B.F.A. and an M.F.A. in Textiles.

UNIVERSITY OF MISSISSIPPI

Fine Arts Center
Department of Art
University, MS 38677

The UNIVERSITY OF MISSISSIPPI offers a B.F.A. and an M.F.A. in Textiles.

UNIVERSITY OF MONTANA

Department of Art
School of Fine Arts
Missoula, MT 59812

The UNIVERSITY OF MONTANA offers a B.F.A. and an M.F.A. in Textiles and Surface Design.

UNIVERSITY OF NEBRASKA
AT LINCOLN

Department of Art
Nelle Cochrane Woods Hall
Lincoln, NE 68503

The UNIVERSITY OF NEBRASKA offers both a B.F.A. and an M.F.A. in Textiles.

UNIVERSITY OF NORTH
CAROLINA AT GREENSBORO

Art Department
Greensboro, NC 27412
(919) 379-5248

The UNIVERSITY OF NORTH CAROLINA offers a B.F.A. and an M.F.A. in Textiles.

UNIVERSITY OF RHODE
ISLAND

Textile and Clothing Design
Kingston, RI 12881

The UNIVERSITY OF RHODE ISLAND offers a degree program in Textiles.

UNIVERSITY OF TENNESSEE

Department of Art
College of Liberal Arts
Knoxville, TN 37916
(615) 974-2369

The UNIVERSITY OF TENNESSEE offers degrees of B.A., B.F.A., M.A. and M.F.A. in Fiber/Fabric Design.

UNIVERSITY OF TEXAS

Art Department
Austin, TX 78712

The UNIVERSITY OF TEXAS offers a B.F.A. and an M.F.A. degree, with various courses in Weaving and Surface Design.

UNIVERSITY OF UTAH

Art Department, AAC 161
Salt Lake City, UT 84112

The UNIVERSITY OF UTAH offers a B.F.A. and an M.F.A. in Design/-Crafts. They also sponsor a Summer Institute in Fibers.

UNIVERSITY OF VERMONT

School of Home Economics
Burlington, VT 05401

The UNIVERSITY OF VERMONT offers a B.S. in Textile Design.

UNIVERSITY OF
WASHINGTON

School of Art
Seattle, WA 98195

The UNIVERSITY OF WASHINGTON offers a B.A., B.F.A. and an M.F.A. in Textile Design.

UNIVERSITY OF WISCONSIN,
MADISON

Department of Art
6241 Humanities Building
455 North Park Street
Madison, WI 53706

The UNIVERSITY OF WISCONSIN AT MADISON offers a B.F.A. and an M.F.A. in Textile Design.

UNIVERSITY OF WISCONSIN,
PARKSIDE

Department of Art
Kenosha, WI 53140
(414) 553-2457

The UNIVERSITY OF WISCONSIN, PARKSIDE offers various classes in fibers and fabric design.

UTAH STATE UNIVERSITY

Art Department
Logan, UT 84332
(801) 752-4100

UTAH STATE UNIVERSITY offers a B.F.A. and an M.F.A. in Textile Design.

VALDOSTA STATE COLLEGE

Art Department
Valdosta, GA 31601

VALDOSTA STATE COLLEGE offers a B.A. and a B.F.A. degree, with various courses in Textile Design.

VIRGINIA COMMONWEALTH
UNIVERSITY

Crafts Department
827 W. Franklin Street
Richmond, VA 23220

VIRGINIA COMMONWEALTH UNIVERSITY offers a B.F.A. and an M.F.A. in Textiles.

WASHINGTON STATE
UNIVERSITY

Fine Arts Center
Pullman, WA 99164
(509) 335-3823

WASHINGTON STATE UNIVERSITY offers a B.F.A. and an M.F.A. in Textiles.

WAYNE STATE UNIVERSITY

Art Department
Detroit, MI 48202

WAYNE STATE UNIVERSITY offers a B.F.A. and an M.F.A. in Textile Design.

WEAVING WORKSHOP

Textile Arts Center
916 W. Diversey Parkway
Chicago, IL 60614
(312) 929-5776

The WEAVING WORKSHOP offers a wide variety of in-depth fiber courses. These include Beginning Rigid Heddle Weaving, Beginning Four-Harness Weaving, Beginning Hand and Machine Knitting, Batik, Spinning and Yarn Design, Beginning Textile Printing, etc. A "Mini Series" of workshops are also offered. The Weaving Workshop also includes a retail fiber supply shop.

WESTERN MICHIGAN UNIVERSITY

Art Department
Kalamazoo, MI 49008

WESTERN MICHIGAN UNIVERSITY offers a B.F.A. and an M.F.A. in Textile Design.

WESTERN WASHINGTON UNIVERSITY

Art Department
Bellingham, WA
(206) 676-3660

WESTERN WASHINGTON UNIVERSITY offers a B.A. and a B.F.A. degree, with various courses in batik and fabric design.

WILKES COLLEGE

Wilkes Barre, PA 18766

WILKES COLLEGE offers a B.A. and a B.F.A. in Textile Design.

WORCESTER CRAFT CENTER

25 Sagamore Road
Worcester, MA 01605
(617) 753-6140

WORCESTER CRAFT CENTER offers courses in all craft areas, including fibers. Worcester also sponsors visiting artist workshops in various subjects. Weaving and spinning supplies are also available at the center.

WOVENWARE

3465 Edgewater Drive
Orlando, FL 32804
(305) 425-7001

WOVENWARE offers a number of fiber arts workshops including Basketry, Beginning Weaving, Natural and Synthetic Dyeing, Navajo Rug Weaving, Rigid Heddle Weaving, Spinning, Tapestry, etc. They also carry a variety of fiber supplies.

CHAPTER
10

Embellishments

This chapter contains all the miscellaneous items that go into decorating or "embellishing" fiber pieces. Listed are sources for handmade buttons, beautiful silk and metallic threads for machine or hand embroidery, shisha mirrors, beads, basic needlework and sewing supplies, patterns, trims, cords, hang tags for items, and more.

AARDVARK TERRITORIAL ENTERPRISE

P.O. Box 2449
Livermore, CA 94550
(415) 443-ANTS

Mail Order; Established in 1976

The AARDVARK TERRITORIAL ENTERPRISE catalog/newsletter is published "rather quarterly" by Ms. Jerry Zarbaugh, "The Aardvark Lady." The newsletter contains many strange and wondrous things, and focuses on fiber artists who work with machine or hand embroidery and stitchery. This amusing publication contains news of new products, books, artists, classes, events, etc.

Ms. Zarbaugh also carries supplies for embroidery — Natesh Embroidery Thread in 336 shades (beautiful), Shisha mirrors in three sizes, beads, tools, and other embellishments — and sells these through her newsletter.

Special sales are offered periodically on supplies throughout the newsletter. Discounts are given to those with resale tax numbers.

Subscriptions to the newsletter are very reasonable, considering all the laughter it provokes — 37¢ for a one year/four-issue, bulk-rate mailing. For $2.00, the newsletters are sent by first class mail. Give it a try — especially if you're fond of aardvarks (and who isn't?).

THE AMERICAN NEEDLEWOMAN, INC.

2946-50 S.E. Loop 820
Ft. Worth, TX 76140
(817) 293-1229

Mail Order, Retail Shop; V/MC;
Established in 1976

THE AMERICAN NEEDLEWOMAN, INC. is an all-around needlework supplier. Some of their products include yarns, kits, DMC Cotton Embroidery Threads, pattern books, machine embroidery threads and books, tatting supplies, wool tapestry yarns, ribbons and fabrics, needlepoint supplies, metallic yarns, knitting and crochet books, rug hooking supplies, and much more.

Send for a free catalog.

BENJANE ARTS

320 Hempsted Avenue
W. Hempsted, NY 11552
(516) 483-1330

Mail Order, Retail Shop;
Established in 1962

BENJANE ARTS has a large variety of seashells, drilled and undrilled, suitable for use in weavings, wearable art, etc.

Quantity discounts are given with a minimum order of $50.00.

Send $3.00 for a color catalog, refundable with order.

BOYCAN'S CRAFT AND ART SUPPLIES

P.O. Box 897
Sharon, PA 16146
(412) 346-5534

Mail Order; V/MC; Established in 1954

BOYCAN'S carries a line of over 10,000 basic supplies for arts and crafts. Fiber supplies include sequins, pearls and beads, macrame braids and cords, accessories, ribbons, stenciling supplies, cotton fabrics and other quilting supplies, rug yarns, knitting and crochet yarns, basketry supplies, needlework accessories, fabric paints, patterns, doll parts, a large number of books, and much more.

Boycan's also carries general art materials such as paints, brushes, and papers.

Send $2.00 for a current catalog; $1.00 is refundable with order.

BOYE NEEDLE COMPANY

4343 N. Ravenswood
Chicago, IL 60613
(312) 472-0354

Manufacturer; Established in
1903

BOYE NEEDLE COMPANY manufactures a complete line of supplies for all needle arts. They supply Boye brand knitting needles, crochet hooks, circular needles, instruction books, embroidery supplies and other accessories.

The company does not sell directly to consumers, but does give school/group discounts with a minimum order of $35.00. Retail establishments can write for wholesale information.

A current catalog is $2.00.

BUTTON CREATIONS

48 Hillcrest Avenue
Chalfont, PA 18914
(215) 822-3648

Mail Order; Established in 1978

BUTTON CREATIONS is owned by the Beck family: John, Molly, Fran and Todd. Their catalog, "1,001 Buttons and other Related Items" contains buttons of leather, horn, wood, ivory, mother of pearl, ceramics, cloisonne, cut glass, hand painted porcelain, pewter, gem stones, and more. Button designs include animals, vegetables, florals, military, Egyptian designs, Indian lore, hearts, etc. Various buckles, findings and rings are available, also.

Send $1.00 for a complete catalog and price list.

COATS AND CLARK, INC.

Box 1966
Stamford, CT 06904
(203) 327-3005

COATS AND CLARK, INC. offers, to educators only, a large number of sewing and needlecrafts products by mail. Included are threads, needles, tapes and trims, sewing aids, and supplies for embroidery, tatting, knitting and crochet. Some books are available as well.

Educators ONLY may write for the Sewing and Needlecraft Products brochure.

THE CORD COMPANY

5611 Virginia
Kansas City, MO 64110
(816) 333-6851

Manufacturer, Mail Order;
Established in 1983

Carol Koebbeman, owner of THE CORD COMPANY, supplies 100% silk cords in many colors and sizes. The cords are made from a beautiful lustrous silk and are dyed with commercial dyes. The ends are secured by binding, either in a matching or contrasting color. Heavier cords and silk ropes are also available. Carol can also create a cord with your choice of colors, or dye the cord so that it goes through a progression of colors.

Quantity or wholesale discounts are available; write for information.

Send for a free brochure and price list. A set of silk samples is $3.50.

DAISY CHAIN

P.O. Box 1258
Parkersburg, WV 26102
(304) 485-6729

Mail Order; V/MC; Established in
1980

DAISY CHAIN carries a line of threads and yarns for embroidery and machine knitting, including DMC cotton embroidery flosses, Balger French metallics, raw silks (10/1 and 10/2 plys) on cones, Tussah, Ping Ling silks, Soie d' Alger, Bouclette, Noppee, Au Ver a Soie French silk yarns for needlepoint, embroidery and knitting, as well as a long list of books, graphs and other accessories for needleworking.

Send $2.00 for a current catalog.

D & E DISTRIBUTING

199 N. El Camino Real #F-242
Encinitas, CA 92024
(619) 436-3262

Mail Order; V/MC; Established in
1983

D & E DISTRIBUTING offers a wide variety of creative threads and supplies for machine embroidery. Paradise Machine Embroidery Threads are available on spools or cones. These 100% rayon threads from Japan come in 230 different shades. Madeira Metallic Thread from West Germany is available in 21 colors, and can be used for hand sewing and machine embroidery. Madeira Metallic Yarns are also offered in 14 colors. Kanagawa 100% pure silk thread from Japan, as well as Kanagawa metallic threads, are available. Synthetic silk ribbons and cotton French twist are sold by D & E, too.

A complete line of machine embroidery supplies are available, also.

Wholesale discounts are given to retailers, write for information.

Send $1.00 for a complete catalog.

THE DESIGNERY

P.O. Box 2887
Kalamazoo, MI 49003-2887
(616) 685-5514

Manufacturer, Mail Order;
Established in 1979

Bobbe A. Luce, owner of THE DESIGNERY, supplies CRAFTags Care Labels for your handmade items. The tags come in your choice of 70 designs covering over 40 crafts and a variety of general titles. All designs are offered in russet ink on champagne parchment. Some designs are offered in other colors, also. Bobbe welcomes custom-design orders and will imprint your name on stock designs.

Quantity and bulk packaging discounts are available. See price sheet for more information.

Send $1.00 for a brochure and CRAFTag Samples (50¢ is applied to first order).

THE DREAMING DEER

P.O. Box 460
Burkittsville, MD 21718

Manufacturer, Mail Order;
Established in 1975

THE DREAMING DEER (formerly The Antler Shed), owned by Rachel and Bud Janse, supplies buttons made of deer or elk antlers. The buttons come in various sizes and in two finishes — polished and unpolished. The buttons are both beautiful and unique.

Professional discounts are given with a minimum order of $40.00. Write for more information and a wholesale price sheet.

Others should send for a free retail price sheet.

ETHNIC ACCESSORIES

Box 250
Forestville, CA 95436
(707) 887-2909

Mail Order; Established in 1978

ETHNIC ACCESSORIES carries the entire line of Folkwear Patterns, as well as several items that can be used to embellish the patterns. Tibetan brass buttons, shisha mirrors, embroidery scrim, goat leather lacing, and fine Kanagawa threads (used in metallic Oriental embroidery) are some of the current offerings. They also carry several books on the fiber arts.

Send $1.50 for a current catalog and price list.

FAIRFIELD PROCESSING CORP./POLY-FIL

P.O. Box 1157
Danbury, CT 06810
(203) 744-2090

Manufacturer, Mail Order;
Established in 1942

FAIRFIELD PROCESSING CORPORATION manufactures Poly-Fil polyester fiberfill in 12 and 24 oz. packages and 100 lb. bales, Fiber King polyester fiberfill, various battings in polyesters and cottons, and covered pillow inserts.

No individual discounts are given. School discounts are given with a minimum order of four cartons (prepaid) submitted on purchase order. Retailers should write for wholesale information.

A free catalog is available to those with a tax resale number.

FASHION BLUEPRINTS

P.O. Box 21141
Minneapolis, MN 55421
(612) 781-8680

Manufacturer, Mail Order; V/MC;
Established in 1980

FASHION BLUEPRINTS produces a line of creative clothing patterns, all of which are based on classic ethnic designs. The patterns are available in 24 different styles which include Chinese jackets, Japanese robes, Pennsylvania Dutch skirts, Thai wrap dress and top, Hippari, Central American top and huipil, and more. Accessory patterns (mandarin collar, tabard vest, obi belt) are included free with every order.

Dealer discounts are available; write for more information.

Send $1.00 for a complete catalog.

FOLKWEAR, INC.

P.O. Box 3859, Dept. CBD
San Rafael, CA 94912
(415) 457-0252

Manufacturer, Mail Order; V/MC;
Established in 1975

FOLKWEAR, INC. currently offers over 60 historically-inspired clothing patterns in two lines: the ethnic line and the "Patterns from Times Past" line. These patterns include designs such as English Smocks, Empire Dresses, Tea Frocks, Prairie Dresses, Kinsale Cloaks, Japanese Hapi and Haori, Guatemalan Gabacha, and many more. All patterns are full size on heavy re-useable paper and contain all sizes in one envelope. The patterns are also educational; many contain sewing, handwork and embellishment techniques, as well as historical lore.

Discounts are available to museums, restorations, shops, retail outlets and legitimate historical groups and associations when purchased for resale. Educators may qualify for discounts on orders of two dozen or more patterns for school use. Inquire on your letterhead.

Send $1.00 for a current catalog illustrating all styles.

THE FREED COMPANY

P.O. Box 394
Albuquerque, NM 87103
(505) 247-9311

Wholesale Distributor, Mail
Order; Established in 1920

THE FREED COMPANY carries all sorts of semi-precious stones, beads from various materials, and coral strands. They also carry pure silk scarves in prints and solids, cowhides, sheepskin and rabbit skins.

Send for a current brochure and price list.

THE HANDS WORK

P.O. Box 386TF
Pecos, NM 87552
(505) 757-6730

Manufacturer, Mail Order; Retail Shop; V/MC; Established in 1979

You are missing out on a treat if you haven't seen the buttons by THE HANDS WORK! The company is comprised of a group of dedicated artisans who make their buttons totally by hand. Each button is totally unique and made with the finest porcelains, stoneware, non-toxic glazes and underglazes. The Hands Work also offers a custom button design service. If you send a fabric swatch or yarn sample to them, they will create the perfect complementary button for it.

Retail establishments can write for wholesale information.

Send $2.00 for a current color catalog and price list.

HELMOR LABEL COMPANY

5143 West Diversey Avenue
Chicago, IL 60639
(312) 237-6163

Manufacturer, Mail Order

HELMOR LABEL COMPANY offers personalized fabric labels stocked in various widths, in a choice of cotton, satin, polyester or nylon. Various type styles and colors are available, and all wording is custom made to your order. Logos from your camera-ready artwork can be printed on the labels.

Quantity discounts are given; write for information.

Send for a current price list.

IMPORTS BY CLOTILDE

237 S.W. 28th Street
Ft. Lauderdale, FL 33315
(305) 761-8655

Mail Order; Established in 1973

IMPORTS BY CLOTILDE is probably your best mail order source for hard-to-find as well as basic sewing notions. Clotilde carries several sizes of Olfa cutters, cutting mats, interfacings, measuring tools, patterns and books, smocking supplies, pressing aids, and a large number of quilting products including those by Nancy Crow. Other supplies include needles, scissors, fusible films, plans for quilting frames, pressing equipment, pin holders, marking devices — and a wonderful disappearing basting tape.

Clotilde, the co-author of *Sew Smart* with Judy Lawrence, is also available for sewing seminars.

Various discounts are given; write for details.

Send $1.00 for a complete catalog.

JOSEPH'S COAT

Cloth of Many Colors
26 Main Street
Peterborough, NH 03458
(603) 827-3205

Mail Order, Retail Shop; AMEX; Established in 1980

JOSEPH'S COAT is a natural fiber fabric store that specializes in patchwork and ethnic clothing design. They handle pewter buttons by Randy Miller, quilting accessories by Nancy Crow, cloisonne buttons from China, quilter's rubber stamps, and a large number of quilting books. Also offered are Folkwear Patterns, scissors, and a large line of natural fabrics by mail (VIP, Concord, Ameritex, Wamsutta, Crompton), including 100% cotton velveteens, flannels and corduroys.

A 15% discount is given on the purchase of a whole bolt of fabric.

Send for a free catalog.

KIMMERIC STUDIO

P.O. Box 664
Pacifica, CA 94044

Manufacturer, Mail Order;
Established in 1983

Carol Carlson, owner of KIMMERIC STUCIO, designs wonderful little craft hang tags for personalization and pricing of handmade goods. The tags include space for your name on the front with the design, and information on care, materials, etc. on the back. Designs included in Carol's catalog can be used by weavers, knitters, batik artists, embroiderers, quilters, cro-cheters, etc. to identify their work — there's a design to please everyone. The tags come in several sizes and colors of stock and ink. Gift certificates are also available.

Bulk prices are available with a minimum order of 300 tags (50 tags minimum of any one design).

Send 50¢ for a complete catalog with price list and samples.

KIRCHEN BROTHERS

P.O. Box C1016
Skokie, IL 60076
(312) 676-2692

Mail Order; V/MC; Established in 1925

KIRCHEN BROTHERS offers a full line of basic craft items. Those of interest to fiber artists include laces, stenciling supplies, feathers, fake furs and shearling, beads, sequins, sewing notions, threads and wires, glues and cements, macrame cords and accessories, etc.

The company also offers a commission sales program and wholesaling program. Write for details.

Send $1.00 for a current catalog (refunded with order).

RANDY MILLER PEWTER BUTTONS

North Road, Box MC
East Alstead, NH 03602
(603) 835-2924

Mail Order; Established in 1978

RANDY MILLER, a member of the League of New Hampshire Craftsmen, creates unique pewter buttons which depict miniature scenes in relief. The button design originates as a small, sculpted engraving cut into wood by hand. A wax impression is then converted into a bronze master button, from which the mold for pewter casting is made. Each button is carefully hand-finished to bring out the natural patina of the metal. The designs include a rose, a bunch of grapes, an apple tree, grazing sheep, folk dancers, yarn basket, a ram, and others.

A 10% discount is given to individuals with an order of 12 or more buttons; wholesale discounts are given with a minimum order of $30.00. Write for more information.

Send a long SASE for a current brochure.

NAME MAKER COMPANY

3938 Shirley Drive
Atlanta, GA 30336
(404) 691-2237

Manufacturer; Mail Order

NAME MAKER COMPANY supplies woven labels with your name imprinted. Special designs for knitters, weavers, macrame artists, crocheters, smockers, etc. are available.

Some discounts are given; write for details.

Send for a free brochure of available designs.

THE NEEDLECRAFT SHOP, INC.

P.O. Box 1406-Dept. MCR
Canoga Park, CA 91304-0406
(818) 882-0759

Mail Order; V/MC; Established in
1965

THE NEEDLECRAFT SHOP, owned by Nancy Tabick, carries a wide variety of needlework supplies, including many threads and yarns: Au Ver a Soie French silks, Zwicky Swiss silk floss, Belding pure silk sewing threads and buttonhole twists, cottons by DMC and Lily, wools by Paterna, Elsa Williams and Medici, metal and metallic threads for embroidery and needlepoint. Nancy stresses personal service in her business, and states, "There really is a Nancy out here in California who cares about your needs. I assure you I am not a machine." Other basic supplies include canvases, needles, hoops, pattern books, etc.

Send $1.00 for a current catalog.

C. M. OFFRAY & SON, INC.

261 Madison Avenue
New York, NY 10016
(212) 682-8010

C. M. OFFRAY & SON, INC. manufactures a line of high quality woven-edge ribbons. Since the company does not handle direct mail orders, write to the address above for the name of the nearest retail outlet which does offer mail orders.

ORNAMENTAL RESOURCES, INC.

P.O. Box 3010
Idaho Springs, CO 80452
(303) 595-4367

Mail Order; V/MC; Established in
1971

ORNAMENTAL RESOURCES, INC. probably carries the largest line of beads, buckles, embellishments and ornaments available anywhere. Some of their extensive line includes Chinese lattice-carved hollow bone beads, Bedouin silver beads, faience Egyptian figures, costume jewelry from the 1930's, facetted crystal ball beads, brass beads and drops, metal bell-caps, abalone shell pieces, old Chinese metal tube beads, old French sequin drops, brass cones, flat-backed facetted rhinestones, glass-based pearls, metallic finish glass beads, mirror buttons, beaded balls and tassels, stones and semi-precious gems (garnet, jade, agate, onyx, quartz, etc.), Chinese porcelains, shell, woods, corals, feathers, horn, and thousands more. A large line of books are also available on beadwork, macrame, jewelry, and other crafts.

The catalog is being updated; write for a current price.

PATTY LOU CREATIONS

Rt. 2, Box 90-A
Elgin, OR 97827
(503) 437-6418

Mail Order; Established in 1982

Patty Fagan, owner of PATTY LOU CREATIONS, is a fabric artist/designer who also sells supplies by mail for machine embroidery and applique. She offers DMC threads, machine embroidery kits, lots of patterns and books, wooden and metal hoops in a variety of sizes, machine needles, Olfa cutters, pins, etc. Patty also offers a bi-monthly newsletter titled *The Stitch in Times* for $3.00 per year. She is available to teach machine embroidery, applique, quilting and fabric stenciling classes.

Discounts are given with a minimum order of $50.00.

Send $1.00 for a current catalog.

SEW CRAFT

P.O. Box 6146
South Bend, IN 46660
(219) 256-6866

Mail Order; V/MC

Gail Kibiger, owner of SEW CRAFT, offers hard-to-find supplies for creative machine stitchery by mail. Gail carries the beautiful 100% rayon Natesh embroidery threads in 336 colors (lightweight) and 40 colors (heavyweight). She also has Madeira metallic threads in 12 colors, Kanagawa metallic threads in 12 colors and Talon metallic threads in gold and silver. Shisha mirrors (both "perfect" and "antique") are also available, as are sewing machine needles, hoops, Olfa rotary cutters and mats, various markers, applique and walking feet for sewing machines and much more. A number of books and patterns are also available.

Some quantity discounts are available; write for more information.

Send 50¢ for a current newsletter/catalog (applied to first order), which also contains book reviews, helpful hints, articles and patterns.

STITCHWITCH

402 Pine Street
Levelland, TX 79336
(806) 894-6459

Mail Order, Retail Shop;
Established in 1975

STITCHWITCH, owned by Pat Grappe, offers a line of embroidery threads including silks, metallics and cottons. Also available are canvases, fabrics, notions, and many out-of-print books on needlecraft.

Pat is also a Certified Embroiderer's Guild of America canvas teacher, and will travel for workshops.

Send a SASE for a current price list.

TEKISON BUTTON COMPANY

P.O. Box 442
Hailey, ID 83333
(208) 788-3107

Manufacturer, Mail Order;
Established in 1971

TEKISON BUTTON CO., owned by Scott and Linda Schnebly, offers a line of beautiful buttons, most of which are handmade. The buttons are all made of such natural materials as horn, woods, antler and walnut shells. The Schnebly's also do custom work in ivory and antler.

Quantity discounts are given with a minimum order of $25.00.

Send $4.00 for button samples and a price list.

THINGS JAPANESE

10845 N.E. 116th
Kirkland, WA 98034
(206) 821-2287

Mail Order; V/MC; Established in 1983

Maggie Backman, owner of THINGS JAPANESE, carries an assortment of supplies for the Japanese needleart form called "rozashi." "Rozashi" is worked on silk canvas with silk threads and incorporates techniques from counted thread, canvas and surface embroidery. Ms. Backman supplies the silk canvas ("ro"), and the highly twisted reeled silk thread ("rozashi-ito"), as well as other silk threads. She has also written a book on the art that is available from her company.

Ms. Backman in addition, gives classes, lectures, and workshops on rozashi.

Quantity discounts are given to teachers; write for information.

Send $1.00 for a current catalog.

TINSEL TRADING COMPANY

47 West 38th Street
New York, NY 10018
(212) 730-1030

Mail Order, Retail Shop; V/MC;
Established in 1933

TINSEL TRADING COMPANY carries metallic embellishments of all kinds (braids, threads, cords, fringes, etc.). The metallic threads were made in the 1930's and consist of real metals. The newer threads are made of Lurex.

Quantity discounts are given to individuals, schools/groups, etc.

Send for a free brochure.

TREADLEART

25834 Narbonne Avenue
Lomita, CA 90717
(213) 534-5122

Mail Order, Retail Shop; V/MC;
Established in 1978

TREADLEART, owned by Janet Stocker, offers a large number of supplies for sewing machine art, including Iris Machine Embroidery Threads from Mexico, Natesh threads from India, DMC cotton threads, Kanagawa metallic threads, silk threads, perle cottons and ribbons. Also offered are books on machine embroidery, quilting, etc. Basic supplies are available, as well as sewing machine accessories, rubber stamps, etc.

Ms. Stocker publishes a bi-monthly magazine which focuses on machine artistry and features hints and tips, new products and books, projects, profiles of fiber artists, class listings, classified ads, and more. The current subscription price of *Treadleart Magazine* is $9.00 per year. A sample copy is $1.50.

A wholesale catalog is available to retailers.

Others should send $1.00 for a current catalog.

TUMBLEWEED

99 Mt. Auburn Street
Cambridge, MA 02138
(617) 492-3279

Mail Order, Retail Shop;
Established in 1974

TUMBLEWEED carries a full line of quilting supplies, including hundreds of 100% cottons and cotton blend fabrics in calicoes, solids, dots, stripes, quilteds, and unbleached muslins. This company handles threads, batting, hoops, books, patterns, etc. for quiltmaking. Special order quilts and quilt covers are available.

Various professional discounts are offered; write for more information.

Send $1.75 for a current catalog and set of fabric swatches.

WACCAMAW LINEN

Hwy. 501
Myrtle Beach, SC 29577
(803) 448-3125

Mail Order; Retail Shop; V/MC;
Established in 1977

WACCAMAW LINEN carries yarns by Phildar and Spinnerin, as well as fabrics by VIP, Wamsutta, Ameritex, Concord, and other craft supplies.

Wholesale discounts are given to individuals with a resale tax number.

Send $1.00 for a recent catalog.

WESTERN TRADING POST

P.O. Box 9070
Denver, CO 80209-0070
(303) 777-7750

Mail Order, Retail Shop;
V/MC/AMEX; Established in
1952

WESTERN TRADING POST is one of the largest suppliers of materials for Indian arts and crafts. They carry many items of interest to fiber artists, too. These include glass seed beads in opaque and transparent colors, glass luster beads, bugle beads, glass facetted beads, pony beads (doughnut-shaped), various wooden beads, bone and glass trade beads, metal beads, cones and conchos, beading looms, storage boxes, tools and accessories, thongs, feathers, bells, leathers, skins, porcupine quills, ermine tails, shells, fabrics, braids, buttons, and a large selection of books. You can even order a tepee from this company!

School discounts are given with a minimum order of $50.00.

Send for a free catalog.

WOOD FORMS

Foster Hill Road
Henniker, NH 03242
(603) 428-7830

Manufacturer, Mail Order

WOOD FORMS manufactures wooden buttons in two styles and three sizes. These are available in your choice of rosewood, bubinga, tulip, or zebra woods. The buttons are sealed with a water-resistant coating, and can be dry-cleaned or hand washed.

Wholesale discounts are available; write for more information.

Send a large SASE for a free catalog.

Index